Tibetan Medicine,
Buddhism and Psychiatry

CAROLINA ACADEMIC PRESS
Medical Anthropology Series

Pamela J. Stewart *and* Andrew Strathern
Series Editors

Curing and Healing
Medical Anthropology in Global Perspective, Second Edition
Andrew Strathern *and* Pamela J. Stewart

Healing the Modern in a Central Javanese City
Steve Ferzacca

Physicians at Work, Patients in Pain
Biomedical Practice and Patient Response in Mexico, Second Edition
Kaja Finkler

Elusive Fragments
Making Power, Propriety and Health in Samoa
Douglass D. Drozdow-St. Christian

Endangered Species
Health, Illness, and Death Among Madagascar's People of the Forest
Janice Harper

The Practice of Concern
Ritual, Well-Being, and Aging in Rural Japan
John W. Traphagan

The Gene and the Genie
Tradition, Medicalization and Genetic Counseling
in a Bedouin Community in Israel
Aviad E. Raz

Social Discord and Bodily Disorders
Healing Among the Yupno of Papua New Guinea
Verena Keck

Indigenous Peoples and Diabetes
Community Empowerment and Wellness
Mariana Leal Ferreira *and* Gretchen Chesley Lang

The Maintenance of Life
Preventing Social Death through Euthanasia Talk and End-of-Life Care—
Lessons from The Netherlands
Frances Norwood

We Have No Microbes Here
Healing Practices in a Turkish Black Sea Village
Sylvia Wing Önder

Of Orderlies and Men
Hospital Porters Achieving Wellness at Work
Nigel Rapport

Lost Selves and Lonely Persons
Experiences of Illness and Well-Being among Tamil Refugees in Norway
Anne Sigfrid Grønseth

Vulnerability and the Art of Protection
Embodiment and Health Care in Moroccan Households
Marybeth J. MacPhee

Genetic Disorders and Islamic Identity
among British Bangladeshis
Santi Rozario

A Tale of an Amulet
Ariela Popper-Giveon

Living Well in Los Duplex
Critical Reflections on Medicalization,
Migration and Health Sovereignty
Anna Waldstein

Wellbeing Machine
How Health Emerges from the Assemblages of Everyday Life
Kim McLeod

Tibetan Medicine, Buddhism and Psychiatry
Mental Health and Healing in a Tibetan Exile Community
Susannah Deane

Living in the Tension
Care, Selfhood, and Wellbeing among Faith-Based Youth Workers
Susan Wardell

Tibetan Medicine, Buddhism and Psychiatry

Mental Health and Healing in a Tibetan Exile Community

Susannah Deane

British Academy Postdoctoral Research Fellow
University of Bristol

Carolina Academic Press
Durham, North Carolina

Library of Congress Cataloging-in-Publication Data

Names: Deane, Susannah, author.
Title: Tibetan medicine, Buddhism and psychiatry : mental health and healing
    in a Tibetan exile community / Susannah Deane.
Description: Durham, North Carolina : Carolina Academic Press, LLC, [2018] |
    Series: Ethnographic studies in medical anthropology series | Includes
    bibliographical references and index.
Identifiers: LCCN 2017044403 | ISBN 9781531001407 (alk. paper)
Subjects: LCSH: Medicine, Tibetan--Treatment--Case studies--Tibet Autonomous
    Region. | Mental health--Treatment--Case studies--Tibet Autonomous Region.
Classification: LCC RC603.T5 D43 2018 | DDC 616.8900951/5--dc23
LC record available at https://lccn.loc.gov/2017044403

e-ISBN 978-1-5310-0488-0

CAROLINA ACADEMIC PRESS, LLC
700 Kent Street
Durham, North Carolina 27701
Telephone (919) 489-7486
Fax (919) 493-5668
www.cap-press.com

Printed in the United States of America

CONTENTS

List of Illustrations   xi

List of Frequently Used Abbreviations   xiii

A Note on Terminology and Tibetan Spelling   xv

Series Editors' Preface   xvii

      Plural Pluralisms: Complexities of Choices, Multiplicities of
         Meanings in Medical Encounters

      Andrew Strathern & Pamela J. Stewart

Acknowledgments   xxi

Introduction   3

PART ONE
THE SETTING AND THE APPROACH

Chapter One · Residents, Migrants and Exiles: A Brief History
                of Darjeeling and Its Communities   15

Darjeeling: History, Geography and Politics   16

Tibetans in Darjeeling: Building a Home in the Darjeeling Hills   21

      Exile and the Tibetan Refugee Self-Help Centre (TRSHC)   22

      Tibetan Identity and the Bhutia Status   26

      Tibetan Organisations and Institutions in Darjeeling   28

Darjeeling Encounters: Conducting Ethnography in Darjeeling   29

      Research Methodology   29

      Roles, Perceptions, and Expectations   33

      Linguistic and Translation Issues   36

Chapter Two · Medicine and Healing in Darjeeling: Practitioners,
                Practices and Institutions in Darjeeling and Around   39
    Biomedicine in Darjeeling   39
    Sowa Rigpa: Tibetan Medicine in Darjeeling   42
    Religious Life and Healing in Darjeeling   45

PART TWO

MEDICINE, MENTAL HEALTH AND HEALING IN THE TIBETAN CONTEXT:
THEORIES AND PRACTICES

Chapter Three · Tibetan Approaches to Mental Illness   53
    Psychiatry and the Subtle Body   55
        Anatomy and the Role of *rLung*   56
            rLung and Consciousness   56
            Fundamentals of Tibetan Anatomy: Humours, Channels,
                Winds and Drops   58
        rLung Disturbance and Mental Illness   59
    Sowa Rigpa in Theory and Practice   62
        Sources of Authority in Sowa Rigpa   63
        History, Learning and Practice in Sowa Rigpa   65
    Religion and Mental Health in the Tibetan Context   72
        'Religion' and the Treatment of Mental Illness   76
    Meeting the West: Western and Biomedical Interpretations
        of Tibetan Medicine   78

Chapter Four · Spirits, Mental Health and Healing   83
    The Role of Spirits and Deities in Tibetan Society   85
    The Role of Spirits and Deities in Mental Illness and Its Healing   88
        Spirits in the *rGyud bZhi*   90
        Management and Treatment of Spirit Afflictions in the
            Tibetan Context   91
    Meeting the West: Western Interpretations of Spirit Affliction   93

Chapter Five · Biomedicine and the Tibetan Context   101
    Biomedical Psychiatry: History, Controversies and Contemporary
        Practice in the West   102
        History and Controversies   103
        Lay Perspectives   107
    Biomedical Psychiatry in Cross-Cultural Context   110
    Biomedicine in Tibetan Contexts: History and
        Contemporary Practice   118

PART THREE
THE CASE STUDIES

Chapter Six · Lobsang: *rLung* and Depression   127
Lobsang's Story   127
Non-Textual Concepts of *rLung* and *Srog rLung* in Darjeeling
    and Beyond   130
Politicisation of the *rLung* Diagnosis   133
The *rLung* of Modern Life: 'Stress', 'Pressure' and 'Depression' 135
Keeping the Mind Calm: Causes of, and Treatments for, *rLung*   138

Chapter Seven · Jigme: Madness and Its Causes   145
Jigme's Story   145
Madness and Its Causation in the Tibetan Context   150
    'Madness', 'Insanity' and 'Psychosis': Examining the Tibetan
        Notion of *sMyo Nad*   150
    Lay Perspectives: Religious Causes of Madness   152
    Lay Perspectives: Non-Religious Causes of Madness   154
Treating and Preventing Madness in Darjeeling   155

Chapter Eight · Wangmo: 'Belief', 'Faith' and Healing   159
Wangmo's Story   159
The Power of 'Belief': Connections, Faith and Healing   163
Karma, *rLung rTa* and *dBang Thang*: 'Causes' and 'Conditions'
    of Illness and Healing   167
Making Sense of 'Madness'   171

Chapter Nine · Dechen: Possession and Mediumship   175
Dechen's Story   175
Luck, Madness and Death: Spirits and Mental Health in
    the Tibetan Context   179
    Spirit-Mediumship   180
    gDon and *'Dre* Affliction in Darjeeling   182
    Lhakpa   182
    Migmar   184
    bTsan, *rGyal Po* and the Dangers of Offending Local Deities 185
    Dorje Shugden   186
Spirit Affliction in Contemporary Tibetan Society:
    Uncertainties and Conflicts   189
Dealing with Spirits in Darjeeling: Treating and Preventing
    Spirit Afflictions   190

Conclusion: Navigating a Pluralistic Medical System in Darjeeling   197
    Mapping Out Boundaries of Mental 'Health' and 'Illness'   200
    Managing Diverse Worldviews in a Medically Pluralistic Context   201
    Pragmatism and the Myth of 'Rationality': Health-Seeking
        Behaviour in Darjeeling   206
    'Integration' and Patient Choice   211

Glossary of Tibetan Terms   217
Reference List   221
Index   241

LIST OF ILLUSTRATIONS

Illustration 1:   Darjeeling hills   17

Illustration 2:   Darjeeling town   18

Illustration 3:   Tea plantation workers in Arya Tea Garden, Darjeeling   19

Illustration 4:   Traditional carpet-weaving at the TRSHC   24

Illustration 5:   One of the residents carding wool at one of the TRSHC workshops   25

Illustration 6:   Amchi Lobsang Thubten at the Darjeeling MTK clinic, July 2012   43

Illustration 7:   Drug Sangak Choling monastery ('Dali Gonpa')   46

Illustration 8:   Lama Karma Shedrup, a local *sngags pa*, at his *lha khang*, June 2012   47

Illustration 9:   Guru-ji, at his temple near Chowrasta, Darjeeling, September 2011   49

Illustration 10:   *Thangka* depicting the Medicine Buddha in the Lhasa Mentsikhang, TAR   66

Illustration 11:   *Thangka* depicting medicinal plants, Lhasa Mentiskhang, TAR   70

Illustration 12:   *brGya bzhi* ritual for *shi 'dre* affliction, Dali Gonpa, July 2012   193

Illustration 13:   Monks conducting a *brGya bzhi* ritual for *shi 'dre* affliction, Dali Gonpa, July 2012   194

List of Frequently Used Abbreviations

APA	American Psychiatric Association
BPS	British Psychological Society
CBT	Cognitive Behaviour Therapy
CST	Central Schools for Tibetans
CTA	Central Tibetan Administration
CTMI	Chagpori Tibetan Medical Institute
DID	Dissociative Identity Disorder
DSM	Diagnostic and Statistical Manual of Mental Disorders
ECT	Electro-Convulsive Therapy
ICD	International Classification of Disease
LAMIC	Low- and Middle-Income Countries
mhGAP	Mental Health Gap Action Programme
MTK	Men-Tsee-Khang
NGO	Non-Governmental Organisation
NICE	National Institute for Health and Care Excellence
PRC	People's Republic of China
PTSD	Post-Traumatic Stress Disorder
TAR	Tibet Autonomous Region
TRSHC	Tibetan Refugee Self-Help Centre
WHO	World Health Organization

A NOTE ON TERMINOLOGY AND TIBETAN SPELLING

As a general rule, I have used the Wylie transliteration system as standard across the book, italicising the Tibetan and capitalising the root letter (rather than prefix or superfix) at the beginning of a sentence or to indicate a proper noun. I have included a phonetic spelling enclosed within double quotation marks in the first instance. Where Tibetan words have come into common usage in English conversation or in the English-language literature (e.g. lama, rinpoche, amchi, Sowa Rigpa), I have used the common phonetic spelling (unitalicised) and included the Wylie transliteration in the parentheses in the first instance. Similarly, for Tibetan names, I have used common phonetic spellings. See the Glossary for a list of commonly-used Tibetan terms referred to in the book.

In addition, I do not add a plural indicator to Tibetan words (neither those transliterated nor spelled phonetically), as this is not used in Tibetan and can create confusion with spelling. Thus Tibetan nouns used in the text refer to either singular or plural forms.

Regarding English terminology, I have predominantly referred to 'mental illness' in the book to refer to illnesses related to the mind, as this is the closest translation of the Tibetan umbrella term of *sems nad* (illness of the mind).

SERIES EDITORS' PREFACE

Plural Pluralisms:
Complexities of Choices, Multiplicities of
Meanings in Medical Encounters

*Andrew Strathern & Pamela J. Stewart**

Susannah Deane's richly documented and thoughtfully analyzed monograph published here resonates with, and makes more complex, many of the stock-in-trade elements in medical anthropology's analyses of therapeutic practices around the world. Her focus is twofold. One is on the indigenous Tibetan ideas as they have come to Darjeeling in India along with Tibetan refugees fleeing from the takeover of Tibet by forces of the People's Republic of China. The other is in the particular complex arena of treatments for the category we call in the English language "mental health" (see for a brief critique of this term Stewart and Strathern 2017: 52–54). Here we find an intensified and layered complexity, first because we are attempting to deal with a concept in English that is itself marked by uncertainty about its meaning and concomitantly its effective treatment and second because we are attempting to match this concept with ideas held in a different social and cultural context, in this case the pluralistic context studied in Darjeeling by Deane.

Deane herself navigates these troubled analytical waters with a deft hand, and we emerge from a bumpy ride with some useful new ways of looking at established problems. Her treatment of the ethnography shows that several different systems coexist in Darjeeling, varying from Tibetan medicine, *Sowa Rigpa*, and versions of indigenous Indian practices, including Ayurvedic ones and a strong mixture of Buddhist philosophies and ideas of the body and personhood. Taken one by one these different contexts show some fundamental differences, but arranged side by side they also show overlaps that can act as bridges when people are trying to decide on what health therapies to use in mental health contexts (or any therapeutic circumstances, but particularly in relation to the intrinsic ambiguities and existential pressures of "mental health").

The first bridge that can link different therapies together is found within a suite of humoral ideas (cf. Stewart and Strathern 2001). Deane points out that three bodily humors are integral to both Tibetan and Ayurvedic systems of thought, and of these the concept of *rlung* or "wind" is crucial to theories of mental disturbance or "madness." "Wind" is a concept of significance in numbers of Southeast Asian systems, as Carol Laderman showed in her striking early study of Malay shamanistic healers (Laderman 1991), so the idea that "wind" may adversely affect the head is one that could be understood across differences among patients and practitioners in Darjeeling. In Darjeeling biomedicine practitioners are also at work and they make efforts further to equate conditions caused by "wind" problems with categories such as depression. However, Deane rightly emphasizes that *rlung* must itself be studied and understood in its own terms rather than simply being translated into "depression." Even using the term "humor" for *rlung* carries with it hazards of translation, because *rlung* in Tibetan usage refers not only to the ordinary body but also to the "subtle body," which is thought to consist of channels of energy (here resembling Chinese ideas of *chi*). Blockages in the flow of *rlung* are said to result in a set of complaints, such as dizziness and headache, and also anger or frustration.

This mention of anger or frustration immediately strikes a chord further afield. In Mount Hagen, in Papua New Guinea, as we have discussed in numerous publications (e.g., Stewart and Strathern 2001 already cited and Strathern and Stewart 2011), anger or frustration is thought to carry the danger of sickness, eliciting corrective therapeutic measures to avoid serious consequences including death. Anger, for the Hageners, is located in the realm of the *noman* or "mind," connected to the system of breath (sc. "wind") within the diaphragm. Mind and consciousness go together in *noman*, as they do also in the Tibetan concept of *rlung*.

Deane draws out here the same conclusion as we do, that investigation of these concepts leads to the transcendence of or a complexification of ideas that would separate body and mind. *Noman* and *rlung* function as mediators or transducers that constantly bring body and mind together, either as causes of illness or as causes of healing and health. They are analytical and experiential bridges that help to make sense of and deal with adverse life experiences, and as such they are surely effective critiques of any scientific or folk system that would seek to explain body and mind in separate terms (see for a thoughtful early explanation Keyes 1985 in Kleinman and Good's edited collection *Culture and*

Depression). Herein lies further the whole problem of the etic versus the emic realms, of questions of translation and translatability, and finally the issue of the validity of indigenous actors' ways of knowing as against those of some specified, but also culturally situated observer(s). In his work, Arthur Kleinman identified the idea of "somatization," i.e., that in certain (Chinese) cultures patients recounted physical, or neurasthenic, symptoms such as headache and dizziness, *rather than* reporting their conditions as ones of "depression." Kleinman called this "somatization," the expression of mental disorder in physical form, resulting from ideas of stigma adhering to mental abnormalities (e.g., Kleinman and Kleinman 1985: 429–490). How to unravel the semantic knots involved here? The approach via *rlung* and *noman* would be to say that all things are connected, and experience encompasses and surpasses the dichotomy of body versus mind, as also does the idea of the involvement of "spirit" in human life processes.

Adding to her exquisitely detailed exposition of her ethnography of Tibetan migrants in Darjeeling, Deane gives us a chapter on current thinking in the biomedical field regarding mental health and illness, and in particular in the field of psychiatry. Here her deconstructionist method also serves her well, as she is able to show that "biomedicine" is not as invariant or monolithic as it might appear to be, since it is practiced differently in different cultural contexts (like Christianity, see Stewart and Strathern 2009). She is able to point out, for example, that biomedical psychiatry is itself a culturally defined set of practices, tied in with ideas of personhood and of the contemporary world at large. Therefore its applicability to other contexts where different ideas of personhood hold sway becomes a point at issue for discussion, if not resolution.

The people Deane studied in Darjeeling were living in the intersections of interpretive issues of this kind. What is heartening about her exposition is to note the pragmatism people brought to their human suffering. Pragmatism is flexible, and Deane astutely replaces earlier ideas in medical anthropology of patients' "explanatory models" with the concept, adapted from the work of other scholars, of "exploratory maps": ways of looking for pathways in forests of illness to clearings where healing may be found.

References

Keyes, Charles F. 1985. The Interpretive Basis of Depression. In Kleinman, Arthur, and Byron Good eds. *Culture and Depression*. Berkeley CA: University of California Press, pp. 153–174.

Kleinman, Arthur and Joan Kleinman 1985. Somatization: The Interconnections in Chinese Society among Culture, Depressive Experiences, and the

Meaning of Pain. In Kleinman and Good eds. *Culture and Depression.*
    Berkeley CA: University of California Press, pp. 429–490.
Laderman, Carol 1991. *Taming the Wind of Desire: Psychology, Medicine, and
    Aesthetics in Malay Shamanistic Performance.* Berkeley, CA: University of
    California Press.
Stewart, Pamela J. and Andrew Strathern 2001. *Humors and Substances. Ideas
    of the Body in New Guinea.* Westport, Connecticut: Bergin and Garvey.
Stewart, Pamela J. and Andrew Strathern eds. 2009. *Religious and Ritual
    Change: Cosmologies and Histories.* Durham, NC: Carolina Academic Press.
Stewart, Pamela J. and Andrew Strathern 2017. *Breaking the Frames: Anthro-
    pological Conundrums.* New York: Palgrave.
Strathern, Andrew and Pamela J. Stewart 2011. *Peace-making and the Imagi-
    nation: Papua New Guinea Perspectives.* St. Lucia, Queensland: University
    of Queensland Press.

* Pamela J. Stewart (Strathern) and Andrew J. Strathern are a wife-and-husband research
team who are based in the Department of Anthropology, University of Pittsburgh and co-direct
the Cromie Burn Research Unit. They are frequently invited international lecturers and have
worked with numbers of museums to assist them with their collections. Stewart and Strathern
have published over 50 books and over 200 articles, book chapters, and essays on their research
in the Pacific (mainly Papua New Guinea and the South-West Pacific region, e.g., Samoa and
Fiji); Asia (mainly Taiwan, and also including Mainland China and Japan); and Europe
(primarily Scotland, Ireland and the European Union countries in general); and also New
Zealand and Australia. Their most recent co-authored books include *Witchcraft, Sorcery, Rumors,
and Gossip* (Cambridge University Press, 2004); *Kinship in Action: Self and Group* (Prentice
Hall, 2011); *Peace-Making and the Imagination: Papua New Guinea Perspectives* (University of
Queensland Press with Penguin Australia, 2011); *Ritual: Key Concepts in Religion* (Bloomsbury
Academic Publications, 2014); *Working in the Field: Anthropological Experiences Across the World*
(Palgrave Macmillan, 2014) and *Breaking the Frames: Anthropological Conundrums* (Palgrave
Macmillan, 2017). Their recent co-edited books include *Research Companion to Anthropology*
(Ashgate Publishing, 2015); *Exchange and Sacrifice* (Carolina Academic Press, 2008) and
Religious and Ritual Change: Cosmologies and Histories (Carolina Academic Press, 2009, and
the Updated and Revised Chinese version: Taipei, Taiwan: Linking Publishing, 2010. Stewart
and Strathern's current research includes the topics of Cosmological Landscapes; Ritual Studies;
Political Peace-making; Comparative Anthropological Studies of Disasters and Climatic Change;
Language, Culture and Cognitive Science; and Scottish and Irish Studies. For many years they
served as Associate Editor and General Editor (respectively) for the *Association for Social Anthropology in Oceania* book series and they are Co-Series Editors for the *Anthropology and
Cultural History in Asia and the Indo-Pacific* book series. They also currently Co-Edit four book
series: *Ritual Studies; Medical Anthropology; European Anthropology* and *Disaster Anthropology*
and they are the long-standing Co-Editors of the *Journal of Ritual Studies* [Facebook: https://
www.facebook.com/ritualstudies]. Their webpages, listing publications and other scholarly activities, are: http://www.pitt.edu/~strather/ and http://www.StewartStrathern.pitt.edu/.

ACKNOWLEDGMENTS

There are many, many people who made this book possible, providing moral, practical and financial support with encouragement, patience and kindness, and I am eternally grateful to all of them. This work is based on doctoral research carried out at Cardiff University, and as such, my first thanks go to my two fantastic research supervisors, Professor Geoffrey Samuel and Dr Tracey Loughran, who inspired and encouraged from our first meetings until the work was completed. Their knowledge, experience and patiently-delivered feedback not only improved this work immeasurably, but inspired me from the very beginning. Particular thanks also to Geoffrey for visiting Darjeeling during the course of my fieldwork, bringing advice and support despite the difficulties of getting there.

During the course of my fieldwork in Darjeeling a number of individuals became good friends, helping me immensely with my research, and also welcoming me into the various communities there and making my time there truly enjoyable. I was endlessly surprised and humbled by the hospitality, openness and patience shown by so many people, who gave up their time to answer questions, help with translations and introduce me to places and people that they thought might be useful in my research endeavour, without ever asking anything in return. The subject of this book—mental health and ill-health—is often a difficult and sensitive topic, and I sincerely appreciated people's willingness to discuss it openly with a relative stranger. Particular thanks to Tsering, who invited me into his family, answered my endless stream of questions on Tibetan society with patience, and helped me with translations. To Chungkyi too, who made me feel welcome in their home; and Sonam, who spent many hours helping me to translate pieces of Classical Tibetan. I am very grateful to all the staff at the Manjushree Center of Tibetan Culture, whose introduction to Darjeeling was invaluable. Special thanks go to Gen Dawa, my ever patient and entertaining Tibetan teacher, who gave many hours in the service of my language learning, in addition to opening a window into the Tibetan community for me.

At the Tibetan Refugee Self-Help Centre, located a few miles from Darjeeling town centre, a small group of *momo-la* (grandmothers) welcomed me into their workshop and their homes, patiently letting me practise my Tibetan, answering my questions about their lives in both Tibet and India and giving me many, many insights into Tibetan society and culture. In addition, a number of Tibetan amchi (doctors) in Darjeeling, Dharamsala and Delhi advanced my understanding of Sowa Rigpa theory and practice significantly. In Darjeeling, Amchi Lobsang Thubten at the Men-Tsee-Khang clinic and Amchi Teinlay Trogawa at the Chagpori Tibetan Medical Institute were hugely helpful and informative, offering me their time and insight, which were much needed and appreciated. Many thanks too to Sujith, who introduced me to the local Nepali spirit-medium tradition, gathering information and translating for me on a number of occasions. Huge gratitude goes also to Helly, who made me feel at home in Darjeeling, introducing me to people and places, helping me to find accommodation, and keeping me going with long chats over cups of coffee and excellent cake. In Gangtok, the help, encouragement and hospitality of Anna Balicki-Denjongpa at both the Namgyal Institute of Tibetology and her home were greatly appreciated.

At Cardiff University, many thanks to those who provided extensive encouragement and feedback during the course of this research, particularly Dr Louise Child, Professor Kevin Passmore and Dr Steven Stanley. In addition, gratitude goes to my doctoral examiners, Professor Kier Waddington at Cardiff University and Dr Joseph Calabrese at University College London. This research would not have been possible without the funding I received from a number of sources: from Cardiff University, the three-year studentship, 125 Award and research grant from the School of History, Archaeology and Religion; a research grant from the Body, Health and Religion Research Group (BAHAR); and a research grant from the Wellcome Trust.

Many thanks to Dr Pamela J. Stewart and Professor Andrew J. Strathern, Ryland Bowman, TJ Smithers and the editorial team at Carolina Academic Press. Their hard work, support and patience during the long journey from proposal to manuscript to publication has been hugely appreciated as I navigated this new world of book publishing.

Finally, endless thanks go to my parents Jenny and John, and my sister Alexa, along with a number of close friends who encouraged me to embark upon this research and then keep going—I would not have got this far without their support.

Tibetan Medicine,
Buddhism and Psychiatry

INTRODUCTION

Appalling, dreadful, inhumane—the worst of words pile on each other to name the horrors of being shunned, isolated, and deprived of the most basic of human rights. But this is not a crisis of the day; it has been the reality of people with mental illness for the four decades that I have been involved in global health and probably for centuries before that. (Kleinman 2009, 603)

To treat smyo nad *[madness], get religious blessings and do* pūjā *[ritual].... Most important is love and care, family and community supports.* (Tibetan informant, Darjeeling, March 2012)

This book examines lay Tibetan perspectives on the causation, management and treatment of mental illness (a category which corresponds broadly to the Tibetan term *sems nad*) within a Tibetan exile community in Darjeeling, northeast India. The book explores common Tibetan understandings and widely divergent perceptions of mental illness and healing, and how these are reflected in health-seeking behaviour in this medically-diverse area, in contrast to 'official' Tibetan textual and biomedical perspectives. In the ethnically Tibetan context,[1] much of the research on the indigenous Tibetan medical tradition, which is commonly referred to as Sowa Rigpa (Tib.: *gSo ba Rig pa*, knowledge/science of healing), has so far primarily focused on the four-volume Tibetan medical text, the *rGyud bZhi* ("Gyu Shi", Four Tantras, Four Treatises), parts of which have been translated into English (see for example Clark 1995; Clifford 1989;

---

1. I use the term 'ethnically-Tibetan' here to refer to Tibetan cultural areas of the Himalayan region and beyond. This geographical area stretches from Ladakh in northwest India, across its contested border with the People's Republic of China (PRC) and Chinese-controlled Tibet, to Bhutan in the east and Nepal in the south.

Epstein and Topgay 1982; Meyer 1998). Much of the ethnographic research in this context has so far tended to focus on the perspectives of traditional medical practitioners, known as 'amchi' (Tib.: *am chi*) (Adams 2001a, 2002, 2003; Adams and Li 2008; Janes 1995, 1999b, 2001; Schrempf 2007), the social and economic context of Tibetan medical provision in the Tibet Autonomous Region (TAR) in the People's Republic of China (PRC) (Hofer 2008a, 2008b) and the history of Tibetan Medicine and its development in exile (Kloos 2010).

In terms of lay and patient perspectives, which have so far received less attention, studies of individuals' health-seeking behaviour have started to give us a picture of Tibetans' navigation of pluralistic medical systems (Gerke 2010; Schrempf 2011; Wangda 1996). However, research on mental health, illness and healing to date has been mainly limited to work on trauma survivors in the form of studies of recent Tibetan exiles in Dharamsala (such as work by Benedict, Mancini and Grodin 2009; Keller et al. 2006; Lewis 2013; Mercer, Ager and Ruwanpura 2005; Ruwanpura et al. 2006; Sachs et al. 2008; Terheggen, Stroeber and Kleber 2001), Ladakhis and Tibetans who have experienced trauma in Ladakh (Schröder 2011) and the politicisation of certain diagnoses (Adams 1998; Janes 1999a; Prost 2004, 2006). Whilst some equivalences have been drawn between a number of Tibetan and biomedical diagnostic categories (Jacobson 2000, 2002, 2007; Millard 2007), the area of what in the West would be termed 'psychotic illness' has remained quite neglected, with very little examination of Tibetan concepts of 'madness' (Tib.: *smyo nad*). Thus overall, so far we know little of the broader lay Tibetan perspectives on mental health and illness, or the utilisation of different treatment approaches in health-seeking behaviour, where religious explanations often predominate.

The two quotations which opened this introduction paint two very different pictures of 'mental illness' in non-Western communities.[2] Indeed, biomedical research often presents a grim vision of mental illness and its treatment (or lack thereof) in non-Western countries.[3] For example, Patel describes the 'ex-

---

2. The delineation into 'Western' and 'non-Western' communities or cultures is of course not ideal. However, other labels are equally unsatisfying and problematic, but perhaps less standard in the literature. Thus in this work, I use the term 'Western' to refer to dominant European, Anglo-American and Australasian approaches to culture and medicine. Here, 'non-Western' refers—very broadly—to communities in Asia, Africa and South America. I also refer to 'local' approaches to illness and healing, in reference to traditions which are indigenous to the communities in which I saw them practised.

3. I use the terms 'biomedicine' and 'biomedical' here to refer to the system of medicine based on the application of the principles of the natural sciences, especially biology and biochemistry (See Merriam-Webster's online dictionary definition: http://www.merriam-webster.com/medlineplus/biomedicine).

tremely scarce' mental health resources in low- and middle-income countries (LAMIC), with a majority of individuals with psychiatric conditions not receiving 'even basic, evidence-based care' (2007, 92). Others note that there is often typically 'one psychiatrist per population of 1 000 000, with little or no multidisciplinary team and few regular drugs' in many low-income countries (McKenzie, Patel and Araya 2004, 1138). In response, many governmental and non-governmental policies, such as those of the World Health Organization (WHO), aim to address this issue, delineating road maps for treatment in both urban and rural areas of LAMIC such as India and China. Such policies are usually based around one of two biomedical classification systems for mental illness: the current tenth edition of the European *International Classification of Disease* (ICD-10, WHO 2005) and the American *Diagnostic and Statistical Manual of Mental Disorders* (either the newly-published fifth edition, DSM-5, American Psychological Association (APA) 2013, or an earlier version). Here, a cross-cultural similarity in terms of the causation and treatment of mental illness is assumed, often in reference back to studies such as the *International Pilot Study of Schizophrenia* (IPSS) and its follow-ups conducted during the 1970s and 1980s (Leff et al. 1992; Sartorius, Shapiro and Jablensky 1974; WHO 1974, 1975, 1979), which purportedly demonstrated the cross-cultural validity of a number of Western psychiatric classifications.

The biomedical approach to treating mental illness assumes relatively clearly defined pathways from cause to symptom to treatment. However, mental illnesses are often viewed by lay individuals and mental health professionals as multifaceted in nature, frequently encompassing multiple causative and contributory factors which can interact in numerous ways to lead to varied outcomes in terms of symptoms and prognosis. Furthermore, the nosological system of biomedicine is constantly evolving and changing, and the shifting ground of biomedical classification throws up its own questions of (intra-cultural) validity. Boundaries between 'health' and 'illness', between 'sanity' and 'madness', are fluid and often culture- and/or time-dependent. The situation is further complicated by the subjectivity inherent in judgements regarding the classification and diagnosis of many mental health conditions, which leads to the boundaries between 'health' and 'ill-health', 'normal' and 'abnormal', 'sanity' and 'insanity' being drawn (by patients, their families and practitioners) in different places by different people. These boundary lines may overlap in places, but—with us each bringing our own backgrounds, experiences and cultural concepts to our summation of the situation—they may well not, and the British Psychological Society (BPS) has criticised the DSM's approach particularly in ignoring 'evidence for the dimensional spectrum of psychiatric symptoms' (BPS 2012, 3). One person's legitimate anger and sadness at a significant bereavement, for example, is another's patho-

logical illness.[4] Furthermore, as we might expect, these questions are only magnified cross-culturally: as Bentall notes, boundaries drawn between 'madness'
and 'normal functioning' 'vary with geography' (2004, 132), and questions of
cross-cultural validity remain. Notions of 'normal' and 'abnormal' behaviour as
well as the rankings of symptom severity vary widely in different contexts. For
example, in Uganda, Bentall tells us, hallucinations and delusions are apparently
far less worrying than alcohol addiction and aggressive behaviour, in stark
contrast to prevailing views in the UK (2004, 119).

Kleinman's well-known distinction between 'disease'—that is, the 'malfunc-
tioning or maladaptation of biological or psychological processes'—and 'illness'—
that is, 'the personal, interpersonal, and cultural reaction to disease'—(1977, 9)
emphasises cultural and experiential components of 'illness'. This lends weight to
his focus on the 'somatisation' of certain illnesses in some cultural contexts, where
physical symptoms may be more culturally 'acceptable' than psychological ones
(Kleinman 1991). Similarly, in the Tibetan context, observing a Tibetan medicine
clinic in Nepal, Millard found that patients rarely referred directly to any psychological condition, describing instead a cluster of physical symptoms (2007, 259).
However, this contrasts with Jacobson's findings in Darjeeling, where he observed
patients diagnosed with various types of *rlung* ('wind') disorder by their Sowa
Rigpa practitioner reporting some psychological symptoms alongside their
physical ones to the amchi they consulted (2000, 2002, 2007).

Comparisons have been drawn between a number of Tibetan and biomedical
categories. For example, Millard has suggested a similarity between the Tibetan
system and the biomedical distinction between 'neurotic' and 'psychotic'
disorders evident in earlier versions of the DSM-5 (2007).[5] Here, he compared
disorders related to *rlung* ("loong", wind, one of the three bodily 'humours' or
'faults')—often likened to 'stress', 'depression' and anxiety'—to 'neurotic' disorders related to depression and anxiety, and those classified as *smyo nad* ("nyö
né", madness) to conditions involving psychosis. Similarly, in Darjeeling, Jacobson described a number of Tibetan patients diagnosed with different types
of *rlung* illness, finding them at least partially analogous with DSM categories
of Generalized Anxiety Disorder (GAD), Major Depressive Disorder and Panic
Disorder (2002, 2007). However, when we start to examine these Tibetan cat-

---

4. Indeed, one contested change of the recently-published DSM-5 is the 'reclassification'
of grief into 'major depressive disorder' (Frances 2012).

5. In fact, this distinction between 'neurotic' and 'psychotic' disorders, which was also
evident in the WHO's ICD-9, has actually been removed from the 10th revision (ICD-10
WHO 1993, 10), and has also been removed from the most recent edition of the DSM
(DSM-5, APA 2013), although is still widely used in practice.

egories in more detail, we see significant differences starting to emerge from the Western categorisations, particularly in relation to the symptoms associated with these conditions, as we shall see in the following chapters.

To date, the Tibetan category of *rlung* illnesses has taken centre stage in much of the ethnographic research on mental illness in the Tibetan context. As noted above, *rlung* is sometimes interpreted as holding similarities to Western notions of 'stress' and 'depression'. It has also been seen as a concept through which to articulate the often very difficult personal and political events experienced by Tibetans in both Chinese-controlled Tibet and exile (see, for example, work by Janes, 1999a). However, I would suggest that in Tibetan communities such as Darjeeling, in areas less defined by the Tibetan political discourse, and where first-, second- and third-generation Tibetan exiles are more integrated with local populations and more exposed to pluralistic healing systems encompassing diverse medical traditions, the situation is rather different. Kleinman described 'explanatory models of illness' (1980), but more recently Williams and Healy proposed instead the notion of 'exploratory maps'. Conducting research in the UK, they found that patients frequently either viewed a number of (sometimes contradictory) possible causes of illness simultaneously, or switched between them over a short period of time (2001, 469). Here, they suggest, understanding mental illness and its causation was an 'ongoing process of making sense and seeking meaning' (2001, 473), often invoking a number of explanatory frameworks rather than a singular 'model' of mental illness as they attempted to understand their experience. Of course, medical pluralism only increases the available explanatory frameworks, and I would argue that attempts to make sense of mental illness are particularly complex in medically pluralistic contexts such as Darjeeling, where a number of different worldviews 'compete' for attention, each with their own explanations of illness, expected health-seeking behaviours and treatment plans. The steady march of biomedicine across the globe forces local explanatory models up against Western concepts of health, illness and disease, leaving patients and practitioners alike to navigate complex webs of explanation, causation and treatment options. Sometimes these explanatory frameworks overlap, and at other times there are clear demarcations between, for example, local or traditional and non-local/non-traditional interpretations of conditions, leaving both biomedical practitioners and non-local researchers struggling to define and describe what is going on. Spirit possession and mediumship are good examples of this, as we shall see in Chapters Four and Nine. Here, biomedical psychiatry tends to favour a diagnosis of 'dissociation' or 'psychosis', compared to the approaches often taken by anthropologists, which have tended to focus on the socioeconomic functions of possession or a discussion of the

relationship between various forms of religious healing and ritual and psychotherapy (Csordas 2002, 2). The study of such conditions—and more
broadly, of mental health conditions in general—can highlight not only significant cross-cultural differences, but also the complex interplay between
health and religion in many contexts.

Psychiatrists Bhui and Bhugra have suggested that more work on
understanding local explanatory models of illness and healing is required *before*
attempts are made to map them onto biomedical diagnostic categories and their
'related care pathways' (2002, 6–7). However, if Williams and Healy are correct
in their suggestion that people often view multiple notions of causation simultaneously, then this will be a particularly complex task. Moreover, I would suggest
that it is especially difficult in the context of mental illness, where cultural differences can demarcate significantly different boundaries between 'health' and
'illness'. Ideas about health and ill-health are often tied up with broader cultural
and religious concepts, and perceptions of 'treatment' and 'cure' can also differ
considerably between cultures. In religious healing, for example, Csordas notes
that the aim is often 'not the elimination of a thing (an illness, a problem, a
symptom, a disorder)' but instead, the 'transformation of a person, a self that is
a bodily being' (2002, 3). This 'transformation' might involve, for example, the
afflicted individual utilising their possession to become a spirit-medium or
shaman within the community. Under other circumstances, the aim may be to
get the patient to accept and manage his symptoms and/or interpret them in a
different way. Such diverse approaches are not restricted to non-Western spheres:
some Western psychological approaches have also taken a similar perspective—
for example some sectors of transpersonal psychology follow Grof and Grof's
interpretation of psychiatric symptoms as part of a 'spiritual crisis' which, when
embraced as such, can lead to personal and spiritual growth (Grof and Grof
1990). These diverse perspectives highlight the significantly different approaches
to 'treatment' and definitions of 'cure' within, as well as between, cultures.

Moreover, Bhui and Bhugra's assertion regarding the need for more research
prior to the 'mapping' of local explanatory models of illness onto biomedical ones,
suggests not only that such an endeavour is possible, but also desirable, when in
fact, neither of these things is yet clear. What it *does* highlight, perhaps, is the predominance of biomedicine in the global mental health discourse—in both
research and practice. Indeed, treatment statistics regarding mental health care
in non-Western countries such as India and China tend to focus overwhelmingly
on simply those receiving *biomedical* treatment. However, this is only part of the
'global mental health' picture. In counting the numbers of 'psychiatrists' in non-
Western countries, as McKenzie, Patel and Araya do, above, the often rich and
diverse local healing traditions and practitioners—medical and/or religious—

who deal with mental illnesses in many cultural contexts are excluded. Traditional healers are often highly affordable, especially in comparison to biomedical services, which in countries without free or low-cost healthcare are often out of financial (and/or geographical) reach for many. Thus, whilst there may have been no 'psychiatrist' where Patel was looking when he described the 'extremely scarce' mental health resources in LAMIC (2007, 92), there may have been instead complex webs of local and traditional healing systems not recognised by biomedicine. As previous research has demonstrated, in many ethnically Tibetan communities, for example, medical and healing services often include a mix of herbal medicines and/or physical therapies (such as moxibustion, bloodletting, bone-setting and massage) offered by Sowa Rigpa, as well as religious healing rituals of numerous kinds, conducted by local monastic or non-monastic ritual specialists (such as spirit-mediums, Tantric practitioners or monks from local monasteries).

Making sense of mental illness and its treatment then, is a complex and often convoluted undertaking for patients and their families as well as for practitioners and researchers, frequently employing numerous explanatory models of illness, perhaps brought together in the form of an 'exploratory map', as Williams and Healy suggest. Kleinman differentiates between 'disease' and 'illness' (1977, 9), and a medically pluralistic environment will certainly offer patients multiple 'diseases' to accompany their 'illness', each one with its own causation, diagnosis, prognosis and treatment pathways. Furthermore, each diagnostic system both represents and encompasses its own theories of the body and the person—and perhaps also the environment—which may be highly culture-specific, and which might have broader implications in terms of a person's understanding of the world and their place within it. As Kirmayer argues, if there is cross-cultural variation in the concept of the person, then surely 'the goals and methods of therapeutic change must also differ' (2007, 233). One example of this is in explanations of spirit affliction, which are common in the Tibetan context, and which are discussed in the coming chapters, where we see wide differences between traditional and biomedical approaches to diagnosis and treatment. Thus, some mental health issues cut to the very questions about personhood and identity which are often viewed so differently cross-culturally, in a way that the majority of physical illnesses simply do not. For example, a broken arm quite clearly renders the sufferer in need of treatment of some kind, and may involve questions about traditional versus biomedical treatment, or the patient's ability to partake in their usual responsibilities within the family or community. However, it is unlikely to provoke questions for the patient about their concept of who they are, their role within the community, and what the condition means for them and their family in quite the same manner that an episode of madness or spirit possession is likely to.

Tibetan understandings of mental health, illness and healing have emerged from uniquely Tibetan concepts of the mind and body—particularly those related to *rlung* and its integral relationship to the mind and consciousness, as I will explore in this work. Thus, the spread of biomedicine in ethnically Tibetan communities and its underlying assumptions of the mind and body lead to questions regarding how individuals and their families make sense of mental illness and healing in medically pluralistic contexts such as Darjeeling. There, multiple models of health and illness—complete with their attendant treatment strategies—compete for attention and business. Moreover, an individual who perceives herself to be suffering from a spirit affliction, but whose doctor determines her to be suffering from a biomedically-recognised psychiatric illness, might find herself in a very difficult position, caught in a complex web of competing explanatory frameworks, at a time when she is particularly vulnerable. What does this mean then for those situated within a web of multiple health systems? Medical pluralism brings forth the possibility, not only as Bentall suggests, 'to be mad in one culture but at the same time sane in another' (2004, 132), but in fact to be simultaneously 'mad' and 'not mad' in one culture but in different parts of town, different treatment or hospital rooms. Here, an individual suffering from one condition may simultaneously inhabit multiple identities of health and illness.

This work thus examines Tibetan perspectives on mental illness in Darjeeling, and how lay understandings—which often differ significantly from 'official' Tibetan textual and biomedical perspectives—inform health-seeking behaviour. It looks at how, in this context, lay Tibetans respond to this pluralistic medical system in the understanding, management and treatment of mental illness, where multiple models of causation and treatment provide different—and sometimes conflicting—theories and treatment options. It focuses on the area of mental illness, as this is a sphere in which local explanatory frameworks often differ significantly from Western and biomedical concepts of health and illness, not only in terms of causation and treatment, but also in terms of symptoms and the boundaries between 'health' and 'illness'. Here, explanations of causation and treatment frequently involve the wider community and/or surrounding environment, are often related to Tibetan religious concepts, and can be uniquely reflective of Tibetan notions of the self. How Tibetans in such communities navigate the often new, plural medical systems in the event of mental illness, where traditional healing methods and medical systems sit alongside biomedical options remains largely unknown in areas such as this. One of the first places to house a Tibetan refugee settlement in the 1960s following the Chinese intervention in Tibet in 1950, Darjeeling remains an area with a fairly settled Tibetan exile population both within the Tibetan settlement (situated a few miles out of town) and living amongst the predominantly Nepali local population within the town itself. Some research has described medical pluralism in the area (see for example work by Gerke, 2010), but research into lay Tibetan perspectives in the arena of mental illness has so far been limited. Myers suggests that ethnographic research may be able to capture the ways in which 'individuals and their families make use of culturally available meanings to make sense of their illness experience and to find relief' (2011, 309–10). This research thus aims to examine how Tibetans understand mental illness and its treatment in a medically pluralistic context, and to investigate the diversity of health-seeking behaviour there. The work builds on the previous research in both Tibetan medicine and cross-cultural psychiatry, contributing significantly to debates within medical anthropology and the 'global mental health' arena.

In terms of what I have included and excluded as 'mental illness' here, I have included conditions defined as 'psychiatric' or 'mental illness' (Tib.: *sems nad*) by biomedicine and/or Sowa Rigpa, as well as those described as such by lay Tibetan informants.[6] This has allowed me to examine a number of diverse conditions, and to be led by informants' perceptions of mental health and illness in this pluralistic context. It has also, of course, led to a number of overlaps— where, for example, both individuals and their healing practitioners perceive a mental illness—and a number of divergences, where there were no easy 'matches' between the different systems, such as in the final case study, described in Chapter Nine, describing Dechen's experience of mediumship. Clearly understood as a case of spirit intervention by Dechen and her family, such situations were described by a local psychiatrist as 'psychosis', highlighting the very different perspectives often evident here.

The research presented here is based on two six-month periods of ethnographic fieldwork conducted in Darjeeling during 2011 and 2012 as part of my doctoral research undertaken at Cardiff University. It utilises four case studies to illustrate some lay perceptions of different mental health conditions and their causes and treatment, juxtaposed with Tibetan textual and biomedical explanations. Both these and the background interviews with lay Tibetans as well as monastic practitioners, Tibetan amchi and biomedical doctors help to draw out the complexities of the situation for individuals affected by different experiences of mental illness. Such cases can highlight the often diverse understandings of mental illness and healing and their implications for health-seeking behaviour for lay Tibetans. If,

---

6. Whilst there is debate over the validity of the various terms used to refer to 'mental illness', as I have referred to research across a number of different disciplines (some of which may disagree over the appropriate terminology), I have chosen to use the term 'mental illness', as it is the closest translation of the Tibetan *sems nad*.

as Bhui and Bhugra suggest, more work on understanding local explanations of illness and healing is necessary (2002, 6–7), then such research is overdue.

Following this Introduction, the book encompasses three parts. In Part One, two chapters provide an overview of the fieldsite and a brief discussion of research methodology, followed by an exploration of medicine and healing in Darjeeling—its practitioners, practices and institutions. In Part Two, Chapter Three introduces traditional Sowa Rigpa and Tibetan approaches to mental health and illness, discussing Tibetan medical literature, amchi practice and Tibetan diagnoses related to mental illness. Chapter Four examines the role of spirits and deities in the causation and healing of various forms of mental illness in the Tibetan context. Chapter Five explores biomedicine and its practice in the Tibetan context and in cross-cultural contexts more broadly, examining the history and controversies of Western approaches to mental illness and its biomedical classification systems and mental health policies, and how these play out in contemporary Tibetan communities. Part Three encompasses four case studies: the first case study in Chapter Six, of a man whom I refer to as 'Lobsang', brings the key Tibetan concept of *rlung* to life, demonstrating comparisons with Western notions of 'stress', 'depression' and 'anxiety', but illustrating the particularly Tibetan perception of the mind and body. The second case study, in Chapter Seven, 'Jigme', illustrates Tibetan understandings of 'madness', and highlights some of the different causation and treatment concepts involved in such cases. In Chapter Eight, the third case study, 'Wangmo', reveals the salience of 'belief' and religious authority for many Tibetans in the face of serious mental illness, as well as illustrating some of the 'causes' and 'conditions' of illness in the Tibetan context, such as karma and 'luck'. The final case study, 'Dechen', in Chapter Nine, highlights the complexities of 'possession' and mediumship, illustrating some of the significant differences between biomedical and Tibetan approaches to this experience. Following these, the Conclusion then draws together the common threads which run through these case studies and the broader interview material, which illustrate a number of common lay understandings of mental illness and its causation and treatment. Often centred around Tibetan religious concepts, in a reflection of broader Tibetan notions of the individual and the environment, these are significantly more comprehensive than Tibetan textual and biomedical perspectives. The highly pragmatic approach to health-seeking behaviour evidenced by this fieldwork material illustrates how these views are reflected in individuals' and their families' search for meaning and treatment in the event of an episode of mental illness, helping us to build up a picture of mental health and illness in this community and beyond.

PART ONE

THE SETTING AND THE APPROACH

CHAPTER ONE

RESIDENTS, MIGRANTS AND EXILES: A BRIEF HISTORY OF DARJEELING AND ITS COMMUNITIES

This research project is based on two six-month periods of ethnographic fieldwork I conducted in Darjeeling, northeast India during 2011 and 2012. The relationship between Darjeeling and Tibet has a long history, with the name 'Darjeeling' thought to come from the Tibetan *rDo rje ling* ("Dorjé ling", Diamond/Thunderbolt place) as a description of the long ridge around which the town is arranged (Jacobson 2000, 243). Today, Darjeeling is home to several thousand Tibetans, first-generation refugees who have followed their exiled leader, the Dalai Lama, into India since the Chinese intervention in Tibet in the 1950s, and their children and grandchildren, members of the growing Tibetan Diaspora. In addition, it is home to thousands of members of the ethnically and culturally Tibetan Bhutia community, whose history in the area can be traced back several hundred years. Bhutias are officially those who arrived from Tibet prior to 1959,[1] in comparison to the Tibetan exiles, who have arrived since then, or been born to exile parents. In this chapter, I will briefly examine the historical, geographical and political context of this fieldsite, including the rather complex history of Tibetans' residence in the area and the issue of Tibetan identity and the Bhutia status, which allows exiled Tibetans to take on Indian citizenship rather than refugee status. I will then move on

---

1. In fact, Bhutia is the Nepali and Hindi term for 'Tibetan', and this topic will be examined in more detail below.

to discuss research methodology, including issues of the ethnographic process which arose during the process of the fieldwork.

When considering potential fieldsite locations, I was aware that Dharamsala—home to the largest population of Tibetans outside Chinese-controlled Tibet—was host to some quite specific mental health issues, resulting from the large number of ex-political prisoners and individuals who have often left family behind in Tibet to come to India alone, at times via a long and sometimes dangerous journey. This often very difficult situation for Tibetans has generated a significant amount of research, much of it focused around coping strategies (Hussain and Bhushan 2011; Lewis 2013; Ruwanpura et al. 2006), the utility of certain Western approaches to treatment (Brock 2008; Mercer, Ager and Ruwanpura 2005) and the politicisation of particular diagnoses (Prost 2004, 2006, 2008). It is, however, a slightly different topic from the one I wished to examine—mainly the less politically-charged area of 'common' mental illness less related to the Tibetan political situation, which has thus far been rather neglected. Darjeeling, with a sizeable (and more settled) diasporic population of Tibetans—many of them now second- and third-generation exiles—seemed like a good location in which to examine these. That is not to say that one is ever really able to escape politics when involved in Tibetan life. In a sense, Tibetan politics pervade into every last corner but, as we shall see in this chapter, the Tibetan political discourse in Darjeeling is rather muted, and I thus expected it to form a smaller part of the discourse on mental health and illness there. In addition, Darjeeling has been the site of some previous research on mental illness (Jacobson 2000, 2002, 2007) which I was able to use as a jumping off point for my own research.

Darjeeling: History, Geography and Politics

Long before commencing this research, my first visit to Darjeeling in 2001 (as a tourist) involved inadvertently arriving in the town on the eve of a planned strike. This resulted in spending approximately five days holed up in a guesthouse (one of the few places open for business), while political tensions ratcheted up through the town, culminating in a midnight armed police-escorted flee back down the mountain road to the safety of the city of Siliguri. This was in fact a good introduction to the political troubles that have plagued Darjeeling since the mid-1980s, and which have only recently started to abate.

At an altitude of 7,000ft, Darjeeling is a growing town situated over a steep hillside in the northern part of the state of West Bengal in northeast India, bordered on three sides by mountains. It is situated between the state of Sikkim

Illustration 1. Darjeeling hills

(with its contested border with China) to the north, Nepal to the west and Bhutan beyond the mountains in the east. To the south lie the plains of West Bengal, with Siliguri the nearest large (and rapidly expanding) city three to four hours' drive away. On the outskirts of Siliguri lie Darjeeling's nearest train station (other than the toy train which travels *very* slowly up the mountain) at New Jalpaiguri, and airport at Bagdogra. Darjeeling's climate sees bitterly cold winters and an annual three-month monsoon from mid-June to mid-September. During this time it rains daily, the seemingly endless damp and fog hanging in the air and permeating everything. Moreover, Darjeeling's lack of infrastructure exacerbates the effects of the weather, where unpaved earth roads become mud pits for weeks at a time, and blocked drains are washed over by torrents of rain. Travel becomes difficult and dangerous during this time of year, and locals frequently advised me against taking any long trips into Sikkim during the monsoon (advice I was happy to heed, having heard frequent reports of mudslides). However, despite such inconveniences, Darjeeling's temperate climate—which attracts both foreign and Indian tourists, especially during India's hot summer season—is a pleasant and welcome relief from the heat of the Indian plains. In addition, the occasional glimpse of the snow-capped mountain top of Kanchenjunga or the other mountains that surround the Darjeeling Hills

Illustration 2. Darjeeling town

and the laid-back, friendly atmosphere of the town make it a pleasant and re-
laxing place to stay, despite its recent political troubles.

In the 1990s, the population of Darjeeling was said to be 60,000 (Jacobson
2000, 250); by the 2001 census, its population was numbered at 106,257 (Gerke
2012a, 39). However, such figures are often said to be rather unreliable low estimates which exclude villages (Gerke 2012a, 39) and, in reality, Darjeeling's
boundaries are rather 'indefinite', making it difficult to get any kind of accurate
statistics (Jacobson 2000, 250). Situated in the Singalila mountain range in the
eastern Himalayas, contemporary Darjeeling is 'the hub of transportation, education, governmental administration, telecommunications, and health care'
for the entire West Bengal Hills region (Jacobson 2000, 252). One of its main
economies, the tea trade, is illustrated by the tea-covered hills and valleys expanding out of town in every direction and the numerous tea shops dotted
around the area. In addition, the large number of hotels and guesthouses—
offering a full range of options from the very basic to very luxurious—indicates
a tourism trade which thrives despite the political problems which have dogged
Darjeeling over the past three decades. Restaurants, souvenir shops and market
stalls, selling everything from jewellery, clothes and traditionally-crafted items
to high- (and low-) end tea attest to this significant part of the local economy

Illustration 3. Tea plantation workers in Arya Tea Garden, Darjeeling

too. Darjeeling is a popular destination for Indian tourists, and to a lesser extent, foreign tourists. As a result, the summers find huge numbers of visitors crowding the market stall-lined streets, as Bengalis particularly make the trip north to escape the heat of the plains.

It was Darjeeling's temperate climate which also attracted the British to the area during the colonial era, leading to its development as a hill station, and its becoming one of India's 'largest and most popular British retreats' (Jacobson 2000, 244). The construction of Hill Cart Road, the main road into Darjeeling from the plains to the south, was completed in 1866, and was followed by a construction boom, as buildings including churches, schools, hospitals and missionary schools were built (Dasgupta 1999, 51). Many of these schools re-main popular and highly-regarded, drawing students from across India and also southeast Asia in addition to local students.

In terms of its population, prior to the British annexation of parts of the region from Sikkim (at that time an independent Tibetan Buddhist state), the Darjeeling hills were rather 'sparsely populated' by Lepcha (who claim to be the indigenous inhabitants of the region), Bhutia, Limbu and Magar; with Nepali Buddhist groups, such as the Yolmo, Tamang and Sherpa resident in the area for 'several centuries' (Gerke 2012a, 46–50). Nepali migrant workers started to arrive in the Darjeeling region from the early nineteenth century onwards, leading to a 'Nepalisation' of the region, and today the majority of the contemporary population is made up of ethnic groups such as the Gurung, Rai and Newar. And, whilst Nepali immigrants continue to arrive in the area, the majority of Nepalis in the region are now Indian citizens (Gerke 2012a, 49–50). In addition, members of numerous Indian social castes who have come to the area for trading and business purposes reside in and around the town.

It is this 'Nepalisation' described by Gerke that has led to Darjeeling's long-running political problems, which have only recently calmed down. The past few decades have witnessed an often violent campaign for independence from West Bengal, as the resident Nepalis call for an independent state of 'Gorkha-land'—a demand which reaches back to 1906 (Gerke 2012a, 51).[2] This campaign has resulted in violence and disruption in the area: the mid-1980s were marked by strikes—during which everything, including businesses and schools, closed—and violence, particularly during the 'agitation' which lasted from 1986 to 1988. This period saw hundreds of deaths and injuries, the destruction of houses, government buildings and vehicles, and significant disruption to the three main local economies of tea, tourism and timber (Dasgupta 1999, 65–6). However, even after the agitation officially ended in 1988, acrimony continued, amid claims that significant economic development had been impossible due to state obstructions (Sonntag 2003, 190). Heavy protests, assassinations, indefinite strikes, interparty violence, and attacks on government offices continued (Middleton, 2013, 618), and in 2010 a prominent Gorkha politician was violently attacked and killed in the centre of town.[3] Certainly, a lack of investment in infrastructure in Darjeeling was obvious during my time there—particularly when compared to nearby Siliguri. Strikes and violence had left the town with limited growth and employment prospects and a damaged tourist industry, and an almost non-existent evening social scene, where everything except perhaps a handful of bars closed by 9pm every night. In addition, power cuts (some scheduled as 'load shedding' off the supply, others unexpected) were frequent, and many of the town's unpaved roads turned to impassable mud during the annual monsoon, as the rain washed away the ground, exposing pipes and cables and thus damaging the

---

2. There are a number of precedents for this in other areas of India, such as a similar campaign in 2000 which was successful in achieving statehood for Uttarakhand, separating it from the state of Uttar Pradesh, within which it had previously been included.

3. http://timesofindia.indiatimes.com/india/Gorkha-leader-Madan-Tamang-hacked-in-public/articleshow/5960365.cms.

water and electricity supply further. Whilst I was in Darjeeling in July 2011, national newspapers reported that the Gorkhaland Territorial Administration (GTA) would replace the Darjeeling Gorkha Hill Council, with '[a]ll major differences ... put to rest'.[4] Nevertheless, whilst Darjeeling no longer experienced the kind of violence seen in the 1980s, intermittent strikes continued, causing disruption to businesses and schools in the area.[5]

Tibetans in Darjeeling: Building a Home in the Darjeeling Hills

In Darjeeling, first-, second- and third-generation Tibetan exiles reside at both the Tibetan Refugee Self-Help Centre (TRSHC) situated a thirty-minute walk down a steep path from Darjeeling town square (or twenty-minute drive along the main road from the bottom of town), and within the town itself, amongst the majority Nepali population, who are usually referred to by Tibetans as 'local people'. According to the Central Tibetan Administration (CTA)'s first demographic survey of Tibetans in India and Nepal conducted in 1998, there were 2,455 Tibetans living in Darjeeling at that time (Gerke 2012a, 56–57). In 2011, the Tibetan Settlement Office accountant, Tsering Dhondup, estimated the Tibetan population to be 'about four or five thousand', but noted that it was difficult to say, as definitive figures were lacking, and a number of school-age Tibetans were studying in other towns and cities.[6] In addition, in Darjeeling, the situation was complicated by the 'Bhutia' issue, and figures may well be much higher than such surveys suggest (Gerke 2012a, 57). These estimates compare with an overall Tibetan population in India of around 94,203 (estimates from the CTA Demographic Survey of Tibetans in Exile 2009, by the CTA Planning Commission 2010).[7]

---

4. http://www.telegraphindia.com/1110709/jsp/frontpage/story_14215656.jsp.

5. Unfortunately, since I completed my fieldwork, the area has again experienced protests and prolonged strikes as a result of this ongoing issue, commencing in June 2017 (see http://www.bbc.co.uk/news/world-asia-india-40491066).

6. Interview conducted with Tsering Dhondup at Keventer's Restaurant, Darjeeling, by the author, 11th August 2011.

7. This survey numbers Tibetans residing outside Tibet at 128,014, with 13,514 in Nepal, 1,298 in Bhutan and 18,999 in rest of the world (http://tibet.net/about-cta/tibet-in-exile/).

Exile and the Tibetan Refugee Self-Help Centre (TRSHC)

Gerke has pointed out the significant dearth of ethnographic research on Tibetans in the Darjeeling area between the work of Beatrice Miller in the 1950s (1956) and that of Tanka Subba in the 1980s (1988, 1990) (Gerke 2012a, 45). It is not entirely clear when Tibetans first settled in the area, although they are thought to have been arriving along the trade route from southeast Tibet into Sikkim and the Darjeeling hills from the latter part of the nineteenth century, some of them taking on Indian citizenship (Gerke 2012a, 48–49).[8] Some of these earlier migrants were highly successful, and Jacobson describes one family who owned 'half of the real estate in the center of the city' until the majority of their property was annexed during the 1986 Gorkha uprising (2000, 244).

In the early twentieth century, the thirteenth Dalai Lama briefly escaped to Darjeeling from Tibet during a Chinese invasion (1910–12) (Jacobson 2000, 246). Following the 1950 Chinese intervention in Tibet and the Tibetan Uprising against the Chinese in 1959, the fourteenth Dalai Lama fled Tibet, followed by a large number of Tibetans who either left soon after, or fled—and continue to do so—in the intervening decades. The Indian Prime Minister at the time, Jawaharlal Nehru, and his government agreed to host the Tibetan refugees, setting aside portions of land for refugee camps. The fourteenth Dalai Lama's 'government-in-exile'—officially named the 'Central Tibetan Administration' (CTA)—was established in Dharamsala, northwest India, and became the centre of administration for Tibetans living across India.[9] From here, an 'elaborate structure of social services' including health, education and welfare programmes for Tibetan exiles is managed (Jacobson 2000, 241). As a consequence, Dharamsala became and remains the most popular destination for Tibetans arriving in India, and is also a focus of foreign tourism for those interested in Tibetan culture, language and/or Tibetan Buddhism and Tibetan aid projects (on which the Tibetan community remains dependent (Prost 2004, 22)). The interest in Tibet's culture and political cause from Westerners has led to both positive and negative consequences for Tibetans: whilst financial aid is often forthcoming, Western expectations of Tibetan culture and religion

---

8. Indeed, Jacobson noted that at least one Tibetan family in the area can trace its arrival to the time of the British Raj (2000, 243–44).

9. The Dalai Lama officially stepped down as Tibet's political leader in 2011, overseeing democratic elections leading to the election of the current *srid skyong* (commonly translated by Tibetans in Darjeeling as 'Prime Minister'), Lobsang Sangay, who hails from Darjeeling, and had attended the Tibetan school there.

can weigh heavily on the community itself. In Dharamsala, for example, I heard several Western tourists voicing surprise and disappointment that young Tibetans were listening to modern 'pop' music rather than Buddhist chants! Such expectations of Tibetan culture's 'spirituality' may ignore the difficult realities of everyday life for many refugees, such as poverty and intra-community tensions. Anand goes so far as to suggest that the Western concept of 'Tibet' operates as 'a physical and imaginative playground for Westerners and their desires', where Tibet is seen to offer 'essential spiritual services to humanity' (2000, 160–1; see also Anand 2002, 2008 and Prost 2004, 2008 for more on this). Over the last sixty years, as more Tibetans have travelled to India, Tibetan settlements have been set up across the country, with 35 Tibetan settlements now located across India (Prost 2004, 16). Similarly, as monastic practitioners have arrived in India, numerous monasteries have been re-established across the country, with 127 established between 1959 and 1976 (Subba 1990, 159).

During the early years of the Chinese occupation, many Tibetans escaped along the old Lhasa-Bengal Hills trade route, with Darjeeling becoming one of their principle destinations (Jacobson 2000, 246). Darjeeling's TRSHC was founded in 1959, one of the first Tibetan settlements established in India, and today has a population of approximately three hundred.[10] The centre encompasses a number of (mostly very small) houses and rooms, a small temple with a resident monk, small infant school, meal hall with space for residents and non-residents to attend religious rituals, a permanent photography exhibition on the history of the centre and on Tibetan wildlife, history and politics, a number of workshops, shop and a small biomedical clinic (founded in 1961). A minority (around 90)[11] of those living at the centre make their living from traditional Tibetan handicrafts in the onsite workshops, such as carpet-weaving, woodcarving, sewing and knitting, items of which are sold in the onsite shop. In return, they receive housing at the centre, some meals and a small wage.

Today, the majority of those working there are first-generation exiles now in their sixties and seventies. Indeed, the vast majority of TRSHC's residents are first-generation exiles who fled Tibet in the 1960s, and some of their children and grandchildren. Many of the younger generation have left the settlement to live and work either in Darjeeling town or in larger Indian cities or

---

10. Estimated by the Secretary of the TRSHC, Chimay Rinchen (interview conducted in his office by the author, 20th September 2011). There is also another Tibetan settlement, the Refugee Cooperative Association of Sonada, approximately 17km away in the small town of Sonada.

11. Estimated by the Secretary of the TRSHC, Chimay Rinchen (interview conducted in his office by the author, 20th September 2011).

Illustration 4. Traditional carpet-weaving at the TRSHC

abroad. A number of older Tibetan residents explained that the younger generation often prefer not to work there, not keen on the hard manual work or the low wages. They described how in the past, the centre had exported large numbers of made-to-order carpets abroad, but these days the operation was significantly smaller. With the low salary difficult to live on, a number of the older residents talked about the 'lucky' ones (themselves or others) who had at least one child working either in a large Indian city or in the USA or Europe, able to send money home for them, and thus putting them in a better financial situation.[12]

However, despite the significant decrease in numbers of residents at the centre, it was evident that it retained a fairly central role in the Tibetan community. Religious and secular events were often hosted here, such as celebrations for the Dalai Lama's birthday (which included speeches, traditional Tibetan dances

---

12. In Dharamsala similarly—despite the international financial aid which often causes friction between the Tibetan community and its Indian neighbours—Tibetans often exist in very difficult economic circumstances: see, for example, some of the 'life stories' described by Vahali (2009).

Illustration 5. One of the residents carding wool at
one of the TRSHC workshops

and music) and Buddhist teachings, generally attended by large numbers of
Tibetans from both the centre and the town. Indeed, while I was there in October 2012, a celebration was held in honour of a very popular (then semi-re-
tired) local biomedical doctor, Dr. Wangdi, to thank him for his many years
of service to the Tibetan community. This event, which lasted most of the day,
included speeches of thanks and performances of Tibetan dance and song.
This sense of community was also evident in other ways, such as the care shown
to one resident unable to look after himself, whose case study is described in
Chapter Seven.

Tibetans living in Darjeeling were involved with varied businesses in town, from the ownership and management of hotels, rooms and restaurants for short- and long-staying visitors to the area, to the running of market stalls and a number of small shops. Indeed, residing there in the 1990s, Jacobson noted that Tibetans were 'economically integrated' — working in the same jobs as the Nepalis (2000, 252–53). In Darjeeling (similarly to Dharamsala) the international support sometimes received by Tibetans has served to increase their economic status, but has also led to Tibetan-Nepali tension (Gerke 2012a, 55). Nonetheless, many Tibetans continued to have little economic stability, moving from sector to sector — and sometimes location to location — depending on the work available. As in many other areas in India, some Tibetans in this situation spent the winter as 'sweater sellers' in other regions of the country, returning home to Darjeeling and seeking temporary work again when the season has finished. Furthermore, the economic (and political) situation for Tibetans living in the Darjeeling area was further complicated by the issue of the Bhutia status, as we shall see.

Tibetan Identity and the Bhutia Status

The Tibetan community in Darjeeling differs significantly from other Tibetan exile communities in India, where there is often a clear cultural, ethnic and linguistic 'divide' evident between the Tibetans and their (usually predominantly Hindu) Indian neighbours. In Dharamsala, home to the Dalai Lama and CTA, as well as a constant stream of new refugees, Prost describes Tibetan identity as focused around the twin focal points of 'religiosity and refugeehood' (2004, 19). In contrast, in Darjeeling, situated amongst a number of Nepali Tibetan Buddhist communities, the Tibetans are less distinguishable from their neighbours and today, many younger Tibetans speak Nepali as a first language (Gerke 2010, 340–41). In addition, due to the historical migration of Tibetans into the area, for Tibetans in the Darjeeling hills, there is an option of officially becoming an Indian citizen through the adoption of the Bhutia status. The Bhutia are classified as one of India's Scheduled Tribes: ethnically and culturally Tibetan, the majority arrived in the area from Tibet as traders over the last few hundred years. However, whilst the Bhutia are officially those who left Tibet prior to 1950 — as compared to the Tibetan exiles or refugees who have left as a direct result of the political situation since then — local Tibetans are in fact free to become Indian citizens through this route, if they so wish.

As recognised refugees in India, Tibetans (whether first- or later-generation) can get a 'Refugee Certificate' (RC), which is issued by the government of India and gives them permission to stay in the country. They may also have a Green

Pass (also known as a 'Green Book' or 'Voluntary Contribution Pass'), which functions as a form of Tibetan identity card, issued by the CTA, and a Blue (Refugee) Pass (Gerke 2012a, 60). However, this refugee status has some limitations: for example, it can be very difficult to get a visa to travel outside of India with only Tibetan 'refugee' documents. Taking Bhutia status can thus make life considerably easier in some areas: as a member of a Scheduled Tribe—and therefore an Indian citizen—not only can one get a passport, but since 1990, Indian government benefits have been available to different ethnic groups, including those under the category of Scheduled Tribes, such as the Bhutia (Gerke 2012a, 58–59). However, those who choose Bhutia status for pragmatic reasons may be viewed somewhat negatively by other Tibetans, particularly as it is impossible to be simultaneously both an 'Indian citizen' *and* a 'Tibetan refugee', meaning that choosing one necessarily means giving up—at least in official documents—the other.[13] Furthermore, despite the cultural (and ethnic) similarities between Tibetans and some of their Nepali neighbours, tensions between the communities are evident, and the Bhutia issue has sometimes contributed to this. During his stay in Darjeeling in the 1990s, Jacobson witnessed an anti-Tibetan demonstration (2000, 269), and Gerke argues that 'anti-Tibetan resentment' has resulted from a number of issues, including the fact that Tibetans (presumably those who arrived after 1950) have been able to secure 'key positions' in Indian administration and police services through their Bhutia status (2012a, 54–55). As Subba suggested, whilst 'physical and cultural similarities' between a refugee and his host community can initially be helpful, 'if he succeeds in improving his lot considerably he becomes an eyesore' (1990, 10). Jacobson argued that in Darjeeling, as in other areas of India, the Tibetan population is:

> at once stigmatized and welcomed, both resented and appreciated for their economic successes and ability to attract aid and tourists, sometimes tolerated as just another of the numerous ethnic minorities which populate India's urban regions, but at other times the focus of sudden mass demonstrations which they are never sure will remain non-violent (2000, 273–74).

Thus Tibetans in Darjeeling and the surrounding area may be simultaneously inhabiting multiple identities, and Gerke suggests that being 'Tibetan' in the

---

13. Indeed, when I asked Dolma, a second-generation exile, about this, she responded indignantly, 'But who wants to do that?!… Everything we have here [in India] is because of the Dalai Lama, so Tibetans don't want to take Bhutia status—not first-, second- or third-generation Tibetans'.

Darjeeling hills often 'primarily means having Tibetan ancestors, adhering to various sorts of popular Tibetan Buddhism, but living a modern Nepali-Indian urban life-style' (2010, 339–40).[14] However, for Tibetans arriving in the area from different parts of India, for example CTA staff or Tibetan medical practitioners, as Gerke notes, this can sometimes be an isolating situation (2012a, 64). Without Nepali language (and depending on their and their new neighbours' knowledge of English), adapting to life in Darjeeling can be quite difficult.

Against this complex backdrop of local Gorkha politics and Tibetan identity politics, Tibetans tend to stay out of the local political discourse, with older generations of Tibetans often also keeping their public statements on Tibetan politics low key (Gerke 2012a, 55–56). However, this is perhaps changing. With the recent—and continuing—wave of Tibetan self-immolation protests across Tibet and China (as well as in India and Nepal), young Tibetans in Darjeeling seemed noticeably politically engaged while I was there. Peaceful candle marches were held frequently, and were well-attended by Tibetans of all ages.

Tibetan Organisations and Institutions in Darjeeling

The Darjeeling Tibetan exile community was generally well-organised, with the 'Tibetan Settlement Office'—a branch of the CTA which deals with the Tibetan community in the Darjeeling area—situated fairly centrally in town. Below the office on the ground floor was a small Tibetan Buddhist temple and community space, used for community gatherings and certain monastic rituals. Nearby was the Tibetan Settlement Diagnostic Clinic and Printing Press. In addition, the community had a further welfare/social system known as the *skyi sdug* ("kidu") system, imported to Darjeeling from Tibet and found in Tibetan communities across India, where it functions as a 'source of aid and comfort' during difficult times for its members (Miller 1956, 150). Whilst *skyi sdug* groups are often arranged around a family's birthplace (for example, Kham in eastern Tibet or Amdo in northeastern Tibet), there are in fact a number of deciding factors bearing on potential membership, including occupation, lo-

---

14. In this research project, all but two of my Tibetan informants described themselves as 'Tibetan'—all either first-generation exiles who had left Tibet after 1950, or the children or grandchildren of those who had. Two informants described themselves as 'Bhutia', and had one first-generation exile parent, and one parent who had left Tibet before this time, whom they described as either 'Tibetan' or 'Bhutia'. Whether any informants had taken Bhutia status for any political, financial or other reason(s) I did not ask, due to the fact that this was clearly a sensitive issue for many Tibetans, which could cause significant tensions within the community.

cation or acquaintance with other members (Miller 1956, 162). Organisations such as the Tibetan Women's Association (TWA) and Tibetan Youth Congress (TYC) were operating in Darjeeling as in Tibetan communities across India.

Darjeeling is home to a number of Tibetan-run institutions. The Manjushree Center of Tibetan Culture is located near the centre of town, teaching Tibetan language to local and foreign students. Staffed by Tibetans (mainly second-generation exiles who had grown up in the area), the centre was founded and financially supported by several local Tibetan families (Jacobson 2000, 263). In addition, funds came from foreign student fees and donations, and hotel rooms run by the centre within the building. While I was there, construction work commenced on a planned museum in the basement of the centre.

Darjeeling also houses one of the Central Schools for Tibetans (CST) which accepts local Tibetan children as well as Tibetan children from poor families all over India, and is funded by the Indian government. With schools across India, CSTs teach in the medium of Tibetan, and the Darjeeling CST was also the site of Tibetan cultural and political events, such as visits by high lamas and celebrations for the Dalai Lama's birthday and suchlike.[15] Admissions at CST have been declining however, as many parents choose the economic and practical advantages of an English language education for their children if they can, sending them to schools where the second and third language options are usually limited to Nepali, Hindi, Bengali and/or Sanskrit. Furthermore, Indian-born Tibetans who have taken on Indian citizenship through the Bhutia status are ineligible for enrolment (Gerke 2012a, 74).

Darjeeling Encounters: Conducting Ethnography in Darjeeling

Research Methodology

This project is based on qualitative research methodology, encompassing participant-observation and in-depth interviews with members of the com-

---

15. I visited the school a few times with one of my Tibetan teachers, who visited weekly to give a small amount of pocket money (either donated by herself or by Manjushree students) to the forty-seven young children aged five to ten from very low families who were living far away from home there, looked after by two 'house mothers'. Some of the girls offered to show us their room, where there were ninety-six beds, made up of two rows of small three-tiered bunk beds pushed up next to each other. The youngest ones slept at the bottom, teenagers at the top. Each student had one trunk of belongings, stacked up neatly against walls and windows, with the older girls allowed a small cupboard each.

munity in Darjeeling, several of whom became key informants over the extended period of fieldwork, as well as a handful in Dharamsala and Delhi. When I arrived in Darjeeling in June 2011, I enrolled as a Tibetan language student at the Manjushree Center of Tibetan Culture. During the initial few months of fieldwork, I focused my attention on language study there, attending Tibetan language classes with other foreigners alongside regular private classes with one of the Tibetan teachers there. As a well-regarded local institution for Tibetan language (teaching both locals and foreigners), affiliation with Manjushree also afforded me an introduction into the Tibetan community. During fieldwork, I also made several trips to the neighbouring state of Sikkim and some other surrounding areas. Sikkim is a restricted area, with travel to different places requiring various permits, and some areas (such as those close to the disputed border with the PRC) closed to foreigners. However, permits to the capital, Gangtok, are easy to acquire and issued in twenty-four hours, although foreigners are required to leave three months between each visit (a rule I found to be enforced rather sporadically).

I thus conducted two periods of ethnographic research, involving a combination of participant-observation, semi-structured interviews, and a vast amount of what is probably best described as 'general chit-chat' as I asked endless questions and initiated discussions as and when they arose during conversations with Tibetan friends and informants. I chose participant-observation as I hoped that it would allow for both the observation of certain 'everyday' behaviours and the opportunity to experience certain situations and events in a manner not entirely dissimilar from that of my informants. This was particularly useful in the sphere of healing rituals, for example, where I was able to observe proceedings and ask questions of those involved (including religious practitioners and lay attendees), as well as experiencing the rituals as an attendee myself, often receiving blessings and/or empowered substances alongside other participants. In addition, due to the lack of research on this topic, I found that semi-structured interviews were able to provide some common starting points, whilst simultaneously allowing space for the interview topics to be shaped by interviewees, leaving room for informants to share illness narratives if they wished. I used chain referral sampling to recruit interviewees, attempting to interview a diverse range of individuals within the community. Some interviews were recorded with a digital voice recorder (especially those more 'official' interviews with medical professionals) and transcribed. However, some individuals were uncomfortable with this, and consequently the majority of interviews went unrecorded, with my taking copious notes during and straight after, recording my own thoughts and observations alongside them.

I conducted twenty-six general interviews with lay Tibetans residing in and around Darjeeling. These varied in length and depth depending on the individuals' time and willingness (although in most cases, they lasted approximately 1–1½ hours), and were generally carried out wherever the interviewee suggested—often in the individual's house or place of work where, in such cases, we were usually alone for the interview duration. In a few cases, a Tibetan friend acted as a translator. Several of these individuals became key informants or friends—often both—with a few people in particular inviting me frequently into their homes, involving me in daily life, and rarely displaying any impatience with answering my endless questions. In particular, I frequently visited a group of four elderly *momo-la*[16] at the TRSHC. Initially visiting to practise my Tibetan language, they showed endless patience with my initially rather mediocre language skills, inviting me into their homes, and letting me sit with them in their workshop while they worked—sometimes chatting in Tibetan, sometimes getting me to translate for them when Western tourists visited the centre and asked questions about the traditional Tibetan crafts they were engaged in. The majority had fled Tibet in 1959 or soon after, and spoke a form of Tibetan I understood more easily from my previous language study in Lhasa than some of the younger Tibetans in town, whose Tibetan language often appeared more influenced by their knowledge of Indian and/or Nepali languages and English. Interactions with these *momo-la* and other key informants sometimes seemed to sit in a kind of no-man's land between general 'chitchat' and 'interview', as we discussed topics as they arose. Participation in the project was of course on a voluntary basis, with special consideration taken due to the often sensitive nature of the research. Excepting biomedical and Tibetan medical practitioners who were interviewed in their official capacity, all informants' names have been anonymised, and certain details (such as place names) have been changed to protect their identity.

I had several main themes which were the focus of the semi-structured interviews: questions surrounding perceptions of the prevention and cause(s) of episodes which might be interpreted by biomedicine or Sowa Rigpa as indicative of mental illnesses; the manifestation of such illnesses and views on various healing and treatment methods and medical systems, and their success in dealing with these illnesses. The interviews themselves, however, were constantly evolving, changing and adapting as a result of the interview process itself, as I experienced fieldwork as a creative process. As informants

---

16. "*Momo-la*" (Tib.: *rmo mo lags*) literally means 'grandmother', and is a polite address to older women. Similarly "*Bobo-la*" (Tib.: *spo bo lags*), meaning 'grandfather', is used to address/refer to older men.

raised new topics, and friends took the time to discuss Tibetan terms and concepts, interview themes broadened in scope. When themes recurred in interviews, I incorporated them into my questions, often returning to interviewees to include them in follow up questions, allowing, as Silverman states, data collection, hypothesis construction, and theory building to interweave with one another (2000, 143), as the research narrowed its focus over its course.

I gathered a number of stories related in some way to mental illness and have included four of these as starting points for four chapters in Part Three, having gathered data through in-depth interviews with either the individuals themselves, or close family or community members. Most of these interviews were conducted in the individuals' homes. I conducted four more formal, semi-structured interviews with Tibetan amchi working in Darjeeling and Gangtok, and two with biomedical psychiatrists working in Darjeeling. In general, these interviews were conducted in the practitioners' clinics, where they were kind enough to give me time during quiet periods of their work. In Dharamsala I interviewed three specialists: Amchi Dorjee Rabten; Amchi Sonam Dolma, at that time head of the Translation Department at the Men-Tsee-Khang (MTK), the Tibetan government-in-exile-affiliated Tibetan Medical and Astrological Institute; and Dr Tsetan Dorji Sadutshang, Chief Medical Officer (CMO) of the local biomedical Delek Hospital. Additionally, in Delhi I interviewed the late Amchi Pema Dorjee at his home in Manju-ka-tilla, the Tibetan area of the city. In Darjeeling I interviewed a number of religious specialists: four local Nepali spirit-mediums, all interviewed in their homes and temples where they practised; one Tibetan *sngags pa* (a particular kind of Tantric practitioner from the Nyingma Tibetan Buddhist tradition), interviewed at his home just outside Darjeeling; and three monks at the largest local Tibetan Buddhist monastery, Dali Gonpa (see the next chapter for a description of the medical and healing facilities in Darjeeling and the surrounding area).

In interviews, I included amongst my topics conditions classified as a mental illness by biomedical classification (according to the DSM-IV TR or ICD-10) or described as 'illnesses of the mind' (Tib.: *sems nad*) or 'madness' (Tib.: *smyo nad*) by Tibetan amchi or the Tibetan medical texts, or in lay perceptions. This allowed for the inclusion of a broad range of conditions, some classified as an 'illness' by only one or the other of these systems. It also enabled an examination of the boundaries of health and illness as perceived by my informants, in a way which also makes sense from Western understandings of mental health and illness, and allowed for some comparison between perspectives in the different systems. Sometimes, interviewees (especially those with a high level of English) felt that psychiatric terms and concepts were translatable across the Tibetan-Western cultural boundaries; at other times, English terms relating to mental illness or symptoms were not known, or were perceived as entirely different phenomena from known disorders in Tibetan culture.

Roles, Perceptions, and Expectations

My position and role within the community changed and evolved, not only over the fieldwork period, as I built relationships with people within it, but also across different sections of the community, adapting to the different situations I found myself in. For the initial months of my stay I was a 'Manjushree student', seemingly given a certain amount of regard as a result of my language study and obvious interest in Tibetan culture. I was frequently assumed to be a Buddhist practitioner and, as I understood it, accorded a layer of respect for this (I frequently overheard the *momo-la* at TRSHC introducing me as a Buddhist, even after I had explained that this was not the case).[17] Seemingly, my interest in Tibetan culture and ability to speak some Tibetan encouraged discussion of Tibetan cultural concepts, and the fact that I had previously studied Tibetan language in Lhasa for one year was often a good starting point. Older Tibetans, such as the *momo-la* at TRSHC, who had mostly left Tibet in their late teens or early twenties, were keen to discuss the current situation there, and on one occasion on a visit to a local monastery, a group of older monks called me over, explaining that they had heard I had studied in Lhasa, and wanted to ask me some questions about my experience there. Furthermore, in asking questions about Sowa Rigpa or medicine in general, and being seen with both Tibetan and biomedical doctors, I was sometimes assumed to be a biomedical doctor, which may have afforded entry into certain situations or places, such as a hospital psychiatric ward, although in such cases, I was careful to clarify my position.

In terms of 'participant-observation', my role often seemed to segue (sometimes intentionally, sometimes entirely unexpectedly) from observer, to participant, and back again. This was often a result of people's willingness to invite me to participate in rituals when I showed an interest in them (this happened both during monastic rituals at Dali Gonpa and at Nepali spirit-

---

17. This is likely due to the fact that the majority of foreigners studying at the institute tend to study Tibetan language as part of their Buddhist study; whilst I was there I was one of only two students engaged in academic research, with the other researcher a practising Buddhist.

mediums' rituals). People's willingness to answer questions or involve an interested stranger in both their daily activities and religious events was a constant source of happy surprise, and I found that sometimes simply an enthusiastic enquiry was enough to open doors which had previously appeared closed.

These different roles, of course, can elicit differing reactions and responses from people: I cannot pretend that those who initially assumed me to be some kind of medical professional may not have reacted differently to my presence than those who had become close friends, and had become inured to my constant questions regarding their daily activities and opinions. Bearing this in mind, I often had to explain what I was doing, and what I was interested in, in different ways, depending on my audience. At times, this meant discussing mental health, illness and healing in the UK with amchi to answer their questions and give some context to my own interest in the topic; at others (particularly when talking to older Tibetans) it was helpful to describe my time in Lhasa and my interest in Tibetan culture. In addition, when discussing cases of illness, I tried as much as possible to be led by the interviewees' own Tibetan or English diagnoses and/or categorisations of illness. Here, as the observer and interviewer, it was inevitable that I, too, shaped the narratives (both intentionally and inadvertently) elucidated from my informants: as Rapport suggests, just as the field started to 'take shape' for me, the field itself was also shaped by my interactions with it (1997, 179).

During the fieldwork, differing views on whether talking about a problem helps or hinders became apparent. Notions of a 'cathartic' approach to psychological pain or trauma are common in contemporary Western culture (reflected, of course, in such sayings as 'a problem shared is a problem halved'). I think it is important to point out that these ideas are not necessarily universal. Discussion of psychological distress is not common in Tibetan culture (Ruwanpura et al. 2006, 191, 196), and I was told several times by informants that talking about a problem might make it worse for the afflicted individual. I was, therefore, mindful of this in my interviews, consistently ensuring interviewees' willingness to discuss their experiences of their own or others' illness. As a non-medical practitioner, I of course never recommended any possible treatments, and was careful to clarify that I had no professional expertise to do so.

In this kind of ethnographic fieldwork, it is of course not possible to include large numbers of informants in the same way as in quantitative research and, as in all forms of social science research, conclusions can be influenced by the researcher's viewpoint and experience of fieldwork, as well as its practicalities (Jacobson 2000, 75–76). However, this kind of methodology can afford a detailed depiction of a community through an in-depth examination of the data through its context (Nurani 2008, 442), and I attempted to include a broad range of views on the research topic, through interviewing a wide range of individuals within the community. I was aware of the possible influence that my presence or participation, as a foreign observer, might have had on the behaviour of my study population, as noted by Nurani (2008, 443). However, I felt that over time, as my presence as a researcher became more frequent and thus more normalised, this effect likely reduced. This is, I would suggest, a particularly pertinent issue in the context of the Tibetan exile situation. Many factors underlie a desire—whether conscious or subconscious—to promote a particular depiction of one's culture, and it would be short-sighted to suggest that Tibetans are not aware of how much of their sponsorship (both financial and political) is reliant on a particular portrayal of Tibetan culture and religion (including concepts of a 'peaceful' Buddhist religion, and the notion of some kind of historical Tibetan 'Shangri-la'). Non-Tibetans have also colluded in both constructing and maintaining this image, which both benefits and constrains Tibetans and their culture (Dodin and Rather 1996; Lopez 1999), and I was aware that my own presence—and interpretations—were situated within this context. This question of identity (both individual and group) construction is an issue for any researcher dealing with narrative (although it may be true to a greater or lesser extent in different communities, as a result of political, socioeconomic, cultural or religious circumstances). However, over my time in Darjeeling I started to read between the lines a little more and adapt my line of questioning when I felt it might elicit the slightly less considered responses I was seeking, often asking hypothetical questions about mental health, illness and its healing, which I found often led to complex replies and lengthy discussions.

In this kind of ethnographic fieldwork, it is very difficult to draw a clear line between the data and its interpretation where perhaps, as Clifford suggested, the 'constructed, artificial nature' of writing ethnography leads to an 'invention' rather than 'representation' of cultures (1986, 2). While it is impossible to escape one's own educational, socioeconomic or philosophical background to access another's perspective, the experience of ethnography itself can thus enhance our understanding of the community within which we are working. Here, as Luhrmann suggests, our very bodily and psychological orientations can affect the judgements we make about others (2010), and 'data' encompasses the ethnographer's own experience as well as what she observes. Within this context, as I attempted to see around the edges of my own views and understand my own experience, I also tried to allow my informants' words to speak for themselves as much as possible in, as Tyler described it, the 'evocation' that is ethnography (1986, 122–23).

Linguistic and Translation Issues

Aside from my interviews with Nepali spirit-mediums, which were conducted entirely in Hindi with the aid of a translator, interviews were conducted in a mix of Tibetan and English, depending on interviewees' and my own linguistic abilities. Conversation with the *momo-la*, most of whom spoke no English, were predominantly in Tibetan, and these were frustrating and rewarding in turn, as a result of my initially rather 'intermediate' language skills, which improved gradually over time.

In Darjeeling, Nepali is the majority language, and many young Tibetans predominantly spoke this. In addition, many attended private English language schools in the area, or in one of the bigger Indian cities, and had a high level of English. As a result, some formal interviews and general conversations were conducted in English, whilst others were conducted entirely in Tibetan (occasionally with the aid of a Tibetan friend, who translated when the conversation got too fast or too technical for me), or a mixture of the two. Several key informants frequently helped with Tibetan language, discussing possible English translations of Tibetan words and medical terms that I had heard spoken.

This, of course, raises several points. The presence of another person undeniably alters the dynamic of an interview (whether positively or negatively), and it is likely that the translator himself adds a layer of his own interpretation to the translation and thus the interview. One such example was when a friend from south India (with similar research interests) translated for me when we met a number of local Nepali spirit-mediums together. His help was invaluable, but his interview approach was quite different to mine, and it served as a reminder of some of the complexities of working with a translator which can, at times, lead to a feeling of being slightly out of control of the interview situation.

Moreover, translation from one language to another, of course, can bring forth as many questions as it answers. A cursory look at a couple of Tibetan dictionaries will provide an insight into the complexities of this, including some widely diverse acceptable translations of many Tibetan terms. This is especially the case with Tibetan medical terms, which may have multiple meanings, may be more or less known by lay Tibetans and sometimes understood quite differently by amchi and lay Tibetans, and may be translated differently by non-Tibetans who have studied Tibetan medicine to a greater or lesser degree. During my fieldwork I embarked on the translation a few chapters of the *rGyud bZhi* Tibetan medical text relating to spirit-caused mental illness. Armed with a dictionary, an online translation tool and a willing Tibetan friend, Sonam, we spent hours over several weeks discussing possible translations of the Tibetan terms, and trying to find an acceptable way to express them in a coherent manner in English. This was not helped by the vast differences between modern spoken Tibetan and the Classical Literary Tibetan verse in which the *rGyud bZhi* is written. Sonam (a student midway through his second master's degree conducted entirely in English, and with an impressive knowledge of written Tibetan, having received his schooling in Tibetan) appeared to find it no less frustrating or difficult than I did. How do we navigate the 'no-man's land' between Tibetan and English concepts which do not translate easily, and come up with acceptable translations? There is no easy answer to this question of course, only an awareness of its complexities, and a system of trial and error, which hopefully over time, will improve our understandings. I have thus included a glossary of Tibetan terms, which aims to further elucidate the meanings of Tibetan words commonly used in the book.

And finally, a note on the ethics of conducting research in the arena of mental health and illness. Due to the often sensitive nature of this topic, where some conditions may be stigmatised, I did not initially intend to interview individuals who had experienced mental illness—only to interview lay Tibetans regarding general perceptions of mental illness and healing. However, several interviewees related stories of relatives or neighbours who had experienced such conditions, and as my research progressed and my relationships with these interviewees developed, they suggested introducing me to the relatives and neighbours they had discussed. Whilst it would be naïve to suggest that my presence or research was able to directly help any of my informants, or indeed improve their situation in the event of illness, I was mindful of not inadvertently hindering it through my activities. This research aids in gaining a comprehensive understanding of concepts of the cause and treatment of mental illness in the Tibetan context, and thus feeds into research in cross-cultural psychiatry. Considering that such knowledge has been rather late in entering the arena, and is still rather scant, I think that this can only be a good thing.

CHAPTER TWO

MEDICINE AND HEALING IN DARJEELING: PRACTITIONERS, PRACTICES AND INSTITUTIONS IN DARJEELING AND AROUND

As a result of its diverse population, Darjeeling is home to a plethora of different medical and healing facilities. In terms of medical institutions and specialists, these include a number of government and private biomedical clinics and hospitals, Ayurvedic clinics, a Homeopathic clinic and two Tibetan medicine clinics. However, in terms of mental health, it was only the biomedical and Sowa Rigpa facilities which were discussed by informants I spoke to in the area, and in terms of non-medical healing services, there were a number of religious specialists in Darjeeling and around who were discussed in relation to the treatment of mental illness. Thus in this chapter, I will explore these three areas of healing and medicine, taking in the various institutions in the area, and exploring the diverse range of services and treatments available between them.

Biomedicine in Darjeeling

Across India, biomedicine (usually referred to by Tibetans as 'Indian medicine') facilities vary from huge, renowned hospitals in the large cities to smaller hospitals and clinics with fewer facilities and resources in smaller towns, villages and rural areas. Similarly to many other towns across India, Darjeeling houses a multitude of private biomedical clinics and hospitals. Of the many private biomedical doctors working in Darjeeling, the now retired Dr. Wangdi—who had been the resident doctor at the TRSHC clinic for approximately forty years—was particularly well-regarded within the Tibetan community. Often described to me using the English phrase that he was 'like a family doctor', he was famous for giving poor Tibetans and locals the free medicines which he received as samples. In 2011, Dr. Wangdi's old biomedical clinic at the TRSHC was now staffed by an Indian doctor and local Nepali nurse in the mornings only. Despite its low consultation fee (Rs.30 for those living at the centre, compared to an average Rs.100–200 in most private biomedical clinics), and the fact that I was told that in-stock medicines were free to patients,[1] I met few Tibetans who had visited there since Dr. Wangdi had left. I understood that the clinic was utilised by the local Nepali population, but it was not popular amongst the Tibetan community, with some discussion of 'greedy' staff charging too much for medicines (claims I was unable to verify).

In town, a biomedical 'Diagnostic Clinic' set up by the TRSHC was managed by Dekyi Dolkar, a second-generation Tibetan exile born and living at the TRSHC. A biomedical nurse, she had previously worked with Dr. Wangdi in the TRSHC clinic. Opened in 2006, this diagnostic clinic included blood testing, x-ray and vaccination facilities, as well as a morning dental clinic run by a resident German dentist. The clinic was open to anyone, with the majority of patients 'locals' (in other words, Nepalis), and Dekyi described the most common complaints: arthritis, asthma, hypertension, diabetes and 'gastric' (a common term referring to a number of different digestive problems and gallstones). Patients at the clinic who required further (non-psychiatric) care were referred to the outpatient department of the government hospital in town, but for those in need of emergency treatment, Dekyi explained that it was usually better to go to one of the private hospitals, as there was often 'lots of queuing' at the government hospital emergency department. Dekyi told me that the clinic pays for itself: although they could claim funds from the Tibetan government for it, they chose not to as, she said, 'others are more needy than us'. In addition, once a year, with the financial support of a Taiwanese medical charity, the International Cooperation and Development Fund (ICDF), clinic staff conducted a 'medical camp', where they, alongside Taiwanese volunteers, travelled to rural areas to deliver medical services and health education. In

---

1. Interview conducted with the Secretary of the TRSHC, Chimay Rinchen in his office by the author, 20th September 2011.

terms of mental illness, Dekyi explained that individuals suffering from any kind of psychiatric conditions were referred to Dr. Sharma, a psychiatrist who visited from Gangtok to practise in a small room at one of the pharmacies in town once a fortnight, although I was told that unfortunately, psychiatric medicines tended to be 'very expensive' to buy.

Clearly then, Darjeeling was not short of medical facilities. Nonetheless, comprehensive biomedical psychiatric services were significantly lacking. The main government hospital was housed in a large building near the bottom of town, but when I initially arrived in February 2011, I was informed that its psychiatric department had been out of action for some time due to a lack of staff. A psychiatrist, Dr. Nirupam Ghosh, arrived in the winter of 2011, but he had only two beds available to him in the psychiatric department. From Calcutta, he was initially unfamiliar with the local area, and used translators to interact with any Tibetan patients (he told me that at that time he had one Tibetan inpatient diagnosed with schizophrenia). With very few medicines available at the hospital, he said that many of his patients would instead take his prescriptions and buy their medicines from pharmacies in town. He explained that he would like to offer psychotherapy to patients, but unfortunately this was not possible due to time constraints, as he was the sole psychiatrist there and was struggling to manage the workload alone. Dr. Ghosh also ran a private clinic in the afternoons—one of several in the town, usually signposted as 'Neuropsychiatrist'. In addition, two private psychiatrists (the previously mentioned Dr. Sharma, from Gangtok, and another from Siliguri, both around 3–4 hours' drive away), who each visited Darjeeling once a fortnight to see patients in rooms at local pharmacies, seemed to be particularly well-regarded by informants.

More comprehensive biomedical psychiatric services were available outside Darjeeling. The STNM government hospital in Gangtok, in the adjoining state of Sikkim, included a psychiatric department, consisting of several wards with approximately ten beds in each, as well as a handful of private individual rooms. Staff included three psychiatrists and two psychologists, as well as several psychiatric nurses. In addition to medication, they were able to offer psychological therapies such as counselling, exposure and response therapy (ERT) for patients with obsessive-compulsive disorder (OCD) and cognitive behaviour therapy (CBT). However, one of the resident psychiatrists explained that since these types of psychological therapy usually required weekly one-hour sessions, accessing them was difficult for many patients, due to financial or geographical considerations. When I interviewed Dr. Sharma, he explained that whilst he viewed electro-convulsive therapy (ECT) as a 'wonder treatment', they were unable to offer it there, due to the lack of an anaesthetist. Patients from Darjeeling could be admitted to the hospital but had to pay fees, in contrast to Sikkimese inpatients, for whom there were no charges for hospital stays.

Finally, Darjeeling—like most Indian towns—was also home to a multitude of private pharmacies, where numerous types of biomedicines could be bought without prescription. Prices varied hugely depending on the medicine, and pharmacists might be more or less knowledgeable depending on the establishment. However, despite this variety of biomedical options in Darjeeling, I was told numerous times by both Nepalis and Tibetans that in cases of serious illness (psychological or physical), anyone who could afford it would travel to a doctor or hospital in a bigger city. Siliguri was the closest and cheapest option, but for those in a good financial position, travelling as far as Delhi was often preferable. However, visiting such hospitals can be a very time-consuming and expensive business, with travel costs adding up as family members stay in an often unfamiliar city whilst relatives are in hospital. Several informants described debts incurred as well as stories of sleeping for days or even weeks on a hospital veranda whilst a relative received treatment. I also heard a handful of distressing stories from Tibetans in Darjeeling, who related being poorly and disrespectfully treated in city hospitals by medical staff whom they felt assumed they could not afford treatment or understand English.

Sowa Rigpa: Tibetan Medicine in Darjeeling

In terms of Sowa Rigpa—commonly referred to as 'Tibetan medicine' by Tibetans and locals in the area—in Darjeeling there were two clinics: the Men-Tsee-Khang (MTK) clinic, staffed by Amchi Lobsang Thubten, a pharmacist and a receptionist, and the Chagpori Tibetan Medical Institute (CTMI), set up by Trogawa Rinpoche (1931–2005) in 1992, and now run by Trogawa's nephew, Amchi Teinlay Trogawa. Both Trogawa Rinpoche and Amchi Teinlay had also travelled to Europe and practised at a clinic in the Netherlands. At both the MTK and CTMI clinics, prices were low compared to biomedical and Ayurvedic clinics. For example, a consultation and 7–10 days' herbal medicine at the MTK and CTMI cost me approximately Rs.100–150 per visit, compared to Rs.300 for a similar service at an Ayurvedic clinic I visited in town.

The Darjeeling MTK clinic is one of the many branch clinics of the MTK system dotted around India, all administered and funded by the Tibetan Department of Health in Dharamsala (see the next chapter for more on this). In the Darjeeling clinic, consultation fees were low (Rs.40), prescribed herbal medicines could be bought immediately from the onsite pharmacy and, as in

Illustration 6. Amchi Lobsang Thubten at the
Darjeeling MTK clinic, July 2012

other MTK clinics, monks, nuns and schoolchildren paid half price, with those
over seventy receiving free medicines. In some MTK clinics both amchi and
patients keep patients' records (see for example Samuel 2001, 253), but in Darjeeling, this was not the case, and instead it was customary for patients to bring
along their previous prescriptions written by the amchi in a small record book
which they kept themselves.

In the Darjeeling clinic, Amchi Lobsang Thubten saw a mixture of Tibetan
and Nepali patients, as well as a few foreigners. Having grown up in another
part of India, he had been learning Nepali since being stationed in Darjeeling
approximately two years previously. However, like many Tibetans who had
lived and studied in Dharamsala, he had a high level of English and often communicated with patients in this. In Darjeeling the clinic was generally open
Monday to Friday all day and every other Saturday morning. In addition, on
alternate Saturday mornings Amchi Lobsang Thubten saw patients at the
TRSHC, and once a fortnight he travelled to the Tibetan settlement at Sonada
(approximately 17km away) and spent the day treating patients there. He was
kind enough to let me observe his clinic one morning in Darjeeling, and to go
with him on one of his day visits to the Sonada clinic. On the morning that I

observed the Darjeeling MTK clinic, he saw ten patients—although he told me that this was often highly variable—and on the Sonada clinic visit he saw thirty-nine patients, which he said was typical of his visits there. At both clinics, he diagnosed patients through pulse diagnosis, questioning and the use of a sphygmomanometer (manual or electronic) to take the patient's blood pressure. The most common complaints were hypertension, diabetes, gastric problems and joint problems such as arthritis.

The CTMI clinic, housed in an old building halfway down one of Darjeeling's steep paths near to the main square, was also open all day Monday to Friday, and Saturday mornings. Student amchi studied at the Chagpori Medical College, situated at Takdah, approximately 30km from Darjeeling. When I arrived in Darjeeling in June 2011, the medical college had twelve students enrolled, with nine recently graduated and approximately ten new students expected to enrol in September 2011. The students study there for five years, and follow this with a one-year internship, before usually setting up their own private clinics.[2]

The CTMI clinic had one resident amchi, Amchi Lobsang Samten, who had been practising there since 2003, and a chief pharmacist, who was a monk. As the director of CTMI, Amchi Teinlay oversaw the running of the clinic (and the entire organisation), and also saw patients who requested him—many of whom had known and been treated by his uncle. Amchi Lobsang Samten saw approximately fifteen to twenty-five patients per day, and told me that they were 'mostly local people'—predominantly Sherpa. He explained that many older Tibetans preferred the MTK clinic, where they received free medicines, whilst the CTMI clinic saw a higher proportion of younger Tibetan patients. Consultation fees were low (Rs.50–70), and free treatment was given to the very poor. He reported the main complaints to be gout, arthritis, back pain, breast cancer, breast cysts, gynaecological problems, kidney problems, high blood pressure and epilepsy. Amchi Lobsang Samten used pulse analysis for diagnosis—occasionally supplemented by urine analysis and/or a sphygmomanometer (manual or electronic) reading. Patients were predominantly treated via herbal medicine—mostly pills but also herbs for tea—but he reported sometimes also performing moxa, cupping using copper and china cups and/or golden needle therapy on the head or feet, and very occasionally bloodletting. Similarly to the MTK clinic, medicines prescribed by the amchi could be bought immediately from the onsite pharmacy.

---

2. If necessary, students may also do two years' preliminary language study of Classical Tibetan prior to commencing their study of Tibetan medicine.

Whilst some Tibetan informants in Darjeeling described a preference for one or the other of these clinics, a significant number reported that they had visited both and felt them to be equally good. At both clinics, the amchi described referring patients to other medical or healing specialists if they felt these would better treat their patients. For example, Amchi Lobsang Samten recommended consulting monastic practitioners for some conditions, either in combination with, or in place of, Sowa Rigpa medical treatment, and it is to these practitioners which I will turn next.

Religious Life and Healing in Darjeeling

Similarly to many areas in Nepal, religious life in Darjeeling often involved an interesting syncretism of Tibetan Buddhist and Hindu[3] concepts and practices. Observatory Hill, for example, a small hill situated close to the main square at Chowrasta, in the upper part of town, was filled with Buddhist and Hindu shrines and small temples, decorated with prayer flags, and was visited on important religious days by local Nepalis, Indians and Tibetans. Darjeeling and the surrounding area are home to a number of Tibetan Buddhist monasteries and Hindu temples of varying sizes, in addition to the Nepali spirit-medium tradition of *jhānkri* and *mata-ji*—male and female practitioners respectively—who conduct ritual and healing practices of various kinds.

In terms of Tibetan Buddhist monasteries, the most famous and most often mentioned monastery in the vicinity of the town was the Drug Sangak Choling monastery—usually referred to locally as 'Dali Gonpa' (Dali Monastery), after the area in which it resides. Home to around three hundred monks from Tibet, Ladakh, Bhutan, Nepal and India, and the largest monastery in the area, this monastery of the Kagyu tradition encompasses a collection of large buildings, situated next to the main road to Darjeeling—approximately 5km from Darjeeling town. The monastery includes a small medical clinic—the 'Gampopa Clinic'—offering medical facilities including x-ray and first aid services to local people, and a home for the elderly staffed by a Tibetan husband and wife, both nurses. In addition, there was an elderly astrologer resident at the monastery, who conducted astrological readings for a small donation. Two other significant local monasteries were the large Sakya Buddhist 'Sakya Gonpa' in Ghoom, approximately 9km from Darjeeling, and the Samten Choling monastery between

---

3. 'Hinduism' itself, is of course a contested concept which refers to a vast array of beliefs and practices found across south Asia. Here, I am referring here to the practices related to Indian deities such as Shiva and Durga which I came across in Darjeeling.

Illustration 7. Drug Sangak Choling monastery ('Dali Gonpa')

Darjeeling and Ghoom. The latter was often referred to by local Tibetans as the 'Shugden Gonpa', as its fifty or so monks were understood to honour the controversial deity Dorje Shugden, whom I shall discuss further in Chapter Nine.

Lay Buddhist individuals often visited these monasteries regularly, attending regular or annual rituals, such as *tse dbang* ("tsé wang", long life empowerments), and sometimes visiting specifically to receive blessings in the event of illness or misfortune. Furthermore, with many monastic practitioners skilled in the management of spirits, they could be commissioned by lay individuals to conduct rituals either at the monastery or at individuals' homes in return for donations to the monastery. A number of informants described rituals that had been conducted on their or their family's behalf by monks from a local monastery.[4] In addition, Tantric Buddhist ritual specialists such as *sngags pa* ("ngakpa", mantra healer, a Tantric practitioner from the Nyingma school of Tibetan Buddhism) were sometimes consulted for help in the event of sickness or misfortune. Indeed, one such

---

4. Indeed, on one occasion after I had been in Darjeeling a couple of months, my landlord and his family commissioned a group of monks from Dali Gonpa to conduct a ritual to placate the local *klu* (Skt.: *nāga*) spirits after their young grandson became afflicted by a skin condition.

Illustration 8. Lama Karma Shedrup, a local *sngags pa*,
at his *lha khang*, June 2012

practitioner, Lama Karma Shedrup (58), lived just outside the main town, and
described a ritual he had conducted for a Tibetan friend of mine, after an unexpected death in the family, which was determined to have been caused by a local
spirit. Such practitioners may be more or less aligned with a local monastery.

Finally, the Tibetan spirit-medium tradition of *lha bzhugs mkhan* ("lha
shuken", spirit-medium, also known as *lha pa*) has been well-documented.[5]
During his research in the 1990s, Jacobson noted that the only Tibetan spirit-
medium in the Darjeeling Hills was one residing in Mirik, a small town approximately four hours' drive away (2000, 303). This same practitioner was
mentioned to me by a few people during fieldwork, but had passed away a few
years previously, leaving no Tibetan spirit-mediums in Darjeeling or the surrounding area. However, with numerous *jhānkri* and *mata-ji* in Darjeeling,[6]
whilst the majority of attendees tended to be Nepali or Indian, I spoke to a few

5. A number of authors have discussed this tradition, but Hildegard Diemberger's work
is perhaps the most recent survey (2005).

6. See Gerke for a description of one of the most well-known local *mata-ji* in the area,
Mataji Kumari Cintury (1999).

Tibetans who had consulted such practitioners. Fees for their ritual services varied from around Rs.100–150 to much more.[7] Whilst some of these practitioners described themselves as 'Hindu', others appeared to operate within a context of religious syncretism. Reflecting this, some Tibetan informants told me that they would not visit these practitioners as they were 'Hindu', with others stating that they were really performing the same service as Tibetan *lha bzhugs mkhan*, with one suggesting that the *jhānkri* are 'Tibetan Bonpos'.[8] These spirit-mediums have been described by a number of researchers (Gerke 1999; Hitchcock and Jones 1976; Miller 1978; Peters 1987), and they vary in their services, with some providing herbal medicines to patients, and others specialising only in the exorcism of unwanted spirits.

I attended the rituals of two local Nepali spirit-mediums: one well-known and highly-regarded local *jhānkri* known as 'Guru-ji' (78), who lived near the town square in the area known as Chowrasta, and Pramila (37), a *mata-ji* living and working in a small town outside Darjeeling. Guru-ji, who was clearly popular and well-regarded, practised in a room inside his house, where he had also built a temple on the roof, housing a large Shiva statue. During his regular and well-attended twice-weekly rituals (which usually lasted approximately three to four hours), he became possessed by the Hindu deity Shiva as part of the process of diagnosing and healing individuals—particularly those afflicted with unwanted spirit possessions. In contrast, Pramila was a Tamang Buddhist who, during rituals, became possessed by the Hindu goddess Durga, of whom she had a statue inside her temple next to the house. Whilst Tibetan and Nepali practitioners such as these are often consulted for these very specific rituals, many such religious specialists are also often consulted in the event of non-spirit affliction conditions, and/or for blessings—often sought concurrently with other medical or healing specialists.

Finally, due to its colonial past, Darjeeling of course has a history of Christian missionary activity. Consequently, there are a number of Christian churches and organisations in Darjeeling, run by locals and/or foreigners. Whilst Gerke mentioned a small Tibetan Christian community in Kalimpong (2012a, 50), I did not meet any Christian Tibetans during my time in Darjeeling (although of course this is not to conclude that there are none in the area), and none of my Tibetan informants mentioned these institutions.

---

7. I heard a couple of stories of *jhānkri* who had charged up to Rs.10,000 (approximately GBP100) for a ritual, although these stories also tended to conclude that such practitioners were either immoral, charlatans, or both.

8. This perhaps, as one informant suggested, reflects the similarity between this term and the other local term for male Nepali spirit-mediums, which is *bombo*.

Illustration 9. Guru-ji, at his temple near Chowrasta,
Darjeeling, September 2011

   Darjeeling is culturally and medically pluralistic. As we saw in the previous
chapter, its history and local political issues provide a complex backdrop for
the Tibetans living there, making it quite a different setting from many of the
other Tibetan Diaspora communities across India. In terms of health and medicine, the rather 'blurry' boundaries between the different Nepali and Tibetan
communities in the area lead to an interesting and complex environment in
which people are often navigating multiple identities and numerous
explanatory models of health, illness and healing. Local political struggles have
affected life for the Tibetan population as well as the Nepali and Indian pop-

ulations in the area, and one of the visible consequences of this was Darjeeling's comparatively quiet Tibetan political movement. However, within this context, Tibetan organisations such as the local branches of the CTA, TRSHC and CST, and *skyi sdug* system continue, and the local Tibetan population celebrates its Tibetan Buddhist holidays and commemorates its political anniversaries as do many other Tibetan communities across India. Over the following chapters, particularly in Part Three, when we explore of a number of case studies and background interviews, I will start to build up a picture of how Tibetans in this area navigated this complex pluralistic environment in their attempts to make sense of and manage mental health and illness.

PART TWO

MEDICINE, MENTAL HEALTH AND HEALING IN THE TIBETAN CONTEXT: THEORIES AND PRACTICES

CHAPTER THREE

TIBETAN APPROACHES TO MENTAL ILLNESS

Mental health is defined as a mind freed from the influence of the afflictive mental factors. (Epstein and Topgay 1982, 68)

Tibetan language has a number of different terms to describe illnesses related to the mind. The most common are *sems nad* ("sem né", illness of the mind, an umbrella term for a number of conditions), *smyo nad* ("nyö né", madness) and *rlung* ("loong"). Commonly translated as 'wind', *rlung* is one of the three *nyes pa*—bodily 'humours'—integral to both Tibetan and Ayurvedic medical theory. In Darjeeling I found these three terms used by lay Tibetans and medical specialists alike, and some appear to share similarities with certain Western psychiatric diagnostic categories in the DSM and ICD classification systems, whilst others demonstrate significant differences. Many of these conditions are traditionally treated with Sowa Rigpa—indeed, the Tibetan amchi Yeshe Donden claims that 'Tibetan medicine' is 'extremely effective' for 'certain types of mental disorders', in addition to a number of other types of illness (1997, 20)—and may be delineated in the *rGyud bZhi*.[1] This four-volume, twelfth-century medical text is considered the main authority on medical theory (Samuel 2001, 247), and forms the basis of many amchi's training. Other conditions may require the intervention of a religious specialist either instead of, or in addition to, any treatment prescribed by an amchi. In this chapter I will examine notions of mental health and ill-health in Sowa Rigpa, outlining the Tibetan concepts

---

1. The full title of this text is often given as *bDud rtsi snying po yan lag brgyad pa gsang ba man ngag gi rgyud*, although in practice the title varies somewhat between different editions.

of anatomy which underlie these, and the sources of authority they reference, in addition to giving an overview of contemporary medical practice. I will introduce the main factors in the relationship between religion and mental health in the Tibetan context, and some of the biomedical interpretations of Sowa Rigpa categories of mental disorders.

The term 'Sowa Rigpa' (Tib.: *gSo ba Rig pa*, knowledge/science of healing) refers to a number of different traditions and practices across ethnically Tibetan areas in the Himalayan region—from Ladakh and Zangskar in the west, across the Tibetan plateau in Chinese-controlled Tibet and the valleys of Nepal, to Bhutan in the east—and beyond. Known in different regions as 'Tibetan medicine', *Bod sman* ("Pö men", Tibetan medicine), 'amchi medicine', 'Mongolian medicine' and 'Buddhist medicine', practices often vary significantly between the different regions (Kloos 2010, 16). In India, Sowa Rigpa was officially legalised and recognised by the Indian government as a 'system of Indian medicine' (alongside Ayurveda, Siddha, Yoga, Unani, Naturopathy and Homeopathy) in 2010, affording it a certain amount of protection and availability in different areas.[2]

Western understandings of 'Tibetan medicine' tend to be based on Tibetan amchi's interpretations of the *rGyud bZhi*, parts of which are memorised by amchi during their medical training. However, with significant differences between textual theory and medical practice, particularly across the diverse medical traditions, the picture that this paints of Sowa Rigpa can be somewhat misleading. Ethnographic research on mental illness in the Tibetan context—both in exile and in Chinese-controlled Tibet—has to date mainly focused on 'wind' (Tib.: *rlung*) illnesses, that is, those related to the *rlung* 'humour' (Jacobson 2002, 2007; Janes 1999a), and those which would be classified in biomedicine as depressive or anxiety conditions or post-traumatic stress disorder (PTSD) (Brock 2008; Prost 2006, 2008; Ruwanpura et al. 2006; Sachs et al. 2008; Schröder 2011). In addition, there has often been a focus on the politicisation of the diagnosis of *rlung* in both Chinese-controlled Tibet and exile (Janes 1995, 1999a; Prost 2006), and the category of *smyo nad* has remained largely unexamined thus far.

---

2. See the Government of India's Ministry of Ayurveda, Yoga and Naturopathy, Unani, Siddha and Homeopathy (AYUSH, previously known as the Department of Indian System of Medicine and Homeopathy (ISM&H)) website for more on this: ayush.gov.in. This is a far cry from the early years of exile in India, when Cantwell notes that Tibetan amchi 'came under attack from Indian biomedical doctors' (1995, 177–78).

Psychiatry and the Subtle Body

[M]uch of Tibetan psychiatry is concerned with the manifestations and treatments of disruptions and blockage in the flow of rLung. (Rabgay 1984, 50)

As stated above, much of the discussion on mental disorders in the Tibetan context—by both Tibetans and non-Tibetans—focuses around the concept of *rlung*, one of the three *nyes pa* ("nyé pa") of *rlung* (Skt.: *vāta*, wind), *mkhris pa* ("tripa", Skt.: *pitta*, bile) and *bad kan* ("bé ken", Skt.: *kapha*, phlegm). The Tibetan term *nyes pa* is a direct translation of the Sanskrit *doṣa*, and is usually translated into English as 'humour', although there are significant problems with this translation. *rLung*, corresponding in this sense to the Sanskrit *prāṇa*, is an important component of the 'subtle (Tib.: *'phra ba*) body' system of anatomy in the Tibetan medical system, and is thought of as a substance or a form of 'energy' which flows through the 'channels' that make up this subtle anatomy. In addition, the term *rlung* is used to denote not only one of the three *nyes pa*, but also the condition which arises as a result of any disturbance in it. This condition is usually characterised by both physical and psychological symptoms, and has been described by Janes as a 'cluster of somatic-emotional complaints, particularly dizziness, headaches, back and neck pain accompanied by insomnia, dysphoria, anger, or frustration' (2001, 211). The term is common in lay parlance as well as that of amchi, with the most commonly mentioned sub-type, *srog 'dzin rlung* ("sok dzin loong", life-holding/sustaining wind)—usually shortened simply to *srog rlung*—often discussed.

rLung stands out from the other two *nyes pa* due to its fundamental role in health and illness. *rLung* is understood to be intimately related to consciousness, and the notion of *rlung* thus links together aspects of the microcosm and macrocosm and the body and mind, and provides a link between Tibetan medical theory and certain Tibetan Buddhist concepts. Therefore, whilst the humours of *mkhris pa* and *bad kan* are related to certain psychological functions and can also be involved in mental disorders—and in fact *rlung* may well act in conjunction with either one or the other (or both) of them, or in conjunction with *gdon* ("dön", spirits)—it is *rlung* itself which is the most relevant here. Due to its integral role in the functioning of the body and mind, where consciousness and *rlung* are interdependent, *rlung* 'can be the cause of every single disease' (Dorjee 2005, 164–8). Moreover, as I mentioned above, one particular type of *rlung* is often the focus here: the *srog rlung*, which is associated with the top of the head, and located in the 'life channel' (Tib.: *srog rtsa*) situated at the heart centre, where it 'serves as the support for the consciousness in the body and the very subtle mind which passes from life to life' (Millard 2007, 270).[3]

rLung has also become a highly politicised concept in the contemporary Tibetan discourse, where it is often used to refer to the difficulties of life within the Tibetan political struggle in both Chinese-controlled Tibet and exile. Thus *rlung* is described by Janes (1999a) as an 'idiom of distress'. Both in this context and in the broader arena of contemporary Tibetan life, the term *rlung* is often used in a similar manner to the English term 'stress', used to denote a heightened state of emotion or cognition. For example, working in Darjeeling, Jacobson described his Tibetan informants' explanations — 'I have wind today' or discussions of having 'high wind' (Tib: *rlung mtho po*) — as indicating a 'temporary condition of moderate irritability or emotional lability due to some adverse circumstance' (2007, 232). In fact, *rlung* is fundamental to Tibetan concepts of anatomy, mind and mental health, as we shall see.

Anatomy and the Role of rLung

rLung and Consciousness

From the perspective of Sowa Rigpa, the body is constituted of the five elements (Tib.: *'byung ba*) of earth (Tib.: *sa*), air (Tib.: *rlung*), fire (Tib.: *me*), water (Tib.: *chu*) and space (Tib.: *nam kha*). From these elements, all animate and inanimate phenomena are composed (Rabgay 1985, 47). In their most subtle form, they are also said to be the 'ultimate basis' of the mind (Tsarong 1991, 46). Out of the five elements arise the three *nyes pa*—the 'basic principles of Tibetan medical physiology' (Gerke 2013, 84), with *rlung*, for example, composed of air and space (Rabgay 1985, 48). And it is *rlung* which is particularly related to disorders of the mind, as a result of its role as the 'foundation' of consciousness (Tib.: *rnam shes*), linking together mind and body (Rabgay 1984, 50). From a Tibetan perspective, there are three levels of consciousness: gross, subtle and very subtle, the very subtle level only accessible through meditation by highly-skilled Tantric practitioners (Ozawa-De Silva and Ozawa-De Silva 2011, 102). Chapter Four of the Second Tantra of the *rGyud bZhi* contains a detailed discussion of the relationship of *rlung* and the mind, and it is often said that the mind rides on the wind as a man rides a horse (Millard 2007, 265–66). In fact Tenzin Wangyal describes this as a *lame* rider and a *blind* horse, explaining, '[w]ithout the mind, the prana [*rlung*] has no direction.

---

3. It is important to note here that in the Tibetan perspective, the seat of the mind (*sems*) is the heart (not the brain).

Without the prana, the mind has no capacity to move. They function as a unity' (2002, 82). With *rlung* tied so closely to consciousness then, it is not surprising that as Epstein and Topgay explain, 'much of Tibetan psychiatry and medicine is concerned with the manifestations and treatments of the disruptions or blocks in the flow of prana [*rlung*]' (1982, 68). Similarly, when I interviewed Amchi Sonam Dolma in August 2012, at that time head of the MTK Translation Department in Dharamsala, she explained, 'Of course there's no denying of the fact that the principle *cause* of all mental problems is *rlung*. And then along with the *rlung* ... there could be other associating factors, like, there could also be *mkhris pa*, there could be *bad kan*'.

Whilst *rlung* naturally varies between individuals as well as across one's lifespan, increasing with age (Janes 1999a, 395), it also can be intentionally manipulated through particular meditative and yogic practices (Samuel 1993, 236–37). Similarly, it can also be *unintentionally* disturbed through such practices (including, for example, yoga or t'ai chi), especially if these practices are conducted incorrectly, as well as through behavioural and dietary factors. For example, fasting, insomnia, physical and mental exertion, vomiting and exposure to cold can all lead to a disturbance in the *rlung* (Rabgay 1985, 49). Furthermore, as Dorjee explains, '[t]he slightest trace of mental stress, tension and pressure will provoke *rLung*' (2005, 165). And in Darjeeling, Amchi Teinlay agreed, explaining that 'a very big shock' or 'mental worry' or a 'burden on the mind' over a long period of time could cause a disturbance to the *rlung*.

Much of Sowa Rigpa's medical theory derives from concepts found in Indian medical and Tantric texts, with Tibetan notions of anatomy, for example, significantly influenced by Tantric cosmology (Millard 2007, 265). One consequence of this has been the conflation of two different Sanskrit concepts— *vāta* and *prāṇa*—and the Ayurvedic and Tantric systems in which they are situated, into the singular Tibetan concept of *rlung*. The former term, *vāta*, refers to one of the three Ayurvedic *doṣa*, mentioned above, which correspond to the three Tibetan *nyes pa*. The latter term, *prāṇa*, is a Tantric concept going back to the Upaniṣadic texts (Samuel 2013), usually translated as 'life force', 'life energy' or 'breath', and the manipulation of *prāṇa* is often a fundamental aspect of Tantric and yogic meditative practices, related to the Buddhist goal of enlightenment. Thus, from a Tibetan Buddhist perspective, the manipulation of *rlung* through Tantric practice is important not only in relation to psychological health, but also in spiritual liberation. *rLung* then, is fundamental in the workings of the body and mind, consciousness, health and illness: as Wangyal explains, *rlung* is 'the energy that powers and is the substance of all things material and immaterial. It is the fundamental energy from which all things arise, the energy of the kunzhi, the basis of existence' (2002, 77).

Fundamentals of Tibetan Anatomy:
Humours, Channels, Winds and Drops

As an integral component of the 'subtle' body, composed of *rlung*, *rtsa* ("tsa", Skt. *nāḍī*, channels) and *thig le* ("tig lé", Skt.: *bindu*, drops), *rlung* is part of the much larger system of Tibetan anatomy which underpins concepts of the mind and body, health and illness. As we have seen, Tibetan medical theory—similarly to Ayurvedic medical theory—describes the three *nyes pa* of *rlung*, *mkhris pa* and *bad kan*, usually translated respectively as 'wind', 'bile' and 'phlegm'.[4] Books on this Tibetan system oriented towards a Western audience often delineate the problem of 'humoural imbalance' and the medical conditions which can arise as a result of this. Indeed, the Tibetan term *nyes pa* is frequently translated into the English term 'humour' (or 'humor') by both Tibetan amchi and Western authors. However, this comparison with Western humoural theory can be misleading (Ozawa-de Silva and Ozawa-de Silva 2011, 104): *nyes pa* actually translates literally into the English terms 'fault' or 'weakness' (Samuel 2001, 255), and has more recently been translated as 'defective energies' by some amchi (Kloos 2010, 17 [note 20]).[5] Furthermore, the aforementioned description of humoural 'imbalance' between the *nyes pa* is also a misinterpretation as, in contrast to the Galenic and Islamic systems—in which such 'humours' can indeed be 'balanced' or 'unbalanced'—it has been argued that in the Tibetan system, these three constituents are actually 'exclusively negative in nature' (Samuel 2001, 255).

With such differences between Tibetan and Western perceptions of physical and subtle anatomy, we should perhaps not be surprised by the diverse range of translations. Furthermore, Gerke notes that differences between Tibetan amchi's translations of Tibetan medical terms can depend on multiple factors, including their education, their exposure to, or personal interest in, biomedicine, or any 'involvement in research studies or clinical trials' (2011, 145; see also Gerke 2012b). With this in mind, I will stick to using the Tibetan terms *nyes pa*, *rlung*, *mkhris pa* and *bad kan* here, except in references to others' use of the English terms. I would note however, that the translation of *rlung* as

---

4. Thus, whilst the Ayurvedic notions of the *doṣa* are unrelated to Tantric theory, because of this conflation of *prāna* and *vāta* in the Tibetan context, *rlung*, which corresponds to *vāta* in the system of *doṣa*, has been drawn into the 'subtle body' system.

5. Gyatso traces this questionable translation of *nyes pa* into the English term 'humour' (or 'humor') back to an 1835 article by Alexander Csoma de Körös who, he points out, was possibly unqualified to make such a translation, bearing in mind his apparent lack of Tibetan medical knowledge (Gyatso 2005, 109–10).

'wind' particularly was common amongst Tibetan informants in Darjeeling, many of whom used these two terms interchangeably.

Moving on to other aspects of Tibetan anatomical theory, we find that the *rlung* is understood to move within the *rtsa*.[6] Similarly to the *rlung*, the *rtsa* have 'gross', 'subtle' and 'very subtle' aspects, in the form of the material/physical body and the subtle body respectively. In fact, the form, location and functions of the *rtsa* have been long debated (Gyatso 2004, 87–89), and today some contemporary Tibetan authors explain them as part of the nervous system (Dorjee 2005, 164) or the blood vessels, nerves and lymphatic system of biomedical anatomy (Wangyal 2002, 81). However, the 'subtle channels' are usually described as 'energetic': undetectable and immeasurable, sometimes said to only be perceivable by accomplished Tantric practitioners (Wangyal 2002, 81).

One *rtsa* which is particularly pertinent in mental health and illness is the *srog rtsa* ("sok tsa"). This has been translated variously as 'aorta' and even 'spine' by different authors (Gerke 2013, 87), however it is usually translated as the 'life-holding channel' or 'central channel'. Within this, the *srog rlung* ("sok loong", life-holding/sustaining wind) flows, and *srog rlung*—referring to a condition resulting from disturbance in this *rtsa*—is a fairly common *sems nad* diagnosis, which I heard mentioned often in Darjeeling. In fact there are three main channels which are particularly implicated in mental health and illness: the central channel and the channels each side of this, one each to the left and the right (Yoeli-Tlalim 2010, 320), which intersect with the central channel at a series of confluence points (Tib.: *'khor lo*, Skt.: *cakra*, energy centres, chakras) from the crown of the head to the base of the spine. Whilst, as mentioned above, some of the channels have been linked to biomedical notions of the circulatory system, when we start to examine Tibetan medical illustrations, we see that many of these channels in fact are not 'circulatory' at all, but linear (Gerke 2013, 92–93).

rLung *Disturbance and Mental Illness*

The effects of *bad kan* and *mkhris pa* disturbances, according to the Tibetan amchi Tsering Thakchoe Drungtso, are mainly physical, though these two *nyes pa* can be involved in some relatively minor psychological symptoms, such as mental 'dullness', confusion or 'mental and emotional instability' in relation to *bad kan*, and forgetfulness or 'aggressive psychological states' such as anger, hatred or jealousy in relation to *mkhris pa* (Drungtso 2004, 175–77, 227–34). Indeed,

---

6. Estimates of the number of *rtsa* in the human body vary widely but are said to count up to 360,000 (Wangyal 2002, 80–81).

in Darjeeling, Amchi Teinlay described how a person with disturbance in *bad kan* may become very withdrawn, feeling 'very sleepy' with no appetite and speaking very little. And in Dharamsala, Amchi Sonam Dolma described some conditions resulting from disturbance in *mkhris pa* as 'like psychosis', describing patients becoming 'hyper … reactive'. Disturbance in the variant *rlung* currents however can lead to a wide range of symptoms: Drungtso lists symptoms from irritated skin, chills, weight loss and stiff joints to insanity, delirium, confusion, depression, hysteria, 'impairment of the sense organs' and a 'feeling of wandering everywhere' (2004, 174, 222–26). In total, there are said to be sixty-three different *rlung* disorders, with disturbances in various different *rlung* currents resulting in psychological and physical symptoms (Epstein and Topgay 1982, 73–75). For example, disturbance in the pervading wind (Tib.: *khyab byed rlung*) (which resides in the heart, but pervades the whole body) can lead to panic attacks and heart palpitations. Disturbance in the descending wind (Tib.: *thur sel rlung*) (which resides in the lower part of the torso and thighs) can result in 'psychological and emotional distress, such as jealousy, fear and worry' (Yoeli-Tlalim 2010, 320). In addition to such overt symptoms, as with other disorders, there will be signs in the pulse and urine which amchi can read in order to make a diagnosis. For example, *rlung* disturbance is usually indicated by a pulse that is 'empty and adrift', with the patient's urine 'clear and watery with no transformation on cooling' (Epstein and Topgay 1982, 74), with *snying rlung* ("nying loong", wind in the heart) indicated by an empty and floating pulse and clear urine containing large bubbles (Dolma 2013). In terms of treatment, this will vary depending on the particular case: at the CTMI clinic in Darjeeling, Amchi Lobsang Samten explained that while some cases are easily treated, others may take months or even years to treat effectively; and Amchi Lobsang Thubten at the MTK clinic noted that for some cases, external therapies, such as massage, moxibustion—and also 'counselling'—were needed alongside herbal medicines.

As I mentioned above, the *srog rlung* is particularly related to mental illness (Millard 2007, 269), and disturbance to this *rlung* current can cause conditions varying in severity from 'slight mental discomfort, anxiety, or mild depression' (Millard 2007, 272), to 'psychosis' (Epstein and Topgay 1982, 74), manifesting symptoms such as loss of consciousness, confusion, auditory or visual hallucinations (Yoeli-Tlalim 2010, 320), 'hysteria' and 'insanity' (Dorjee 2005, 168). As such, a diagnosis of *srog rlung* can indicate quite variant psychological conditions. Exploring this in Darjeeling, for example, Jacobson described a number of case studies of patients diagnosed with *srog rlung* at the local MTK clinic. Patients described physical symptoms such as dizziness, reduced appetite, difficulty breathing, fatigue and headache, and psychological symptoms such as difficulty concentrating, sadness and an 'agitated mind' (2007, 235–37).

If we turn next to look at the category of *smyo nad*, (also *smyo(n) pa*), there has been far less textual or ethnographic exploration of this to date. The Tibetan term *smyo nad* is usually translated into the English words 'madness' or 'insanity' by both amchi and lay Tibetans, and its symptoms share some similarities with Western understandings of 'psychosis' (Millard 2007). In Darjeeling, Jacobson noted the use of *smyo pa* as a 'generic term for conditions marked by obvious hallucinations, delusions, and disruptive speech and behaviour' (2002, 261). As we have just seen, such symptoms can be the result of disturbance in one or more of the *rlung* currents. Epstein and Topgay describe a number of factors understood to 'encourage the development' of *smyo nad*, including depression, mental discomfort or exertion, a weak heart, poor diet and a number of 'behavioural patterns' (1982, 76).

However, *smyo nad* can also result from spirit affliction, and this was certainly the cause that was most discussed by informants in Darjeeling in relation to this condition. This reflects what we find in the *rGyud bZhi*, where *smyo nad* is included in the Third Tantra, the *Man ngag rGyud* (Oral Instruction Tantra) under two sections: the general category of *rlung* disease, where it is discussed as the result of disturbance in the *rlung,* and the category of *smyo byed kyi gdon* ("nyö ché gyi dön", spirits that cause madness).[7] This could also be translated as 'spirit *disturbances* that cause madness', changing the emphasis slightly. Similarly, Namkhai Norbu uses the term 'provocations', describing *gdon* as not only 'a disturbance caused by one of the classes of non human beings', but also as 'the provocation of an imbalance in the energy sphere of an individual made possible by his condition of weakness and proneness to receiving negativity' (1995, 143). The text describes the multiple factors which can be involved in the causation of *smyo nad* in addition to disturbance in the *nyes pa*, such as karma, poison, spirits (Clifford 1989, 137), mental discomfort or exertion, a weak heart, poor diet or certain behavioural patterns (Rabgay 1985, 48). Such cases are frequently treated through religious means, such as the making of offerings to local spirits, lama's blessings and/or rituals to appease local spirits and/or deities, and these will be discussed in more depth in the next chapter.

Thus we see that whilst any of the three *nyes pa* can be involved in *sems nad*, due to its relationship with consciousness, it is the *rlung* which is most often associated with mental health and ill-health. In its role as one of the *nyes pa*, the *rlung* currents (and corresponding *rtsa*) are fundamental components of

---

7. In addition, mental illnesses related particularly to children and the elderly are delineated in separate sections of the *rGyud bZhi* (Clifford 1989, 129).

the 'subtle body' anatomy, which encompasses the five elements, *nyes pa*, *rtsa* and *thig le*. Disturbances in the flow of *rlung* can lead to a combination of physical and psychological symptoms which vary significantly in severity, from mild symptoms such as dizziness to hallucinations. However, with the manipulation of *rlung* a fundamental aspect of certain Tantric practices, the functions of the *rlung* in the body are related not only to health, but also to the Buddhist goal of enlightenment. The concept of *rlung* thus locates the origins of a number of Sowa Rigpa notions of the mind and body in diverse Indian Tantric and medical theories. It is to the sources of authority in these theories of the mind and body, health and illness which I will turn next.

Sowa Rigpa in Theory and Practice

The Sowa Rigpa conceptions of the mind and body described here developed across a number of different periods in history, influenced by diverse sources, including earlier Asian and Himalayan ideas and Indian Tantric concepts (Gerke 2013, 89). As mentioned above, there are descriptions of various types of *sems nad* in the *rGyud bZhi*, the text often referred to as the 'root' medical text, and described by Dorjee as the 'heart-essence text of Tibetan medicine' (2005, 227). This text is used in teaching across the Tibetan plateau (Ga 2010, 1–2), and has been described as the 'single core text' which forms the syllabus of the MTK training (Kloos 2010). However, as we shall see in this section, in reality this is a composite text which contains a number of 'internal cleavages' due to the inclusion of material from multiple diverse sources (Samuel 2001, 257). In addition, the text in fact only forms part of the medical knowledge and training of Sowa Rigpa practitioners, with much of amchi's practice actually influenced by other sources, and much of their learning taking place during apprenticeship (Samuel 2001, 261). Furthermore, there are often broad differences in medical practice across different geographical areas, as a result of local ecologies (that is, the availability of plant, mineral and animal products for the manufacture of medicines) and local 'distributions' of medical knowledge (Schrempf 2007, 105).

Whilst there are a multitude of practitioners who deal with mental disorders across ethnically Tibetan areas of India, Nepal, Bhutan and the PRC, in this section I will focus on amchi—in other words, those practitioners who specialise in Sowa Rigpa—rather than ritual healers, who will be discussed in the next chapter. Up until the seventeenth century, the majority of amchi are thought to have been male 'hereditary' (or 'lineage', Tib.: *rgyud*) village amchi who studied in private lineages under the tutelage of a teacher—often for many years—before working independently.[8] Unsurprisingly, this tradition was characterised by a lack of standardisation, with broad differences in diagnosis and practice from place to place (Kloos 2010, 61). However, Tibet also has a long history of institutionalised medical training, and the last century has seen a centralisation of institutionalised Sowa Rigpa in both Chinese-controlled Tibet and exile, with the majority of contemporary amchi now training in institutions. That is not to say that the hereditary amchi lineages have entirely disappeared—certainly not, and they are more evident in some areas than others,[9] but today, in India for example, the vast majority of Tibetan practitioners are trained under the syllabus of the Tibetan government-in-exile-affiliated MTK Tibetan Medical and Astrological Institute in Dharamsala, whose training is based on the *rGyud bZhi* (Kloos 2010, 16) and supplementary texts (Samuel 2001, 258). And, as we saw in the previous chapter, whilst Amchi Teinlay had trained entirely under the tutelage of his uncle, Trogawa Rinpoche, he now heads a medical college teaching medicine in an institutional setting. Tibetans I spoke to in Darjeeling had mixed views on which system was superior. In this section then I will briefly examine the main sources of authority in Sowa Rigpa, the predominant institutions, and the practice of Sowa Rigpa across the Himalayan region.

Sources of Authority in Sowa Rigpa

Accompanied by commentaries, the *rGyud bZhi* text covers anatomy and the nosological framework of medicine, as well as diagnostic and treatment methodology (Ga 2010).[10] Thought to date from the twelfth century, the text

---

8. Such practitioners were not necessarily blood relatives: the focus here is on *household* continuity, and consequently it is possible for such 'hereditary' amchi to be adopted into the family and continue the lineage.

9. In Amdo, Schrempf notes that lay Tibetans often have more trust in the medical knowledge of the hereditary amchi than the amchi who has trained at one of the medical institutions, as such practitioners are viewed to have been less influenced by Chinese state policies and 'Chinese medicine' (*rgya sman*) or 'party medicine' (*tang sman*) (2007, 97). Similarly, in Spiti, northwest India, Besch describes the importance of an amchi's lineage, and the knowledge and skill that this long unbroken line of knowledge and practice is understood to confer on him (2006, 69–73).

10. Parts of the *rGyud bZhi* have been translated into English and German (mainly the first and second sections, see Clark 1995, Donden 1997), with Terry Clifford's work perhaps one of the first publications to bring the sections on mental illness to a Western audience (1989). When I interviewed Amchi Sonam Dolma at the MTK Translation Department in August 2012, she informed me that they were at that time working to translate the whole *rGyud bZhi*, with the large Third Tantra set to be published in several sections.

is understood to be a composite work influenced by multiple sources including Sanskrit and Chinese texts, as well as original Tibetan medical concepts (Emmerick 1977; Ga 2010; see also Ga 2014 and Gerke 2014; and Gyatso's recent and very comprehensive 2015 work on the development of medical theory in Tibet in the 12th–18th centuries). Much of it is understood to be a translation of a seventh century Sanskrit text, the *Aṣṭāṅgahṛdayasaṃhitā*—one of the most important Ayurvedic medical texts—translated into Tibetan in the eleventh century.[11]

The *rGyud bZhi* comprises 156 chapters across four sections:

1. *rTsa rGyud* (Root Tantra): Six chapters
2. *bShad rGyud* (Explanatory Tantra): Thirty-one chapters
3. *Man ngag rGyud* (Oral Instruction Tantra): Ninety-two chapters
4. *Phyi ma'i rGyud* (Additional or Final Tantra): Twenty-five chapters (Samuel 2001, 256).

Mental disorders, referred to in the text by the umbrella term *sems nad* (Millard 2007, 247), are covered in two sections of the *Man ngag rGyud*: under the general category of *rlung* illnesses in Chapter Two, and under the category of *smyo byed gyi gdon* in Chapter Seventy-Eight. Thus in Chapter Two of the *Man ngag rGyud* we find descriptions of sixty-three *rlung* disorders differentiated by their physical and psychological symptoms, including: pain in the back, chest, jaw bones and *rlung* points; restlessness; insomnia; anger and tinnitus (Epstein and Topgay 1982, 73–74), and more serious psychological symptoms such as 'mental instability' (Clark 1995, 36).

The authorship of the text was traditionally attributed to the Medicine Buddha, Bhaiṣajyaguru, and its written style suggests a traditional Buddhist teaching between a buddha and the interlocutor, as in Tantric texts (Samuel 2001, 256; see also Ga 2010, 152–3). Nonetheless, it has long been known to many Tibetan scholars that large parts of the *rGyud bZhi* are translations of the Ayurvedic *Aṣṭāṅgahṛdayasaṃhitā* text (Ga 2010, 85), and it is thought that much of the *rGyud bZhi* was codified in the twelfth century by Yutok Yanton Gonpo (Tib.: *gYu thog Yan ton mGon po*, often referred to as 'Yutok the Younger') and his students. Indeed, Gyatso argues that some scholars considered this Buddhist 'frame story' a 'pious fiction, added merely to give legitimacy to what really is a compilation of the knowledge of historical

---

11. See Yang Ga for a description of the translation and dissemination of this text, the translated Tibetan version of which spawned a number of teaching lineages in Tibet and which was used as a textbook in numerous medical schools throughout the eleventh to thirteenth centuries (2010, 75–85).

physicians' (2015, 35). The text later became the 'root' medical work in Tibet (Gyatso 2004, 84), used at the Chagpori (Tib.: *lCag po ri*) medical institution, which was established in central Lhasa under the reign of the fifth Dalai Lama in the seventeenth century by Desi Sangye Gyatso (Tib.: *gDe sri Sangs rgyas rGya mtso*) (Meyer 2003), a well-known politician and scholar who wrote a number of works on Tibetan medicine (Ga 2010, 142), in addition to revising the *rGyud bZhi* (Meyer 2003, 105). In addition, a number of other medical traditions developed in other regions of Tibet, each adding to the *rGyud bZhi* text with its own commentaries. Some of these developed curricula that were 'at odds with the medical orthodoxy' of Chagpori (Gyatso 2004, 85), although there also seems to have been a certain amount of 'borrowing' between them, with some of the texts from the Zur medical tradition copied into Desi Sangye Gyatso's commentaries, for example (Ga 2010, 142–44). In addition, there is also a class of commentary texts called *nyams yig* ("nyam yig", writing from experience), authored by amchi, on the basis that experience was often superior to learning medicine from texts. Over time, these commentaries began to supplant the *rGyud bZhi* text itself (Gyatso 2004, 86). Indeed, in Desi Sangye Gyatso's own *nyams yig* he suggests that the utility of the *rGyud bZhi* is limited to the recognition of medical plants and the basic structures of medical knowledge (including the locating of the channels in the body), and was actually of very little use for treating patients. This sentiment was echoed by a nineteenth century amchi, Kongtrul (Tib.: Kong sprul), who also suggested that the diagnostic methods laid out in the *rGyud bZhi*—pulse and urine diagnosis— were 'not sufficient to diagnose disease' (Gyatso 2004, 86).[12]

History, Learning and Practice in Sowa Rigpa

As noted above, medical knowledge has traditionally been disseminated via two methods in Sowa Rigpa: through 'hereditary' lineages, where knowledge was passed on directly from teacher to student,[13] and through institutionalised study. Both of these traditions continue to this day, and there are sometimes overlaps between them with, for example, hereditary amchi teaching at medical institutions (Schrempf 2007, 97). However, in many contemporary ethnically

---

12. Gyatso notes that by the twentieth century, amchi 'almost always used recent *nyams yigs* as their actual handbooks, usually Blo gros mtha yas, Kong sprul, *Advice to Novice Physicians*, or one of the ones by Mkhyen rab nor bu' (2013, 381 [note 20]).

13. See particularly Florian Besch's description of hereditary amchi lineages in Spiti (2006).

Illustration 10. *Thangka* depicting the Medicine Buddha in the
Lhasa Mentsikhang, TAR

Tibetan contexts, the remaining hereditary amchi are often far outnumbered
by those who have trained at one of the main institutions. In Tibetan areas of
the PRC, there are a number of contemporary centres of medical study, such
as the Mentsikhang, the Tibetan Medical School at Tibet University, and a separate Tibetan Medical College, all in Lhasa (Ga 2010, 144), and the Tibetan
Medical College at Qinghai University in Xining,[14] in addition to a number of
private, non-governmental medical schools (often sponsored by international
NGOs) in different areas (Hofer 2008b, 504).

The history of institutionalised medicine in Tibet is thought to go back to
the eighth century, with the first medical college established in 763 CE in
Kongpo (Kloos 2010, 61), and a number of schools specialising in medical
learning established over the centuries since (Gyatso 2004). In 1696, Desi
Sangye Gyatso established the medical institute at Chagpori in Lhasa, a
monastic institution and functioning medical clinic which trained monks from
across Tibet. However, Chagpori's patient population was mainly limited to

---

14. See Adams, Dhondup and Le for a description of this very modern institution (2011).

Tibetan religious and political aristocracy, whilst the majority of the Tibetan population continued to rely on local medical and healing traditions until the early twentieth century, when the Lhasa Mentsikhang (Tib.: *sMan rtsis khang*, Department/House of Medicine and Astronomy) was founded in 1916 as part of the thirteenth Dalai Lama's drive to 'modernise' Tibet. This institute took a greater focus on public health, and collated some of the variant branches of Tibetan medical knowledge, training lay as well as monastic amchi (Kloos 2010, 62–64).

However, the mid-twentieth century brought great changes to Tibet. During the Cultural Revolution the Chagpori building was destroyed, and the institute was officially merged with the Mentsikhang, which continues to operate today in central Lhasa. In addition, in response to the steady growth of the Tibetan exile population in India since the 1950s, a number of Sowa Rigpa institutes have also been founded there. The first Tibetan exile clinic was established in Dharamsala in 1961, not long after the Dalai Lama's 1959 flight into exile in India. Over the decades since, this establishment has struggled,[15] but has endured and expanded, and today the MTK Tibetan Medical and Astrological Institute has over fifty branch clinics across India staffed by both lay and monastic, male and female amchi,[16] busy with Indian as well as Tibetan and foreign patients. In addition, the MTK has become a symbol of cultural survival—an 'important placeholder of Tibetan culture'—for Tibetans in exile (Kloos 2010, 126).

In addition to the MTK, there are a handful of other Sowa Rigpa institutions in India: the CTMI in Darjeeling, founded in 1991 by the Tibetan amchi Trogawa Rinpoche; the Department of Sowa Rigpa (founded in 1993) within the Central Institute of Higher Tibetan Studies (CIHTS), now the Central University of Tibetan Studies (CUTS) in Sarnath, near Varanasi; and the medical facility (founded in 1989) at the Central Institute of Buddhist Studies (CIBS) in Choglamsar, Ladakh. Kloos notes that there have often been tensions between the MTK and private amchi (2010, 83–84) and the other institutions of Sowa Rigpa, which have often taken different approaches to medical theory and practice. At the CTMI for example, following the tradition of the original Chagpori Institute in Lhasa, Trogawa Rinpoche placed a greater emphasis on religious practice, giving Buddhist transmissions to the students, and passing

---

15. Indeed, Stephan Kloos has described significant 'periods of internal discord, mismanagement, or weak administration' over the history of the Dharamsala MTK (2010, 67–71).

16. See the MTK website for a list of branch clinics: http://www.men-tsee-khang.org/branch/main.htm.

on his own traditional methods for the manufacture of medicines.[17] Kloos suggests that the founding of the Dharamsala-based Central Council of Tibetan Medicine (CCTM, Tib.: *Bod kyi gSo ba rig pa'i Ches mtho'i sMan pa'i Lhan tshogs*) in 2004 eased some of the tensions between these different parties, not least because seats on its executive board are held by a number of private amchi as well as MTK staff (2010, 106).

Treatment for *sems nad* and *smyo nad* often encompasses a broad range of approaches. For example, Epstein and Topgay describe treatment for mental disorders as encompassing diet, behaviour, medications and physical therapies such as massage, moxibustion and enema (1982, 76). Similarly, Amchi Pasang Y. Arya describes a number of physical therapies for mental disorders including medication, nutrition, change of lifestyle, golden needle therapy, moxibustion, use of incense and massage in addition to a number of 'religious' treatments.[18] Above I mentioned the central role of the *rGyud bZhi* in amchi's training at the MTK.[19] However, as I suggested, there are in fact a number of other texts also integral to students' learning (at both the MTK and other institutions), and in fact, amchi do not necessarily memorise the full text of the *rGyud bZhi*. So, whilst memorisation of the first, second and fourth sections is usually required of students, the third section is often rather neglected (Samuel 2001, 261), frequently considered to be the 'least relevant' section (Besch 2006, 50), with only a tiny minority of the chapters memorised or even included in the amchi's copies of the *rGyud bZhi*. Indeed, Gyatso argues that whilst medical colleges continued to insist on its memorisation in the seventeenth to nineteenth centuries, the *rGyud bZhi* 'fell out of clinical use' at this time (2013, 368). Other medical texts that are highly significant in Sowa Rigpa practice include two sixteenth-century supplementary texts by Desi Sangye Gyatso, and a recently published three-volume textbook from the MTK, which covers the standard topics of the *rGyud. bZhi* as well as some supplementary material (Samuel 2001, 256–58).

Sowa Rigpa has also been influenced by its encounter with biomedicine. The MTK syllabus has included some teaching on Western science since the 1990s—despite the classes' often 'mediocre' attendance by students (Kloos

---

17. See their website: http://www.chagpori.org/college.htm. In contrast, the department at CUTS focuses on textual research and publication projects, as well as its teaching college, medical clinic and pharmacy. Independent from the MTK and funded by the Indian Government, it has its own syllabus, examinations and certificates. Finally, the CIBS in Ladakh is also an autonomous institution, focused on training Ladakhis in Sowa Rigpa (Kloos 2010, 91–93).

18. http://www.tibetanmedicine-edu.org/index.php/psychology-and-psychotherapy.

19. See the MTK syllabus on their website: http://www.men-tsee-khang.org/college/course/med-course/medcollege.htm.

2010, 87)—and in practice, sometimes Western-derived categories (for example, tuberculosis) take the place of Tibetan ones in amchi's practice (Samuel 2001, 258). This is often also the case in Chinese-controlled Tibet, where 'Tibetan medicine' institutions may well offer both biomedical and Tibetan diagnostic categories and treatments (Schrempf 2007, 119; Hofer 2008a).

An amchi's practice is often significantly influenced by not only the apprenticeship which follows initial study at the MTK, but also practical considerations of resources and/or time. Thus some of the *rGyud bZhi* material on pulse and urine diagnosis (Tib.: *rtsa la brtag pa* and *chu la brtag pa* respectively) for example, is often less relevant in contemporary practice, where some of the pulse diagnosis material is utilised and other parts are neglected, and urine diagnosis is often omitted altogether. Instead, diagnosis often centres on pulse diagnosis and questioning, in addition to an amchi's use of a sphygmomanometer to take the patient's blood pressure (Samuel 2001, 252–53). In Ladakh, Besch described pulse diagnosis as the most important skill for amchi (Besch 2006, 66), and I found that this was also the focus for amchi in Darjeeling, where Amchi Lobsang Thubten used only pulse diagnosis and questioning (alongside use of a sphygmomanometer) at the MTK clinic, and Amchi Lobsang Samten mainly used pulse diagnosis and questioning (and a sphygmomanometer), occasionally supplemented with urine analysis, at the CTMI clinic.

In addition, different traditions often prevail in different geographical regions, and may either focus on different texts, or accompany study of the *rGyud bZhi* with other, perhaps more 'local' knowledge (for example, local herbal knowledge), and amchi may specialise in different practices. This is often particularly true in the case of hereditary amchi, who may make their own medicines and/or be distinguished by their particular medical expertise (Schrempf 2007, 101). In Gangtok, I interviewed Amchi Sonam Topda at the independent Gangjong Sorig Clinic. He had trained at the MTK College in Dharamsala, but now made his own medicines, from plants collected for him from the surrounding area. In Amdo, northeast Tibet, Schrempf describes the focus on external therapies such as bloodletting (Tib.: *gtar*) and administration of purgatives (Tib.: *bshal*)—treatments rarely used at the Lhasa Mentsikhang. She also notes that many of the hereditary amchi in Amdo continue to produce their own medicines, rather than buy those produced in large factories (2007, 100).[20] In terms of textual learning there, she found that contemporary Bonpo

---

20. In fact, these are frequently preferred to the medicines produced in Lhasa factories by patients too, and are often particularly sought after (Schrempf 2007, 100–1).

Illustration 11. *Thangka* depicting medicinal plants,
Lhasa Mentiskhang, TAR

amchi in Nagchu often focus on the 'standard' Bon[21] medical text, the *'Bum bZhi*, considered by the Bonpo tradition to be the 'original' Tibetan medical text from which a number of hereditary lineages result, and from which the *rGyud bZhi* is adapted (2007, 98–99). Thus, whilst these amchi study the *rGyud bZhi*, this is in addition to other texts, and it is often the relationship with the local teacher and the transmission of medical and pharmacological practice that is in fact 'considered to be of most importance' (2007, 97; see also Besch 2006, 67–68). Here then, as Schrempf concludes, these amchi's models of 'Tibetan medicine' often overlap with, or even 'exist outside of', the 'institutionalised and modernized Tibetan medicine' represented by the Mentsikhang system (2007, 93).

---

21. Whilst debate continues in regard to whether or not the contemporary Tibetan tradition of Bon constitutes a 'fifth school' of Buddhism or is, in fact, another tradition entirely (see Bjerken 2001; Kvaerne 1976 and Samuel 1993), there is a small amount of literature on Bonpo medical traditions, such as the research mentioned here by Schrempf (2007) and work by Millard (2013).

Broad differences in practice within both Chinese-controlled Tibet and exile are also evident. For example, in a Tibetan medicine hospital that I visited in the Chinese city of Xining in 2010, there was a heavy focus on physical therapies such as moxibustion, herbal baths, acupuncture and massage,[22] whereas in the MTK clinic in Dalhousie, Samuel found that herbal medicine treatments—which differed significantly from those described in the *rGyud bZhi*—predominated, with two or three different kinds of pills prescribed to take at different times of day (2001, 251–58).[23] In terms of such medicines, Tsarong describes some of the most commonly-prescribed Tibetan medical formulations and their uses, including *Srog 'dzin 11*, *Shing kun 25* (Devil's dung 25) and *A gar 35* (Eaglewood 35), described in the *Bods man gyi Tsad gZhi* text as for use in the treatment of *srog rlung*, in addition to a number of other formulations described in other medical texts, a number of which are related to the treatment of *rlung*-related 'madness' (1991, 50–59).[24]

Finally, in terms of mental disorders particularly, there may be significant differences evident between treatments laid out in the *rGyud bZhi* and amchi's practice. For example, the text describes many herbal medicines for treating *smyo nad*, and Tibetan doctors I interviewed echoed this—especially in cases of *rlung* (or other *nyes pa*-related) disturbance. Indeed, the MTK's Tibetan Medicine Museum in Dharamsala displays many plants, precious stones and medical compounds labelled (in English) for use in the treatment of 'psychosis' and 'insanity'. Nevertheless, in reality, I found in Darjeeling that amchi were rarely consulted in the first instance for such conditions, and instead ritual and religious specialists were normally consulted in cases of disorders such as this.

As we can see then, Sowa Rigpa, practised across the Himalayan region, is by definition a 'complex and heterogeneous system of thought and practice' (Samuel 2001, 263). This is not surprising when we consider the multiple influences which have impacted on the different variants of this tradition. Today,

---

22. These types of therapies were marketed particularly towards potential affluent Chinese patients, with new private hospitals building hotel-like accommodation to house them (at high cost) during short periods of treatment.

23. Samuel notes that in contrast, the amchi at the Delhi clinic he observed offered cupping and gold needle moxibustion (2001, 264 [note 11]).

24. Millard also describes a number of medical compounds prescribed for patients suffering from various types of *rlung* disorder presenting at Amchi Dhonden's Tibetan medicine clinics in the UK (2007), as does Jacobson in Darjeeling (2000, 498), and the principal formulations recommended for the treatment of *srog rlung* disorders by the chief pharmacist at the Tibetan Medical Center Pharmacy in Upper Dharamsala are listed by Epstein and Topgay as *Agar-Gayba* (Eaglewood-8), *Agar-Chonga* (Eaglewood-15), *Agar-Nyshu* (Eaglewood-20) and *Agar-Songna* (Eaglewood-35) (1982, 78).

the vast majority of amchi in India train at the MTK. The *rGyud bZhi* remains the main textual authority in Sowa Rigpa across the Himalayan region, and the focus of much Western scholarship on 'Tibetan medicine', despite its questionable utility in certain aspects of clinical practice. In reality, this text is only one of many sources of knowledge for contemporary practitioners of Sowa Rigpa, and significant differences between what is laid out in the *rGyud bZhi* and medical practice are often evident across the region.

Illnesses related to the mind are often a particularly clear example of this diversity. As we have seen, mental disorders are included in two sections of the *rGyud bZhi*, delineated by the Tibetan amchi Pasang Y. Arya as '[m]ental disequilibrium (mild psychological disorders mainly, belonging to wind disorders in Tibetan medicine)' and '[i]nsanity (psychopathic and psychotic disorders)'.[25] However, in practice, whilst amchi commonly treat *rlung* conditions, they may in fact be the last specialists to be consulted in the event of a severe mental disorder such as *smyo nad*. In such cases, it is more usual to consult—at least initially—an astrologer or a ritual specialist such as a local lama or *sngags pa*. Such conditions are considered more than likely to include a religious component of some kind, such as a spirit affliction, and it is the religious practitioners who are thus the experts in such cases, as will be explored in the next chapter. Moreover, there are numerous additional ways in which religious beliefs and practices can be involved in the causative explanations and treatment of illness—particularly illnesses pertaining to the mind—and it is to this topic which I turn next.

Religion and Mental Health in the Tibetan Context

'Mental health' is defined by Epstein and Topgay as 'a mind freed from the influence of the afflictive mental factors'. These three 'mental factors' (Tib.: *nyon mongs*, Skt.: *kleśa*) of the Buddhist tradition—delusion (Tib.: *gti mug*, Skt.: *moha*); attachment (Tib.: *'dod chags*, Skt.: *rāga*) and aversion (Tib.: *zhe sdang*, Skt.: *dveṣa*)—are not only the ultimate underlying causes of both physical and mental diseases (Epstein and Topgay 1982, 68), but are also said to give rise to the *nyes pa*, disturbances in which lead to illness. As Clifford summarised: '[e]motional imbalance produces humoral imbalance that is manifested as a psychiatric disturbance' (1989, 139).

---

25. http://www.tibetanmedicine-edu.org/index.php/psychology-and-psychotherapy.

I have already mentioned some of the links between health, illness and religion in the Tibetan context, such as the frame story of the *rGyud bZhi* and the tradition of monastic amchi. In addition, in pre-modern Tibet,[26] there was often a dearth of medical practitioners in many areas, leaving many people reliant on ritual intervention (Cantwell 1995, 167–68). Medicine's relationship to Buddhism is emphasised in some amchi's clinics through a plethora of Buddhist imagery (Jacobson 2000, 417), although this may vary significantly in different clinics: Samuel notes, for example, that in the clinics he studied in Dalhousie and Delhi there was very little of this, but in the clinic in Dharamsala (which catered mainly to Westerners), there was far more.[27] Indeed, as we saw from Illustration 6, in the MTK clinic in Darjeeling, religious iconography (in the form of a Medicine Buddha *thangka* on the wall) was clearly visible here too. In this section I will consider what has been described as the 'Buddhicisation' of the Sowa Rigpa tradition, as a result of the 'Buddhist hegemony' in Tibet (Gerke 2013, 94). More recent influences on this 'Buddhicisation' of medical theory and practice include the contemporary political situation in Chinese-controlled Tibet and exile, and the marketing of 'Tibetan medicine' for a Western audience. Furthermore, the multiple ways in which this relationship between religion and medicine plays out in the Tibetan context results in a number of 'religious' treatments for mental disorders, from the increasing of individual merit (Tib.: *bsod nams*) through Buddhist activities (such as circumambulating stupa or monasteries) to the making of offerings to deities thought to be involved in the causation of illness, and I will introduce these here. As Jacobson noted in Darjeeling, and as I found here too, for many lay Tibetans, religious and medical matters often remain 'deeply intertwined' (2000, 511).

The fundamental role of the *nyon mongs* in the formation of *rlung* is described in two places in the *rGyud bZhi*: Chapter Two of the *Man ngag rGyud* and Chapter Eight of the *bShad rGyud* (Ga 2010, 182). Moreover, the *nyon mongs* are also implicated in the formation of the other two *nyes pa*, as Epstein and Topgay explain:

> Tibetan medicine ultimately attributes imbalances in any of the three
> nyes-pa to psychological causes. The three nyes-pa owe their arising
> to the three afflictive mental factors that serve as the roots of all un-

---

26. This term indicates the period of Tibetan history right up until the Chinese intervention in Tibet in 1950.

27. In conversation with the author, 10th July 2014.

wholesome states of mind and that in Buddhist theory serve as the
basis for birth in cyclic existence (1982, 71).

Thus certain psychological states can be both cause and consequence of disturbance to the *nyes pa*, where this disturbance may manifest in mental illness.

This idea has been discussed by Western authors, some of whom have suggested an English translation of *nyon mongs* as 'destructive emotions', discussing their role in mental health from a more Western perspective, with Goleman, for example, defining them as those emotions which 'cause harm to ourselves or others' (2004, xx). However, I would argue that this link between the *nyon mongs* and the formation of the *nyes pa* is not at the forefront for most Tibetans; it was certainly never mentioned in Darjeeling, where discussions—with amchi and lay Tibetans alike—around the causation of mental illness focused on more immediate concepts such as karma, adverse life events and spirit affliction. Moreover, such competing theories of causation (for example, karma versus humoural disturbance) reflect the 'discrepancies' between notions of anatomy in the Tantric and medical systems (Gyatso 2004, 87), as a number of Indian Tantric ideas were 're-worked' 'into a workable Tibetan medical body' (Gerke 2013, 89). This is also evident in the continuing (and perhaps unresolvable) debate over the *rtsa* mentioned above, the principal problem being the attempts to match up the Tantric theory of the *rtsa* with the medical perspective on anatomy (Gyatso 2004). Nonetheless, whilst the debate over whether the *rGyud bZhi* was in reality authored by a buddha or a Tibetan medical specialist 'played out over centuries of Tibetan medical thinking' (Czaja 2005/2006, 132), Samuel notes that there is in fact little in the text itself to indicate a close connection with Tantric Buddhism (Samuel 2001, 256). Indeed, Gyatso argues that the focus of treatment in the *rGyud bZhi* is very much on 'a kind of care that is very much distinct from the ritual approaches to healing emphasized in Buddhist sources' (2015, 101). Thus whilst canonical Buddhist texts on healing describe 'the powers of meditation, ritual and faith', the medical *rGyud bZhi* only 'briefly' mentions ritual and magical healing (Gyatso 2015, 98–99).

Interestingly, more recent history has seen a move towards the secularisation of 'Tibetan Medicine' in Chinese-controlled Tibet simultaneous to an emphasising of its Buddhist dimensions in India and beyond. The beginning of the twentieth century marked a shift 'from the spiritual to the pragmatic', overseen by the thirteenth Dalai Lama as part of his 'modernisation' initiative (Samuel 2001, 262). Following this, as I mentioned briefly above, the Cultural Revolution brought broad changes to Tibetan medicine and its learning in Tibet. Janes describes how during this time the Lhasa Mentsikhang was 'brought under the direct control of Chinese health bureaucracy', with restrictions brought in banning monk-physicians from practising, and the more Buddhist aspects of practice (such as the use of the root Tantra texts) de-emphasised and later banned, Buddhist healing rituals denounced as 'feudal superstition', and many medical texts destroyed. Many students who had to study solely from 'hastily prepared, secularized textbooks' in training later derided them as 'worthless' (Janes 1995, 17–20). The 1980s then brought further change: Tibetan medicine was recognised as valuable again—this time by the Chinese government as part of 'the family of Chinese traditional medicines'—and was provided with state financial and political support (Janes 1995, 21). Unfortunately, by this time, much medical knowledge—and numerous medical texts—had been lost, and religious aspects of medicine were still on the margins of medical theory and practice. This governmental support continues to this day however, and a certain amount of reintroduction of selected Buddhist aspects of Sowa Rigpa has been allowed in teaching and practice. Nevertheless, Sowa Rigpa has become significantly secularised and 'rationalised' not only as a consequence of this history, but also contemporary state policies and the influence of biomedical theory and practice (Janes 1995, 2002; Adams 2001a, 2001b), and amchi themselves may sometimes play down the religious aspects of Tibetan medicine (Adams 2002, 211–12). In addition, internal and external interests and pressures, such as those from the PRC government to 'internationalise' Tibetan medicine, and that from international development organisations (Adams 2002, 215–16) often compound this situation. In Amdo, Schrempf quotes an amchi who explains, 'In the past, the most famous doctors were both lama and physician. Nowadays, many physicians are like one-eyed doctors, since they do not believe in religion' (2007, 103). Meanwhile, for lay Tibetans, the use of this ('Buddhist') 'Traditional Tibetan medicine' can also be one of the few remaining means through which Tibetan (Buddhist) identity can be expressed 'safely' in contemporary Tibet (Janes 1999a, 407).

In contrast, for Tibetans in exile, there has often been an *emphasis* on the Buddhist aspects of 'Tibetan medicine'. For example, when I interviewed Amchi Dorjee Rabten, senior consultant physician in the Tibetan Medical Centre in Bangalore and ex-Director of the CCTM, in Dharamsala, he described the 'important role' that Tibetan Medicine can play in mental illness, particularly in contributing to our 'understanding the nature of the mind, how suffering comes about, how you can help yourself'—presumably here referring to Buddhist notions of the mind.[28] I would suggest that some of this emphasis on Ti-

28. Interview conducted with Amchi Dorjee Rabten at Kunga's Guesthouse restaurant, Dharamsala, by the author, 28th July 2012.

betan Buddhism's role in Sowa Rigpa is occurring as part of Tibetans' fight for cultural survival—where Tibetan 'culture' more often than not means Tibetan Buddhism—and 'Tibetan medicine' is often marketed as a 'holistic' health system to Westerners.[29] Thus, whilst representations of Sowa Rigpa aimed at Westerners often focus on the 'spiritual' aspects of Tibetan medical theory and practice, such as the role of the *nyon mongs* in the arising of disease (Samuel 2001, 262) and an emphasis of the 'Buddhist' motivations of good amchi (Besch 2006, 103–4), such factors are often of less concern to Tibetan patients.

'Religion' and the Treatment of Mental Illness

As I noted above, historically Tibetan doctors have also often been religious specialists. In both the old Lhasa Mentsikhang and the first years of the MTK in Dharamsala, the majority of doctors, students and staff were Tibetan Buddhist monks (Kloos 2010, 74 [note 67]). Today, this varies significantly across different regions. In Spiti for example, Besch found that a number of amchi were renowned ritual specialists who performed religious practices 'based on the *Rgyud bzhi*' as part of their medical practice (2006, 156–61). Whilst I was in Darjeeling in 2011, a number of nuns had recently graduated from CTMI, although at the Darjeeling MTK the resident amchi was non-monastic, as were several other amchi I visited in Gangtok. Similarly, in Dalhousie in the 1990s, Samuel found that only a minority of the Tibetan doctors were monks or nuns (2001, 252). Nonetheless, strong links between the two spheres remain, particularly in regard to the manufacture of medicines, where herbal compounds are often still produced and empowered through Tantric rituals related to the practices of specific deities (Donden 1997, 215–18). Moreover, in Ladakh and Spiti, some amchi may mark the end of their training with a ritual empowerment (Tib.: *dbang*), which serves to both confer spiritual power to the amchi (and allow him to receive particular restricted Tantric teachings) and to initiate him as a full member of the amchi community (Besch 2006, 67).

In this context, from a lay perspective, for an individual and her family, a case of *sems nad* can bring forth multiple explanations of illness which span both the 'medical' and 'religious' spheres, taking in notions of the *nyes pa*, karma and spirit affliction, for example. This supports Williams and Healy's notion of 'exploratory maps' of illness, whereby sufferers attempt to make sense of their experience of mental illness—particularly in its initial stages—through com-

---

29. This is evident in many English language books on Sowa Rigpa, which have titles such as Pema Dorjee's *The Spiritual Medicine of Tibet* (2005) or Terry Clifford's *The Diamond Healing: Tibetan Buddhist Medicine and Psychiatry* (1989).

binations of 'external', 'internal' and 'direct' causes as they seek meaning in their illness experience (2001). Not surprisingly, Tibetans' health-seeking behaviour often reflects this plurality, and an individual may consult a number of medical and religious specialists concurrently or in short succession in the event of illness. Similarly, whilst an amchi may prescribe medicines (and perhaps also physical therapies of some kind) for a case of *sems nad*, depending on the perceived cause, she might also simultaneously advise the patient directly on some religious activities, or alternatively, suggest the consultation of a particular kind of religious specialist. Arya describes treatments for mental illnesses including mantra recitation, rites and rituals, 'soul retrieval', meditation, Tibetan Yoga, the cultivation of bodhicitta, receiving of initiations and wearing of amulets.[30] In Dharamsala, Wangda found that patients and their families predominantly consulted religious practitioners for conditions such as 'anxiety, depression and psychosis' (1996, 126–27), and in Darjeeling, Jacobson described a number of 'treatment' activities reported by patients diagnosed with *srog rlung* including recitation of mantras and prayers, prostrations, circumambulation and pilgrimage (2000, 508). Where a condition is thought to be related to some kind of spirit affliction, whilst the main recourse for the patient will likely involve the consultation of a monastic or non-monastic ritual specialist (perhaps in addition to the making of offerings to the offending spirit(s)), the amchi may be able to prescribe medicine to deal with, for example, an underlying *rlung* condition, which may have facilitated the immediate spirit problem.

Finally, we turn to qualities and skills of the amchi where, even for non-monastic practitioners, Buddhism is often seen as an integral factor in the likely success of their practice and prescribed treatments. In Dharamsala, Ozawa-De Silva and Ozawa-De Silva were told by Tibetan amchi that a medical practitioner with a 'deep knowledge of Buddhist philosophy' is 'better equipped to help his or her patients' (2011, 103). Indeed, the *rGyud bZhi* states the importance of compassion and the manifestation of a 'mind of enlightenment' during amchi's practice (Clark 1995, 224–33; Phuntsok and Lhamo 2009, 385–90). Furthermore, the compassionate profession of the medical specialist is viewed very positively in Tibetan Buddhism, with the *rGyud bZhi* explaining that 'a physician who has abandoned deceit and desire and who engages in healing will proceed to the unsurpassed state of Buddhahood' (Clark 1995, 233). Thus Ozawa-De Silva and Ozawa-De Silva tell us that 'healing the mind' (Tib.: *blo-gso*) involves:

> showing kindness, compassion and general friendliness to the patient, as well as giving advice that can help the patient to achieve a calm and

---

30. http://www.tibetanmedicine-edu.org/index.php/psychology-and-psychotherapy.

healthy mind, which is especially important for patients suffering from rlung disorders, since these disorders are especially connected with mental disturbances. Often this advice is in the form of, or based on, Buddhist teachings (2011, 109).

Thus, with the *nyon mongs* delineated (at least in the *rGyud bZhi*) as underlying causes of illness, and the notion of *rlung*—with its twin origins in medical and Tantric theory—integral to the understanding of the functioning of the mind, religion and mental health are never far apart in Sowa Rigpa. With the 'secularisation' of Sowa Rigpa in one geographical and political arena and the emphasising of Buddhist aspects of 'Tibetan medicine' in another occurring simultaneously alongside the politicisation of *rlung* illnesses, constructing meaning in the event of illness and health-seeking behaviour is a complex, multifactorial endeavour. Furthermore, in places such as Darjeeling, whilst overtly religious treatments are often a preferred method of managing certain forms of mental ill-health, the required practitioners are not necessarily available, as we saw in Chapter Two. In addition, perhaps there has been a growing divide between the spheres of religion, health and medicine here which has not occurred to the same extent in other areas, such as Spiti, where we saw that a number of amchi were also renowned ritual specialists. In their place are often a multitude of local and biomedical options, bringing Tibetan concepts of health, illness and anatomy into an often uncomfortable meeting with contrasting and contradictory explanatory models and, as we shall see next, forcing medical specialists to navigate between them.

Meeting the West: Western and Biomedical Interpretations of Tibetan Medicine

I mentioned above that some attempts have been made to equate particular Tibetan medical and Tantric concepts with biomedical ones, for example the linking of the *rtsa* to the blood vessels, nerves and lymphatic system of biomedical anatomy. A number of comparisons and equivalences have also been drawn between some of the Sowa Rigpa and biomedical diagnostic categories of mental disorders, by both Tibetan and non-Tibetan authors and practitioners. For example, Millard has suggested that Tibetan words which convey 'depression' (for example *skyo snang, sems pham pa, sems sdug*) and 'anxiety' (for example *sems ngal, sems 'tshab pa, sems khrel*) or 'panic' (for example *'jig skrag zhad snang, dngags skrag*) correspond to the biomedical concept of 'neurotic' states, whilst various Tibetan terms denoting 'madness' (for example *smyo nad, sems rnyog dra, sems skyon nad rigs*) correspond to the bio-medical concept of 'psychotic' states (2007, 247). Similarly, as I mentioned briefly above, *rlung* has often been equated with the Western notion of 'stress' by Tibetans and Westerners alike. Furthermore, a number of Western authors in the field of psychology have drawn comparisons between Tibetan conceptions of the body and mind and certain Western theories, such as Jungian psychology and psychiatry.[31]

However, Samuel notes the problematic 'uncritical' use of biomedical equivalents of Tibetan diagnostic categories by Western authors, when there is 'no reason to assume a one-to-one correspondence' between them, and there is in fact 'no consensus about these translations' (2001, 253). I described above some of the problematic translations of Tibetan concepts such as *rlung, nyes pa*, and *rtsa*, and Loizzo, Blackhall and Rapgay suggest that Tibetan medicine's models, methods, and predictions actually differ so significantly from biomedical ones as to make them 'completely incompatible' with biomedicine (2009, 224). In this section I will briefly introduce some of the Western interpretations of the main Tibetan mental illness categories. These will be examined in more detail as I turn to a number of case studies in Part Three in order to illustrate how these concepts and categories play out for Tibetans living in Darjeeling.

In Darjeeling and Gangtok, Jacobson observed Tibetans diagnosed with *rlung* conditions presenting at a Sowa Rigpa clinic, and drew comparisons to biomedical diagnoses in the fourth edition of the DSM (DSM-IV, APA 1994). He suggested that in five out of the six cases he examined, the patients with a diagnosis of *srog rlung* 'qualified for both major depression (MD) and general anxiety disorder (GAD), or missed full comorbidity by only a single criterion symptom' (2007, 235). He noted however, that patients tended to present with a number of somatic traits, which are not included in the DSM-IV criteria for either diagnosis, and he highlighted the fact that there was no mention in the DSM or ICD systems of the specific somatic symptoms listed in the *rGyud bZhi*. Based on this research, Jacobson suggested (albeit with the caveat that it was a very small sample) that 'the closest DSM equivalent for *srog rlung* may be "highly somaticised comorbid depression and generalized anxiety"', thus placing *srog rlung* 'in the company of similar syndromes of highly somaticised, comorbid anxiety and depression which have been described in several other cultural settings' (2007, 236). However, conducting research at a Tibetan Medicine clinic in Edinburgh (UK), Millard found that Western patients diagnosed

---

31. Examples of this include Radmila Moacanin's *The Essence of Jung's Psychology and Tibetan Buddhism: Western and Eastern Paths to the Heart* (1986) and Anodea Judith's *Eastern Body, Western Mind: Psychology and the Chakra System as a Path to the Self* (2011).

by the resident Tibetan amchi as having *srog rlung* (rather than, for example, *smyo nad*) had been diagnosed by biomedical psychiatrists with 'schizophrenia' and 'bipolar disorder' (2007, 257–59), often regarded as more 'severe' types of mental illness than, say, generalised anxiety disorder or depression. Furthermore, other researchers have equated certain cases of *srog rlung* with PTSD in exiled Tibetans (Benedict et al. 2009). PTSD, of course, is characterised by quite specific symptoms including the repeated re-living of a traumatic event in intrusive memories ('flashbacks'),[32] setting it apart from depressive and anxiety disorders. Such findings clearly indicate the difficulties of comparing these Tibetan and biomedical categories.

Srog rlung then, appears to be a rather complex and problematic category for such endeavours. In the Tibetan understanding of this condition, whilst mild cases of disturbance to this *rlung* current tend to produce 'neurotic' symptoms such as sadness, depression or anxiety, more severe cases can produce very severe symptoms—often those which biomedicine classifies as defining 'psychotic' states—including hallucinations, delusions and/or confusion, and some amchi have even described or translated such cases as 'schizophrenia' (Rosenbush 2013). It is clear then that *rlung* conditions are on a continuum, whereby symptoms can range from the very mild to the severe. This of course contrasts sharply with the biomedical distinction between 'neurotic' and 'psychotic' disorders.

The Tibetan category of *smyo nad* may be easier to equate with biomedical categories. Millard and Jacobson both argue that this Tibetan term translates quite easily into the English terms 'madness' or 'insanity', and concepts of its symptoms share similarities with Western understandings of 'psychosis' (Millard 2007). In Darjeeling, Jacobson described the symptoms of those diagnosed with *smyo nad*: hallucinations; delusions and 'disruptive speech and behaviour' (2002, 261), which echo some biomedical descriptions of schizophrenia and other psychotic disorders.[33] We will explore this further in Chapters Seven and Eight, when I describe two case studies where *smyo nad* and 'madness' were discussed.

In addition to the differences in symptomatology between Sowa Rigpa and biomedical diagnostic categories, common Tibetan and Western perceptions of illness causation only highlight these differences further. As I mentioned above, from a Tibetan perspective, fasting, insomnia, physical and mental exertion, vomiting and exposure to cold can all lead to a disturbance in the *rlung*

---

32. http://apps.who.int/classifications/icd10/browse/2010/en#/F40-F48.
33. http://apps.who.int/classifications/icd10/browse/2010/en#/F20-F29.

(Rabgay 1985, 49), and depression, mental discomfort, poor diet and certain 'behavioural patterns' can contribute to the causation of *smyo nad* (Epstein and Topgay 1982, 76). In this chapter we have also seen the significant role of the *nyes pa* as an underlying factor in all manifestations of illness, and the often strong focus on religious factors such as karma. In reference to *smyo nad, gdon* often play a significant role in perceptions of causation, and I will explore this in more detail in the next chapter. These explanations of mental illness and its causation are reflected in health-seeking behaviour which often encompasses a broad range of religious and medical activities, and some of these Sowa Rigpa notions of mental health and illness, its causation and treatment, clearly demonstrate the difficulties of equating its categories with those of biomedicine. This will be explored further through a number of ethnographic case studies in Part Three. There, an examination of some particular cases of mental illness which I encountered in Darjeeling will help to illustrate the complex ways in which individuals and their families make sense of and treat episodes of mental illness in the context of a medically-pluralistic system, where Sowa Rigpa and biomedical practitioners offer often very different explanations and treatment pathways.

*   *   *

I have given in this chapter an overview of Sowa Rigpa approaches to anatomy and the subtle body, where the role of *rlung* is integral to the healthy functioning of the mind and body, and disturbance in its functioning is implicated in mental ill-health. As we have seen, such disturbance can result in symptoms ranging from sadness and anxiety to hallucinations and 'insanity'. These professional perspectives on mental illness—from both amchi and the medical texts—can serve as a counterpoint to lay Tibetan perspectives, which have often been neglected in the research to date, and which will be examined in Part Three of this book through a number of case studies and interviews from my fieldwork in Darjeeling.

As has become clear, whilst the *rGyud bZhi* remains the main textual authority for Sowa Rigpa, in reality medical practice often diverges significantly from what is laid out in the text. Historical and contemporary attempts at the 'secularisation' and 'Buddhicisation' of Sowa Rigpa highlight the complex relationship between religion, health and medicine in the Tibetan context, particularly in the arena of mental health and illness. Here, concepts such as *rlung* can represent much more than diagnostic categories—where the survival of 'Tibetan medicine' is seen as fundamental to the survival of Tibetan culture for exiled Tibetans, 'Traditional Tibetan medicine' is viewed by the Chinese state as a new revenue stream, and *rlung* can be a safe way in which to articulate distress or express a Tibetan identity in a complex political situation, notions of mental 'health' and 'illness' become much broader than we might expect. However, within this complex political arena, the personal experience of *sems nad* and its healing has not yet fully been explored, and the category of *smyo nad* particularly has been neglected. Attempts to correlate Tibetan and Western approaches to mental health and illness are complex and often frustrating, and may often be played out on an individual level through the consultation of a number of biomedical and Sowa Rigpa practitioners and religious specialists in attempts to manage and treat mental illness when it occurs. In Part Three I will use a number of case studies and material from interviews to examine this process in more detail; however first, in the next chapter, I will focus on the often important role of spirits in mental illness.

CHAPTER FOUR

Spirits, Mental Health and Healing

In the previous chapter, I described some Tibetan approaches to mental health and illness, including a number of 'religious' aspects of Tibetan notions of health, illness and healing. One significant way in which the relationship between mental illness and religion is evident is through causative explanations involving various types of spirit affliction. Indeed, in the Tibetan context, different types of spirits and deities can be involved in mental illness in a number of ways, from the *smyo byed kyi gdon* ('spirits that cause madness') mentioned in the *rGyud bZhi* to the period of 'madness' which often precedes recognition as a spirit-medium, often understood to be caused by uncontrollable possession by a deity and/or spirit (see for example Day 1989; Diemberger 2005; Gutschow 1997; Rösing 2006). Such explanations of illness reflect the fundamental role which spirits and deities play in everyday life for many Tibetans and, as we shall see in the following chapters, in Darjeeling, such different types of non-human entities were often discussed by Tibetan informants, particularly in relation to mental illness. I will refer to 'possession' and 'mediumship' here rather than 'trance' states, as I think these terms better reflect the Tibetan conception of this, although all of these terms have been used in the ethnically-Tibetan context.

In this chapter I will explore the place of spirits and deities in Tibetan society, and the different roles they can play in the causation and healing of various forms of mental illness, where the boundaries between 'illness', 'possession' and 'mediumship' are not always clear cut. Here, as Day notes, possession practices frequently 'straddle important local boundaries between sickness and health' (1989, 11). I will highlight the often significant differences between textual and professional perspectives on the role of such entities, providing a backdrop from which to examine lay notions of spirits and deities and their role in mental health and illness, and how these are reflected in health-seeking behaviour. As we shall see, whilst in the Tibetan context, there are understood to be certain types of spirit affliction related to mental illness—particularly *smyo nad*—there are also experiences of relationships between humans and deities which do not fall under the category of *sems nad*, and are instead understood as experiences of mediumship. Despite this, biomedical practitioners working in Darjeeling and the surrounding area may interpret such episodes as evidence of a biomedically-diagnosed mental illness, and this complex issue is explored here. I will also outline here some of the Western anthropological and biomedical approaches to possession and mediumship, where explanations often focus around notions of 'dissociation' and the supposed 'functions' of possession and mediumship for those involved.

In Tibetan society, non-human entities are understood to cause harm and misfortune in a number of ways—not all of them related to mental illness—through both possession and non-possession spirit afflictions. In relation to mental illness, it is possible for individuals to become inadvertently possessed by a (usually lower order) spirit such as a *gdon* (usually translated as 'spirit') or *(shi) 'dre* ("(shin) dré", generally translated as 'ghost' and understood to refer to the spirit of someone recently deceased).[1] The consequences of this can be varied, but such possessions often result in mental illness of some kind for the afflicted person. In such cases, ritual intervention is usually required in order to subjugate the spirit/deity involved and bring it under control, 'exorcising' it out of the body/consciousness. A variety of practitioners can be consulted to conduct such ritual intervention, including monastic ritual specialists and independent Tantric practitioners such as *sngags pa* and *lha pa* (spirit-mediums).

This last group of specialists, the *lha pa*, highlight the fact that in the Tibetan context, 'possession' is not exclusively undesirable or 'negative', as for example in cases of possession by *gdon* or *'dre*. Possession can also be viewed in a 'positive' light, as in the case of spirit-mediumship, where the practitioner is able to control and manage a possession through ritual in order to make predictions and/or heal others through various techniques. As the Tibetan amchi Lobsang Rapgay explains, 'In the Tibetan view, there are many different kinds of possession, some deliberate, healthy, and functional, and some inadvertent and dysfunctional' (1985, 51). I will examine these different forms of involvement with spirits and deities, and through this, a picture will start to emerge of some fundamental Tibetan notions of the person and their relationship to the environment and the deities which reside within it which underlie many explanations of mental health and illness.

---

1. Millard quotes one geshe's description of *shi 'dre* as 'spirits of the dead who because of some unfulfilled task, such as an existing vendetta, remain attached to the place where they lived' (2007, 261).

The Role of Spirits and Deities in Tibetan Society

As in many societies, the spirits and deities which populate the Tibetan landscape play an important role in Tibetan society, able to help or hinder one's daily life in a number of ways, from causing misfortune and illness or protecting against harm, to affecting the weather and crops. Samuel describes the 'embedded ecology' of Tibetan life (2007, 221), whereby Tibetans have a 'direct and intimate' relationship with the local deities (Samuel 1993, 191). The first Western account of such Tibetan entities was Nebesky-Wojkowitz's work focusing on protective deities (1956), and a number of more recent works have examined these particular deities in more detail (see for example, Blondeau 1998). Descriptions of the vast array of non-human entities, from protective deities to water spirits, differ within both Tibetan and non-Tibetan works. Samuel and Cornu describe, for example, a delineation into 'eight classes' (Tib.: *lha srin sde brgyad*), often found in Tibetan Buddhist Nyingma texts, which usually in fact includes ten classes of deities: *klu* ("lu", Skt.: *nāga*); *sa bdag* ("sa dak"); *gnyan* ("nyen"); *btsan* ("tsen"); *rgyal po* ("gyelpo"); *bdud* ("du", Skt.: *mā ra*); *ma mo* (Skt.: *mātrika*); *gza'* ("sa"); *gnod sbyin* ("nö jin", Skt.: *yakṣa*) and *lha* (Skt.: *deva*) (Samuel 1993, 161–63; Cornu 1997, 247–53). These entities are situated within a 'pantheon' of Tibetan deities, delineated by Samuel into four different components from the *yi dam* (Tibetan Buddhist Tantric deities) down to malevolent spirits. However, as he notes, the boundary between these categories can be a little blurred (1993, 166–67), with this 'pantheon' a 'series of intermeshing patron-client relationships' rather than a 'rigid hierarchy' (1993, 191), indicating the delicate nature of negotiating relations with these spirits and deities. A critical point here is the position from which Tibetans are dealing with such entities, with lay Tibetans negotiating from a position of inferiority—given the deities' greater spiritual power—and Tibetan lamas negotiating from a position of superiority—their greater spiritual power provided by their Tantric Buddhist accomplishments. Thus whilst the lay population need to politely request the assistance of the deities, lamas are instead able to compel the deities to assist them when necessary (Samuel 2012, 170–71).

Underscoring humans' relationships with these entities is the Tibetan understanding of the environment and its historical 'taming' by Buddhism. In the current Tibetan Buddhist understanding, many of these deities were originally opponents of Buddhism, thought to have been subdued by the historical Indian Tantric Buddhist teacher Guru Rinpoche (Tib.: *Gu ru Rin po che*, Skt. *Padmasambhava*). Visiting Tibet in the eighth century, he subjugated the local gods and spirits using his superior spiritual power, which he held as a result of his Buddhist practice—understood to be stronger than all other forms of (non-Buddhist) spiritual power. A number of these deities were thus converted into protectors of Buddhism and its teachings. As a result, there are understood to be particular guardian deities who can be invoked to deal with problems related to some of the 'lower classes' of deities listed above. For example, Cornu describes a particular class of deities known as *btsan*—'the spirits of erring monks of earlier times'—noting that, '[w]hen they are subdued by a great practitioner, the Tsen often become the guardian of [Tibetan Buddhist] temples, shrines, and monasteries' (1997, 250–52). However, crucially, despite their subjugation, deities such as *btsan* and *rgyal po* are not necessarily positively disposed towards humans. As unenlightened deities (Tib.: *'jig rten pa*), they are subject to worldly emotions, and some in particular are characterised by arrogance and pride (particularly the class of spirits known as *rgyal po*), and may be easily offended and/or wrathful in nature—although they can be 'induced by ritual to be helpful and to prevent misfortune' (Samuel 1993, 161). As Calkowski notes, such deities are often 'at once easily offended and readily appeased' (1985, 70). Thus *btsan* and *rgyal po* are sometimes regarded as *lha* (gods),[2] at other times as malevolent spirits. Furthermore, *rgyal po* in particular are understood to be particularly dangerous: as a result of their previous lives as religious practitioners, they are understood to hold significant knowledge and power (Calkowski 1985, 107).

Despite the vast number of Tibetan deities and spirits described by different authors, in Darjeeling only a handful were discussed by Tibetans I spoke to— particularly in relation to mental health and illness—and I shall therefore limit my discussion to these. These were *lha* (this term was mainly used to refer to local protective deities, sometimes also called *yul lha*); *gdon* and *(shi)'dre* (sometimes used interchangeably) and *btsan* and *rgyal po* (often also described as 'local deities'). Due to their status as 'worldly'—that is unenlightened—deities, it is imperative for lay people to be highly cautious in their dealings with these kinds of entities. Such deities and spirits can be dangerous should you encounter them, especially if you have offended them, whether purposefully or inadvertently. Certainly such entities should not be relied upon for soteriological purposes in any way: as deities of this world, they may be able to help

---

2. The Tibetan term *lha*, which refers to both benevolent and malevolent entities, is a translation of the Sanskrit *deva* ('god'), and is used to refer to three different categories in the Tibetan context: local (unenlightened) deities, enlightened gods of the Buddhist heavens and Tantric deities (Samuel 1993, 165–66).

one achieve secular gains in *this* life, but are entirely useless when dealing with issues related to the next life and the Buddhist path towards enlightenment.

The presence of such entities, of course, necessitates individuals skilled in dealing with them—particularly when it is ascertained that they are responsible for causing harm within a community. Above I mentioned the superior power of Buddhism in comparison to the lesser spiritual power of such unenlightened deities, but in fact there are a number of different monastic and lay specialists who may be called upon to help in this sphere. Often it is spirit-mediums— usually referred to as *lha pa* (male) and *lha mo* (female) or *lha bzhugs mkhan* ("lha shuken")—who are consulted here, able to use the stronger spiritual power of higher level deities to subjugate *gdon*, *'dre*, *btsan* or *rgyal po* (see for example Day 1989 and Rösing 2006 in Ladakh; Diemberger 2005 in Tibet; Gutschow in Zangskar 1997 and Berglie (in a Tibetan refugee community) in Nepal 1976). In Ladakh, for example, Rösing describes 'shamans' (sometimes also referred to by the English word 'oracle'), who may be 'monastic oracles' or 'village shamanic healers' (Rösing 2006). Such practitioners often have a variety of areas of speciality, including divination, exorcism, various types of healing (for example sucking illness out of a patient's body) or recalling a wandering *bla* ("la", spirit, soul, life force).

In some areas, many spirit-mediums, whilst lay rather than monastic practitioners, come under the auspices of local monastery to some degree, or have the local lama's blessing for their work (Berglie 1976, 93). Furthermore, whilst the history of these types of spirit-mediums likely pre-dates the arrival of Buddhism in Tibet, today they are 'well integrated' into the Buddhist system (Samuel 1993, 194), as are the spirits and deities of the Tibetan pantheon mentioned above. Moreover, the very narrative of the 'taming' of Tibet by Guru Rinpoche through the superior power of Buddhism, and the hierarchical relationship between human and non-human entities which resulted from this, is re-enacted again and again through rituals conducted in response to spirit afflictions. Here, afflictions related to lower-level spirits can be treated (through their ritual exorcism or subjugation) by either a spirit-medium—through the stronger spiritual power of the higher-level deity possessing him or her—or a monastic practitioner, who is able to access and utilise the highest level of spiritual power due to his or her Buddhist Tantric skills.

In addition, another form of mediumship in the Tibetan context occurs in the form of officially-sanctioned 'oracle-priests', the most famous and high status of whom is the state oracle—the Nechung (Tib.: *gNas chung*) Oracle— who acts as a medium for Pehar, one of the protector deities of Tibet. These types of oracles perform divinations and are duly consulted on regular occasions by monastic and state authorities (Samuel 1993, 195), and such monastic practices 'have been integrated into discussions of religious salvation and state affairs' (Day 1989, 29). Indeed, whilst in contrast, incidences of possession by *gdon* themselves may appear to be very locally-situated, in fact as we saw, the larger system in which they are an integral part—the hierarchical relationship between humans and various non-human entities, both enlightened and unenlightened—is fundamental to not only Tibetans' understanding of the world, but also to Buddhism itself.

The Role of Spirits and Deities in Mental Illness and Its Healing

The rather complex relationship between spirits and mental illness in the Tibetan context may be more or less explicit in different situations. For example, *gdon* possession can cause *smyo nad* (madness), manifesting in sudden behavioural change, particularly out-of-character aggressive and/or violent behaviour. In Darjeeling, Amchi Lobsang Thubten described an afflicted individual becoming 'very aggressive' and restless, unable to sit still, perhaps also aggressive towards others, 'sweating, and talking non-stop'. In contrast, the inadvertent offence of a deity such as a *btsan* or *rgyal po* might cause a slow escalation of diverse symptoms related to the mind (such as confusion and/or nonsensical conversation), where the spirit cause may be less immediately clear. In Ladakh, for example, Day found numerous illnesses attributed to 'local gods, lu, tsan and a host of other figures' when they were 'thought to be angry, at a neglected rite or a polluted site, or greedy, for people's food or wealth'. Here, most cases of 'madness' were attributed (at least initially) to *gson 'dre* ("söndré", living demons) (1989, 278). In Dhorpatan, Nepal, Millard found that all the cases of mental illness he saw were related to the action of 'harmful spirits', and he reports that this kind of 'harm' was common amongst both Tibetans and Nepalis living in the area (2007, 259). Illnesses related to spirits may therefore occur as possession or non-possession afflictions, and the likelihood of a person being affected by spirits is also linked to a number of other Tibetan concepts, such as *rlung rta* ("loong ta", luck), *dbang (thang)* ("wang (tang)", spiritual power) (Calkowski 1985, 219–21), *bla* and *bsod nams* ("sonam", (Buddhist) merit). Thus for example, the Tibetan amchi Yeshi Donden explains that when *bla* or *bsod nams* are low (in other words, weak), it is possible for a spirit to 'come in and take over' (1997, 103), whilst Calkowski notes that *rlung rta* can offer some protection against spirit affliction (1985, 220). In addition, Rösing suggests that an episode of *smyo nad* may sometimes be the first sign of possession by a *gdon* or *lha* which often precedes recognition as a *lha bzhugs mkhan*. In such cases, 'madness' frequently plays a 'fundamental role at the outset on the path towards a vocation in shamanism' (2006, 128–29), as she describes:

> [D]escribed primarily as a kind of "madness" (*tsha ba tshu ba, nyon pa song* are the most commonly used terms for it), manifesting as erratic roaming around, various aches and pains, vivid dreams, confused visions and hallucinations, or perhaps indecent or nonsensical behaviour and running away (Rösing 2006, 114).

Initially, she argues, 'these people are always looked upon as "mad", until it gradually becomes clear that they are not suffering from a nondescript "normal madness" but from a shamanic illness', caused by a 'dramatic struggle between a *lha*, a god, that wants to possess the body, and the *de*, the demons' (2006, 114). Similarly, in Nepal, Berglie outlined the 'strange experiences' of one Tibetan *dpa' bo* medium, whom he described as being 'just like a "madman" (Tib. *smyon pa*)' (1976, 89). Of course, as this suggests, not every individual manifesting 'madness' is experiencing it as the first step of a shamanic calling—some people are simply suffering from what we might call 'normal madness'.

Moreover, the Tibetan notions of *rlung* ('wind') and *rtsa* ('channels') which were discussed in the previous chapter may also be involved in possession and mediumship, where disturbance in the *srog rlung* can be caused by a non-human entity. As Rapgay states: '[p]sychosis is said to result when the space or channel containing the subtle life-bearing *prana* is forcefully entered by another energy, usually a spirit but sometimes merely another increased *nyes-pa* (disturbing the relationship between *pranic* flow and mind)' (1985, 48). He explains:

> Invasion by spirit or *nyes-pa* ... creates a blockade in the inferior site [channel], occluding or reversing the current of *prana* upon which the mind rests. Thus, control over the functioning of mental processes is lost, with loss of memory and hysterical behaviour preceding full-fledged psychosis ... the spirit forcefully enters the site of the life-bearing current, de-localizing it and functioning itself in that space. This is akin to "two people forcefully living together in one room", when one becomes more powerful, the other loses control and struggle becomes commonplace. No longer does the affected person's mind bear its original nature, but that individual has not totally lost his mind either (1985, 49–50).

As Rapgay suggests here, spirits or deities usually enter through the *rtsa*—often through openings located in the fourth finger of each hand. In fact, the location of entry can indicate the type of spirit or deity involved (Berglie 1976, 90).

Spirit afflictions are usually understood to be fairly common: as Donden states, '[t]here are many occurrences; I could not even count the number of people who have been affected by spirits' (1997, 103). However, as I noted above, spirit affliction does not always involve possession and, in the same way that humans are understood to sometimes inadvertently cause harm or offence to local deities (through polluting the water source or earth that they reside in, for example), it is said that sometimes spirits themselves also inadvertently cause harm to humans, by becoming attracted to and involved with them (Donden 1997, 103).

Spirits in the rGyud bZhi

As we saw in the previous chapter, *smyo nad* is included in the *rGyud bZhi* in two different sections, the second of which is under the category of *smyo byed kyi gdon*: spirits that cause madness. In fact, the Third Tantra, *Man ngag rGyud* describes a number of spirits which can cause both mental and physical illnesses:

- Chapter 77: *'Byung po'i gdon* (elemental spirits)
- Chapter 78: *sMyo byed kyi gdon* (spirits that cause madness)
- Chapter 79: *brJed byed kyi gdon* (spirits that cause forgetfulness or epilepsy)
- Chapter 80: *gZa' yi gdon* (spirits that cause strokes or partial paralysis)
- Chapter 81: *kLu'i gdon* (water spirits, which usually cause skin conditions)

Some of these have been described in some detail by a number of Tibetan amchi (see for example: Donden 1997, 101–2, 233; Drungtso 2004, 53), and are described by the amchi Pasang Y. Arya as 'the five major, mild and aggressive mental disorders' related to possession.[3] In reality, spirits actually take up little space in the text of the *rGyud bZhi* as a whole (Samuel 2001, 262) and, as I noted in the previous chapter, the *Man ngag rGyud* is one volume of the text not necessarily learned by heart by student amchi at the Men-Tsee-Khang (MTK) medical colleges (Samuel 2001, 258). Indeed, in Darjeeling, Jacobson was told on a number of occasions by Tibetan amchi, 'We don't really understand some of these verses, because they are not really practiced anymore' (2000, 116), and when I initially asked Amchi Lobsang Thubten about what

---

3. http://www.tibetanmedicine-edu.org/index.php/psychology-and-psychotherapy.

kinds of illnesses might be caused by *gdon*, he told me that he was unsure, and would have a look in the text and tell me next time I visited. This highlights the fact that much knowledge held by amchi regarding spirits derives from non-*rGyud bZhi* sources. However, the chapters on pulse and urine diagnosis (Chapters One and Two respectively) in the *Phyi ma'i rGyud* are also relevant here, as they describe characteristics of the pulse and urine which indicate spirit causation, as well as the specific spirits involved (Millard 2007, 260). For example, Donden explains that in a 'spirit pulse', the beats are 'uneven' and the pulse 'changes suddenly and frequently ... sometimes pausing, sometimes jerky, and sometimes double' (1997, 101–02). He describes the different types of pulse which characterise possession by different entities (1997, 88–89, 101–05; see also Drungtso 2005, 295–97), as well as the diagnosis of spirit possession through urine analysis (1997, 126–30). However, often in reality spirit afflictions are diagnosed through the nature of the affliction, rather than through such diagnostic techniques, as Samuel found in Dalhousie (2001, 259–60), with divination often used to determine the nature of the problem (Samuel 2009, 93).

Moreover, as Samuel argues, these categories of spirits in the text do not necessarily correspond that closely to how contemporary Tibetans understand and manage illness, with Chapters 78 and 79 seemingly reflecting Indian rather than Tibetan concepts. Noting his own findings within a Tibetan community in Dalhousie in the 1990s, as well as Ortner's findings amongst Sherpa in Nepal in the 1960s, he suggests that Chapters 80 and 81 however, discuss spirits which remain very much part of contemporary Tibetan ideas about illness-causation (Samuel 2007, 214–15). This further illustrates the problematic nature of attempts to compare biomedical and Sowa Rigpa concepts, when *rGyud bZhi* notions of spirits are not necessarily shared by amchi, religious specialists or lay Tibetans.

Management and Treatment of Spirit Afflictions in the Tibetan Context

How then are these different forms of spirit affliction managed and treated in the Tibetan context? A visit to the MTK's Museum in Dharamsala highlights the use of herbal medicine ingredients and compounds in the treatment of a number of mental illnesses including those related to *smyo byed kyi gdon*. For example, on a visit there in August 2012, I saw precious stones such as agate, tiger's eye and quartz labelled for use in the treatment of 'disorders caused by naga spirits', 'elemental spirits' and 'demonic possession'. Others have discussed some of the herbs used in the different herbal medical compounds: for example, Arbuzov mentions the herbs *acorus calamus*, *sinapis alba* and *commiphora mukul* in the treatment of 'provocations and madness' (2013). In Darjeeling, Amchi Lobsang Thubten explained that, as most spirit possession is related to *rlung*, it is possible to give medicine to 'balance the *rlung*'. However, cases of spirit possession may require personal Buddhist practices and/or ritual intervention in addition to medicine—Amchi Thubten suggested that the afflicted individual's family should recite Medicine Buddha prayers in such cases. Indeed, Donden suggests that it is imperative that the religious activities are conducted *first*—'[o]therwise, no matter how much medicine is given, it cannot be effective' (1997, 103). Similarly, Rapgay explains that for Tibetans, 'the first line of therapy for disorders presumed to be caused by spirits is religious' (1985, 51). In Dalhousie, Samuel found that in cases of *gza'* spirit intervention—which were quite common there—whilst most afflicted individuals used Tibetan medicine, they generally had little confidence that it would offer anything other than 'limited relief', favouring instead *rin chen ril bu* ("rinchen rilbu", precious [ritually empowered] pills) and other 'empowered substances' (Tib.: *byin rten*) (2007, 217). In Dhorpatan, Millard reports a clear 'division of labour' between the local amchi—who treated patients with herbal medicines and external therapies—and the head lama of the community, who treated patients in need of ritual intervention. Here, he found that patients who suspected a spirit cause to their condition sometimes consulted the lama in the first instance (2007, 260).

In Tibetan societies, there are numerous different religious rituals which might be conducted to subjugate, exorcise or destroy the different types of *gdon* and *lha* in cases of spirit affliction. In addition, there are a number of so-called 'tricks': more secular activities which can serve to 'confuse and turn away' spirits, such as the changing of a person's name or clothes, or the offering of a 'substitute' in the form of an effigy (Tib.: *glud*) (Calkowski 1985, 135–212). Furthermore, Calkowski notes that in Dharamsala, *sngags pa* were able to 'trap' *rgyal po* in *nam mkh'a* ("namka", spirit trap, thread cross) through their ability to manipulate the *rgyal po*'s perception (1985, 135–212). Some such rituals are conducted by monastic practitioners, and may be performed either at the monastery, or at the home of the afflicted individual. Other rituals are conducted by spirit-mediums, who may work independently or under the auspices of a local monastery, and in some ethnically-Tibetan areas, such as Ladakh, there has been a significant increase in the number of—often female—spirit-mediums over the last few decades (Kressing 2003, 8). Interestingly, in Darjeeling, both Amchi Teinley and Amchi Thubten suggested that for a case of possession by *gdon*, it was best for the afflicted individual to consult a monastic or tantric practitioner experienced in dealing with such things—usually a lama or *sngags pa* (rather than a *lha bzhugs mkhan*) although, as Teinley noted, these days there were far fewer Tibetan *lha bzhugs mkhan* around anyway.

Clearly, the borderline between 'good' and 'bad' possession can sometimes be rather 'blurred' (Diemberger 2005, 132), with the symptoms often similar—at least initially—in cases of both possession and mediumship. Thus, whilst as we have seen, *smyo nad* can be caused by *gdon*, a *lha bzhugs mkhan's* journey into mediumship also frequently commences with a period of *smyo nad* (or something akin to this), which is eventually revealed to be the symptoms of a *lha* possession (see for example Day 1989; Diemberger 2005; Gutschow 1997; Rösing 2006). In both contexts, a non-human entity enters the individual's consciousness (Tib.: *rnam shes*). Rösing describes the medium's experience (which she refers to as 'trance') in Ladakh: '[T]rance ... is first of all a complete loss of consciousness. The only thing remaining is the body, an outer shell. And secondly trance is the process of a god taking over this empty body' (2006, 158). Indeed, as Halperin suggests, 'the essence of possession rites for most participants is not that of "entering" a trance, but rather of being entered by the spirit, of being "incorporated," literally, by a force outside oneself' (1996, 37).

Whilst some have suggested that possession states, mediumship and 'altered states of consciousness' are a 'universal' across human societies (Bourguignon 1973; see also Kleinman 1991; Somer 2006; Winkelman 1997), often occurring more frequently amongst female rather than male members of many societies (Spanos 1994, 148), their manifestations often vary widely (Boddy 1994, 408–9)—sometimes within societies as well as between them (Spanos 1994, 148). These experiences have been explored in a number of ways in Western literature where, writing in the late 1980s, Csordas noted that there had been a trend towards the medicalisation of possession (1987), and it is to these differing interpretations which I turn next.

Meeting the West:
Western Interpretations of Spirit Affliction

The anthropologist Janice Boddy suggests that 'possession' is in fact a 'broad term referring to an integration of spirit and matter, force or power and corporeal reality'. Here, boundaries between individuals and their environment are 'acknowledged to be permeable, flexibly drawn, or at least negotiable' (1994, 407). Anthropological interpretations of possession and mediumship have so far tended to focus on the social and political aspects of the healing process

(Samuel 2010, 9), viewing spirit affliction as a way to manage 'structural inferiority and vulnerability' (Samuel 2007, 219). For example, in Nepal, Jones discusses the sociopolitical functions of possession, whereby it acts not only as an explanatory system for misfortune, but also as a means by which individuals from lower castes are able to achieve social positions and respect which would be otherwise denied to them (1976, 7–8). In both Nepal and Ladakh, unwanted 'possession' has been linked to a young woman's negotiation of her changing role as she gets married and moves into the marital home with her husband and his family (Gellner 1994; Crook 1997), and this has also been discussed in other cultures (see, for example, Spanos' work on north American female spirit-mediums in the late nineteenth century, whose 'adoption of the medium role was a vehicle through which women could circumvent some of the restrictions associated with the female role and earn an independent living' (1994, 148)). However, such interpretations do not explain the variety of spirit afflictions which may be found in the Tibetan context, where spirits and deities can affect humans in a number of very different ways, and spirit afflictions may or may not include possession by another entity. Here, spirit afflictions are understood to lead to very serious consequences — even death — which are not necessarily explained by these social and political explanations.

Others have argued that religious healing, shamanism, and psychotherapy are 'versions of the same thing', with the spirit-medium and Western psychotherapist invoking similar psychological processes, named by Moerman as 'symbolic healing' (Dow 1986, 56; see also Csordas 2002; Jones 1976). Similarly, Hitchcock suggests that '[b]oth shamans and psychiatrists achieve results by ordering clients' experiences in a meaningful way' (1976, xvi). This perspective suggests a psychodynamic interpretation of possession and mediumship, where possessing spirits and deities are no more than psychological processes: part of the unconscious mind, as opposed to independent entities. Thus whilst, as Samuel notes, from a biomedical perspective, 'explanations in terms of spirit action are radically unacceptable' (2010, 9), it seems that from some anthropological perspectives too, this is also the case. In addition, this kind of analysis clearly ignores the perspectives of afflicted individuals, and thus their very understanding of the world and their place within it. In Darjeeling, many Tibetan informants very clearly perceived spirits and deities as entities in their own right, and perspectives on their involvement in health and illness were a clear reflection of fundamental Tibetan notions of the individual and the environment.

Biomedical interpretations of spirit possession and mediumship have taken a variety of approaches, from psychodynamic understandings of spirit affliction to explanations based around the concepts of psychosis and/or dissociation. Much of the contemporary psychiatric literature has taken what Seligman and

Kirmayer describe as a 'functional' approach to possession and mediumship (2008, 35), where explanations of these practices often include discussion of various types of biomedically-categorised 'dissociation', including 'Dissociative Identity Disorder' (DID, formerly 'Multiple Personality Disorder' (MPD)), which I shall discuss here.

Looking at cases of involuntary or 'negative' possession by *gdon* and *'dre*, Clifford's early work on Tibetan approaches to psychiatry drew comparisons with certain biomedical diagnostic categories, using the third edition of the DSM (DSM-III) (APA 1980). Clifford also explained the 'spirits' in terms of psychological or emotional states, characterising them as 'primarily a psychological phenomenon', and suggesting that, to 'learned Tibetans', 'demon' was a symbolic term, representing 'a wide range of forces and emotions ... normally beyond conscious control' (1989, 148–49). This interpretation is reflective of some of the psychodynamic theories of psychology which focus on the unconscious mind and its role in the causation of mental illness which were more popular in Western psychiatry prior to the 1980s. This perhaps fits into some common Western concepts and cultural tropes too, where talk of 'battling' or 'overcoming' one's 'demons' is common in discussions around psychological or emotional aspects of the person. In fact, from a strictly Buddhist philosophical perspective, *gdon* do *not* have any intrinsic existence; but from this perspective, neither do you nor I, making this rather a moot point for anyone other than Buddhist philosophers concerned with Madhyamaka Buddhist philosophy. For everyone else, *gdon* and *lha* are *as real as* you or I and thus, for the majority of Tibetans, such entities are indeed as tangible as humans, able— and likely—to cause harm quite directly when angry or offended. Clearly, it is too simplistic to suggest that for Tibetans, *gdon* are purely 'psychological' and/or symbolic, with only 'the common Tibetan' 'misunderstanding' them as entities in their own right. For many 'learned' amchi, as we saw above, these entities are also 'real', and the effects they have on those afflicted equally so. As Donden—a Tibetan amchi—argues, '[e]ven though spirits cannot be seen, they definitely do exist and bring harm' (1997, 102–3). Similarly, in Nepal, Millard found that many lay Tibetans discussed their experiences of seeing spirits or witnessing their presence in some way, describing them as an 'everyday reality' for his informants (2007, 261). In Darjeeling, I saw this too, when two amchi discussed with me the possibility of seeing certain types of spirits, and their relative sizes, and one lay Tibetan, Phurpu (50) related a story of his father having seen a spirit on the road ahead of him one day many years previously. Furthermore, as we saw above, spirits of different kinds are integral not only to the Tibetan conception of the environment, but also to Tibetan notions of the individual, and his or her relationship to the wider world.

What then of the 'intentional' or 'positive' possession experience of spirit-mediumship? For many spirit-mediums—in both ethnically Tibetan societies and beyond—their path into this role often starts with a period of 'madness', followed—usually after a long period of training under another spirit-medium—by acquiring the ability to control the incoming deity. In Ladakh for example, Rösing tells us that '[t]he calling always begins with a mental problem' (2006, 114). From a biomedical perspective, such states have often been categorised under a number of different Western diagnoses. In the 1960s, for example, Silverman suggested a five-stage cognitive model to 'explain the etiology and elaboration' of behaviours associated with both 'shamanism' and 'schizophrenia' (1967, 21). This model was strongly disputed by Noll who, writing in the 1980s, concluded that the psychological states involved in these two experiences were definitively not the same (1983, 455), although he noted that psychosis, neurosis, epilepsy and hysteria had all variously been compared to 'shamanism' (Noll 1983, 448–49).

More recently, 'possession' has often been viewed as a form of 'dissociation', described by Somer as 'the experience of having a mind in which there can be at least two independent streams of consciousness flowing concurrently' (2006, 213). (Of course, as we saw above, from a Tibetan perspective, there are *not* 'two independent streams of consciousness flowing concurrently', but *one* consciousness displaced by another.) Seligman and Kirmayer have explored the nature of possession and trance through an understanding of dissociative mental states, delineating 'dissociation' as 'both a set of behaviors and experiences involving functional alterations of memory, perception and identity as well as the psychophysiological processes presumed to underlie these phenomena' (2008, 32).

Over the last few decades then, possession states have been included under separate categories in the ICD and DSM systems, sometimes under broader categories of 'dissociation', often with more or less accession to cultural differences. Both the ICD and DSM currently include possession states as subsections of dissociative disorders. The ICD-10 (Version: 2010) specifically lists 'Trance and Possession Disorders' under Section F44.3 (a sub-category of 'F44—Dissociative (Conversion) Disorders'), defining them as 'Disorders in which there is a temporary loss of the sense of personal identity and full awareness of the surroundings. Include here only trance states that are involuntary or unwanted, occurring outside religious or culturally accepted situations' (WHO 2010a).[4] Similarly, the DSM-5 discusses 'possession-form' DID, stipulating that its man-

---

4. Available online at: http://apps.who.int/classifications/icd10/browse/2010/en#/F40-F48.

ifestation should not be 'a normal part of a broadly accepted cultural or religious practice' (APA 2013, 292), and describing DID as 'characterized by a disruption of and/or discontinuity in the normal integration of consciousness, memory, identity, emotion, perception, body representation, motor control, and behavior' (2013, 291). Further, it notes that the 'fragmented identities' of DID 'may take the form of possessing spirits, deities, demons, animals, or mythical figures' (APA 2013, 295). It suggests that,

> Possession-form identities in dissociative identity disorder typically manifest as behaviors that appear as if a "spirit", supernatural being or outside person has taken control, such that the individual begins speaking and acting in a distinctly different manner.... Or an individual may be "taken over" by a demon or deity, resulting in profound impairment (2013, 293).

However, taking into account cultural differences, it advises that 'the majority of possession states around the world are normal, usually part of spiritual practice, and do not meet criteria for dissociative identity disorder' (APA 2013, 293–94). Nonetheless, despite the emphasis on culturally-normative experiences of possession here, this is not necessarily the stance taken by biomedical practitioners, as I witnessed in Darjeeling. In addition, as we shall see, it is not always easy to demarcate a clear boundary between a practice which is 'a normal part of a broadly accepted cultural or religious practice' and one that is not, in a sphere where 'involuntary or unwanted' possession may also occur *within* 'religious or culturally accepted situations'.

Moreover, DID is itself a fairly contentious diagnosis—indeed, Hacking calls it 'the most contested type of diagnosis in psychiatry' (1998, 9)—with some psychiatrists arguing that it is not a valid clinical diagnosis at all (Somer 2006, 213; see also Merskey 1992), others delineating it a 'culture-bound syndrome' (Spanos 1994, 152), and some arguing that a misdiagnosis of MPD/DID can even hinder access to the most appropriate treatment for patients (Merskey 1992, 338). Spanos, a clinical psychologist, suggests that what he refers to as 'multiple identity enactments' occur 'in most human societies' (1994, 160), and concludes that both possession and DID are learned behaviours, where individuals may be encouraged to create and maintain a number of separate identities or 'multiples' by well-intentioned medical or religious practitioners. Thus, in cultures where possession is normative, some patients are likely to manifest a possession of some kind, whereas in Western cultures where possession is not normative, patients are more likely to manifest with DID (1994). As with many learned behaviours, he tells us, there are likely benefits to this 'parcelling off' of 'identities':

[T]he idea of being a multiple, like the idea of suffering from peripheral possession or demonic possession, may provide some people with a viable and face-saving way to account for personal problems as well as a dramatic means for gaining concern and attention from significant others (Spanos 1994, 154).

Of course, dissociation is in fact a continuum, with, as Seligman and Kirmayer suggest, 'everyday experiences of absorption like "highway hypnosis"' at one end, and 'more profound dissociative phenomena that include various forms of dissociative amnesia and alterations in identity' such as DID at the other (Seligman and Kirmayer 2008, 32). Within this context then, we might ask how medical and/or healing practitioners determine whether an individual is experiencing a 'possession' which may not require biomedical treatment, or a biomedically-diagnosable 'dissociative' condition which might. If we turn to the DSM-5, we are told that,

Possession-form dissociative identity disorder can be distinguished from culturally accepted possession states in that the former is involuntary, distressing, uncontrollable, and often recurring or persistent; involves conflict between the individual and his or her surrounding family, social, or work milieu; and is manifested at times and in places that violate the norms of the culture or religion (APA 2013, 295).

However, as I mentioned above, the reality is that possession experiences do not always fit easily into such categories. It is perfectly possible, for example, for a 'culturally accepted possession state' to *also* be 'involuntary, distressing, uncontrollable, and often recurring or persistent', or to involve 'conflict between the individual and his or her surrounding family, social, or work milieu'. And an afflicted individual may experience an uncontrollable possession which does *not* violate the norms of the religion and her, her family and/or local community may disagree over whether she is 'possessed' or 'sick'. These issues will become more pertinent when I discuss the case of Dechen in Chapter Nine, which clearly illustrates some of these complex issues.

* * *

I have delineated in this chapter a number of ways in which non-human entities can be involved in mental illness in the Tibetan context, from unwanted *gdon* possession to the experience of spirit-mediums, whose path most often commences with a period of 'madness'. In the former, we find possession unwanted and uncontrollable, entirely negative; in the latter it may (or may not) be desirable and controllable, and useful to the surrounding community. Furthermore, in Tibetan society, spirits can cause 'harm' in diverse ways, from mis-fortune or crop failure to (mental) illness, and spirit afflictions may or may not involve possession. Indeed, as we have seen, such entities have a fundamental place in the Tibetan conception of the cosmos. As Boddy notes, possession prac-tices 'have to do with one's relationship to the world, with selfhood—personal, ethnic, moral, and political identity' (1994, 414). The particular myth of Tibet's 'taming' by Padmasambhava allows for the ritual subjugation of deities through both spirit-mediumship and Tibetan Buddhist ritual, and there are often nu-merous ritual specialists who may be consulted in the event of spirit affliction. Thus, whilst we see herbal medicines recommended for the treatment of such problems, in reality, it is usually to religious specialists of various kinds that lay Tibetans turn when spirit causation is suspected.

Both anthropology and biomedicine appear to struggle to deal with posses-sion and mediumship. Certainly, I would argue that the ICD and DSM de-scriptions present rather unrealistic boundaries between 'culturally normal' possession and 'illness', into which many instances of possession and medi-umship will not easily fit. In Chapter Nine I will examine a case study of pos-session/mediumship in Darjeeling which, alongside a number of other possession narratives from the fieldsite, illustrates some of these complexities in more detail. In the next chapter however, I explore the biomedical tradition, and its use in the Tibetan context.

CHAPTER FIVE

Biomedicine and the
Tibetan Context

[M]edicine is not a coherent whole. It is not a unity. It is, rather, an amalgam of thoughts, a mixture of habits, an assemblage of techniques. (Mol and Berg 1998, 3)

I have described already some of the equivalences which have been drawn between certain Tibetan and biomedical classifications of mental illness. Such comparisons highlight the predominance of the biomedical model which often dominates the research and discourse on mental illness in both Western and non-Western contexts. This biomedical approach also drives the majority of global mental health policies, such as those of the WHO and individual governments. Cross-cultural comparisons of mental illness often utilise the American Psychiatric Association (APA)'s classification system, the *Diagnostic and Statistical Manual of Disease* (DSM). In fact, the WHO's *International Classification of Disease* (ICD) is the official coding system in many countries, and programmes such as the WHO's *Mental Health Gap Action Program (mhGAP) for Low- and Middle-Income Countries*[1] are based on this system, although some argue that the successive iterations of the DSM may actually be used more frequently by mental health professionals around the world (see for example, research by Andrews, Slade and Peters 1999, 3; and Littlewood 1991, 260). This biomedical model of mental illness assumes that mental disorders are 'biologically-based brain diseases' (Deacon 2013, 847), leading to the broad use of pharmacological interventions in the treatment of diverse mental health conditions. While the benefits of biomedical psychiatry for many suffering from

---

1. http://www.who.int/mental_health/mhgap/en/.

severe mental illnesses cannot be denied, it remains a contested system and draws criticisms from many quarters, as we shall see here.

In this chapter, I will explore some Western approaches to mental illness, taking in the two main biomedical classification systems and the model(s) of mental illness which they derive from, before giving an overview of some of the controversies and alternative narratives in the field, as well as lay perspectives on mental illness. This will build up a picture of the complex field of contemporary mental health care in countries such as Britain and the United States of America, where a number of different perspectives coexist within this field. I will then explore the use of biomedicine and its diagnostic systems in non-Western contexts to argue that its practice in mental health care is often based around pharmacological interventions, despite the best intentions of health planners to provide more comprehensive treatment strategies. This illustration of biomedical mental health care provides some context for the practice of 'Western medicine' in Tibetan communities, and will provide a backdrop for the practice and utilisation of biomedicine in Darjeeling. What becomes clear, is that what is often referred to rather monolithically as 'biomedicine', is in fact a complex field of contemporary mental health care, within which a number of different perspectives coexist. In addition, its practice may be significantly influenced in different geographical contexts by a number of financial, pragmatic or political factors, as we shall see.

Biomedical Psychiatry: History, Controversies and Contemporary Practice in the West

Western psychiatry is—and always has been—an evolving system, replete with disputes, disagreements and challenges, from both within and outside the system, where illness categories and treatments appear and disappear over time in line with prevailing cultural attitudes. The enterprise of delineating the 'abnormal' from the 'normal', in terms of mental states and behaviour is, perhaps unsurprisingly, highly subjective, constantly shifting as a result of cultural and political changes. As notions of 'normal' and 'abnormal' change, so too do doctors' and patients' ideas about mental 'health' and 'illness' and, as a result, their aims in terms of treatment. Over the last few decades, these changes have been delineated in one or both of the two major biomedical classification systems used in Western psychiatry: the APA's DSM, (the current edition being the DSM-5, APA 2013) and the WHO's ICD (currently in its tenth edition, the ICD-10, WHO 2005). These texts are both results and representations of the biomedical approach to mental illness, which is based on the concept that each classified condition exists 'out there'—'independently of the gaze of psychiatrists or anyone else' (Summerfield 2001, 95). Here, diagnostic categories are assumed to describe disorders which are universal across time and space (Thakker and Ward 1998, 502).

From this biomedical perspective then, serious illnesses are expected to occur in identical or similar formats both intra-culturally and cross-culturally, with psychiatric conditions diagnosable, classifiable and treatable across different contexts, in the same manner as physical diseases such as tuberculosis or cancer. In many (although not all) physical conditions, a 'diagnosis' indicates specific underlying biological abnormality or dysfunction (Moncrieff 2010, 373), suggesting a clearly-defined treatment pathway and/or enabling the prediction of disease outcome within an understood range of outcomes for that diagnosis. In the biomedical model, mental illnesses are assumed to follow the same path. Of course in practice, this is not necessarily the case, and disagreements—between doctors or between doctors and their patients—are not uncommon in cases of both physical and mental illness. Moreover, definitive causes for many mental illnesses are yet to be found and, overall, they remain unpredictable in terms of prognosis and treatment response.

In fact, as a product of Western cultural ideas born out of the Enlightenment and contemporary European philosophy (Hepburn 1988, 60), biomedical psychiatry is a rather culturally-defined endeavour. It is tied to cultural concepts of the person and the surrounding world and follows trends in scientific theories or knowledge (see for example the current emphasis on genetics in much Western scientific research). This raises serious questions about its relevance in other contexts, where individuals often hold significantly *different* concepts of the person and their relationship to the surrounding world, particularly for example in theories of causation that involve spirits or deities such as those we saw in the previous chapter.

History and Controversies

The history of Western psychiatry and psychology has been well-documented elsewhere (see for example Shorter 1997; Waddington 2011), and so I shall restrict myself here to an overview. First and foremost, the contemporary biomedical approach to mental illness is usually traced back to Emil Kraepelin, the German psychiatrist (1856–1926) who hypothesised a finite number of categories of mental illness, each with its own pathophysiology and aetiology (Bentall 2004, 42). Kraepelin's theories remain evident in contemporary psychiatry and psychology textbooks, in both the DSM and ICD classification systems (which continue to use some of his diagnostic concepts, such as 'manic depression' and 'paranoia'), and in contemporary mental health research, all of which are organised around his assumptions about mental illness to a greater or lesser degree (Bentall 2004, 42–43).[2]

However, during the same historical period that Kraepelin was formulating his hypotheses, Sigmund Freud (1856–1939) put forward his theory of 'psychoanalysis', proposing that mental illnesses were caused by unconscious and repressed feelings and desires, leading to the advent of 'talking therapies' as treatment. With its origins in European philosophical and religious traditions (Richards 2000, 186), psychoanalysis became particularly popular in Britain in the aftermath of the First World War (Richards 2000, 188); and in the USA, by the 1960s, 'dynamic psychotherapy' had become the focus of training and treatment for psychiatrists in some hospitals (Kandel 1998, 457–58). Whilst psychoanalysis per se does not have a significant presence in contemporary British or American public sector mental health treatment, it has had a long-term effect on psychiatric thinking and practice (Burns 2013, 96–97), as well as on cultural ideas in the West (Richards 2000).[3] In addition, it, and its antecedents, such as psychodynamic psychotherapy, retain a presence in the spheres of contemporary psychology and psychological therapy.

Whilst the 1970s saw the rise of the 'biopsychosocial' model in Western psychiatric treatment, which is perhaps best illustrated by George Engel's 1980 position, stressing the significance of the psychosocial context within which the individual exists (Pilgrim 2002, 585), the 1980s marked a shift in orientation towards biological approaches (Angel 2010; see also Moncrieff 2010; Pilgrim 2007; Wilson 1993), alongside the rise of neuroscience (Healy 2004, 219). Advantages of this new perspective included a shift away from the placing of blame for a child's illness on particular family members (the focus of much psychodynamic theory of schizophrenia), and advances in pharmacological treatments, which were no doubt a vast improvement on the 'hazardous and irreversible' treatments which were a feature of asylums in earlier times (Waddington 2011, 335). However, this welcome change of focus also brought with it unintended consequences, as the 'biological' perspective gave schizophrenia the 'inevitable degenerating course' Kraepelin had originally out-

---

2. See Bentall (2004) for a more in-depth examination of Kraepelin and his influence on contemporary psychiatric practice.

3. Indeed, Richards argues that Freudian concepts have been accepted into everyday language since the 1930s (2000).

lined for it many years before, leaving any treatments supposedly powerless against this 'incurable' illness (Luhrmann 2007, 140).

Over the last few decades, a number of alternative theories of mental illness have also been proposed, either focused on specific disorders or on mental illness more generally. For example, back in 1966, Siegler and Osmond described six models of schizophrenia: medical; moral; psychoanalytic; family interaction; conspiratorial and social (1966). More recently, in 2013, Tyrer and Steinberg delineated five models of mental disorders more broadly: disease; psychodynamic; cognitive-behavioural; social and integrated (2013), and in a study of trainee psychiatrists at a London hospital, Harland et al. came across eight models through which psychiatric illnesses were classified and treated: biological (often also referred to as 'medical' or 'biomedical'); cognitive; behavioural; psychodynamic; social realist; social constructivist; nihilist and spiritualist (2009, 269). Similarly, the psychiatrist Tom Burns tells us that contemporary psychiatrists draw on biological, pharmacological, psychological, physiological and sociological theories, depending on the patient presenting before them (2013, xxvii). These diverse models of mental illness illustrate the broad range of views within the mental health field, where different approaches have become more or less popular amongst mental health professionals at different times, in part as a reflection of broader cultural changes. Yet despite these changing 'trends' in Western approaches to mental illness, it seems that biological explanations of illness have been a continuous and significant presence (Moncrieff and Crawford 2001). However, this biomedical model has been challenged from a number of different directions—from those within the profession, as well as those outside it. One of the most significant of these critiques was the 'anti-psychiatry' movement of the 1960s and 1970s,[4] which voiced the 'increasing disquiet about the nature of psychiatry' (Waddington 2011, 336), and was headed by key figures such as Szasz (1960a, 1960b) and Bateson (see Bateson et al. 1956, 1963) in the USA and Laing in the UK (despite, as Crossley (1998, 878) notes, Laing disowning the 'anti-psychiatry' label). Many of the anti-psychiatrists' criticisms have resurfaced within the more contemporary 'critical psychiatry' (Pilgrim 2002, 590), and 'post-psychiatry' (Thomas and Bracken 2004, 368) movements.[5]

---

4. See Crossley (1998) and Dain (1989) for interesting examinations of the anti-psychiatry movement in Britain and the USA respectively.

5. See for example, the 'Council for Evidence-based Psychiatry' (CEPUK), whose members include psychiatrists, psychologists and medical anthropologists amongst others, and which aims to 'reduce psychiatric harm by communicating the latest evidence to policymakers and practitioners, by sharing the testimony of those who have been harmed, and by supporting research into areas where evidence is lacking': http://cepuk.org/.

In addition, despite the fact that the enduring Kraepelinian paradigm has encouraged a reliance on antipsychotic drugs, and discouraged the use of psychological treatments (Bentall 2004, 504–05), psychological approaches to mental illness and its treatment often sit alongside psychiatry in the West, as evidenced by the diverse models mentioned above. In the UK for example, the National Health Service (NHS) offers therapies such as Cognitive Behaviour Therapy (CBT), applied relaxation, psychotherapy (such as interpersonal therapy, family therapy, arts therapy and mindfulness-based cognitive therapy) and/or counselling services alongside drug interventions for mental health conditions, and stresses the importance of 'person-centred care,' with such therapies usually conducted by psychologists (rather than psychiatrists).[6] In Europe, Finland's 'alternative' 'Open Dialogue' approach[7] to psychosis has received a certain amount of publicity in recent times.[8] In the UK, CBT is often the treatment of choice for non-psychotic conditions; for example, it is favoured over psychodynamic treatments for 'moderate to severe depression' (National Institute for Health and Care Excellence (NICE) 2009, 45).[9] Research has also demonstrated the utility of CBT in treating psychosis and schizophrenia in some cases (Bentall 2004, 508–9; Morrison et al. 2014), and some psychiatrists have reported that patients' engagement with their 'voices' can enable them to cease (Luhrmann 2012, 33)—and so we find CBT also recommended in the prevention and treatment of psychosis under the NICE clinical guidelines (NICE 2014). Thus perhaps contemporary Anglo-American psychiatric practice can be best described, as Pilgrim suggests, as a number of 'different disciplines (and groups within them), who favour different approaches to mental health work, negotiating a form of mutual tolerance' (2002, 590).

However, whilst the different models are employed to different degrees by both practitioners and patients, it seems that the biomedical model often still predominates, in part due to its enshrinement in the more recent versions of the widely-used DSM. Indeed, Keen (1999) argues that in practice,

---

6. See the National Institute for Health and Care Excellence (NICE) clinical guidelines for treating 'depression' (NICE 2009), 'Generalised Anxiety Disorder and Panic Disorder' (NICE 2011).

7. http://opendialogueapproach.co.uk/.

8. See, for example, research on this approach by Seikkula and Olson (2003) and Seikkula et al. (2006), as well as some of the news articles on a UK play and 2011 film based on this approach: http://www.theguardian.com/lifeandstyle/2014/mar/24/play-mental-illness-eradication-schizophrenia-western-lapland-open-dialogue-hallucination; http://beyondmeds.com/2011/03/17/opendialogdoc/.

9. See Hofmann et al. for a review of mindfulness-based therapy for anxiety as well as physical illnesses (2010).

antipsychotic medications often remain the first line of treatment for patients with psychosis, and Pilgrim describes the biomedical model as the 'hardy perennial' of the psychiatric arena, where junior psychiatrists often learn biodeterminism 'by assumption', and the model is often 'instinctively favoured' by doctors (2002, 590–91). Others have suggested that recent years have seen a 're-ascendancy' of the biomedical model (Pilgrim 2002, 593), where the 'Kraepelinian construct of psychosis resulting from illnesses' retains its dominance in much psychiatric practice 'despite the evidence to the contrary' (Sapey and Bullimore 2013, 629).

Of course, regardless of mental health professionals' disagreements over explanatory frameworks, they need to be able to treat their patients. As Kleinman notes, '[e]ffective treatment and prevention require a usable diagnostic system' (1991, 16), and the need for a usable system stipulates at least a certain degree of cohesion. In addition, due to the necessity of adhering to the DSM or ICD classification system, as is required by peers, publication stipulations and insurance companies, psychiatrists must abide, at least to a certain extent, by a biomedical bias. Moreover, in day-to-day practice, whatever mental health professionals' own perspectives, their practice is often significantly constrained by financial and practical factors beyond their control, such as the limitations of local resources and services, as well as any political interests:[10] external influences on the situation come from a number of directions—it is not only a question of 'Does it work?', but also, 'Can you/we afford it?' and 'Is it available here?'. This is often particularly the case in non-Western contexts, as we saw in Chapter Two: in Darjeeling, for example, I described how mental health services were mainly limited to drug interventions, and there were simply not the resources for government-funded non-pharmacological treatments, despite the resident psychiatrist's view on their significant value.

Lay Perspectives

Within this complex web of explanatory frameworks, how then do patients and their families—and indeed the broader lay population—understand mental illness and its causes and treatment? Furthermore, how do patients and their families navigate this multi-faceted medical system in what Shah and Mountain describe as the 'active process involving seeking help, evaluating options and making

---

10. Whilst there is not the space here to discuss the 'politics' of psychiatric diagnosis and treatment, Summerfield's (2008) examination of PTSD and the 'evolution' of this diagnosis within particular political and cultural circumstances provides a good example.

decisions about treatments' that is 'getting better' (2007, 376)? Shaw argues that no one now is 'unaware of professional explanations' of health and illness (2002, 293), and indeed, a number of DSM concepts have become part of everyday language and understandings in the West (Moncrieff 2010, 370). Nevertheless, misunderstandings and misconceptions of psychiatric illness abound.[11]

Shah and Mountain state that biological explanations and treatments for diseases such as epilepsy have reduced stigma, superstition and fear, and increased 'understanding, hope and humane methods of treatment'. They conclude that '[l]ogically a biological perspective in psychiatry should do the same' (2007, 375). However, some research has suggested that 'biogenetic' perspectives on schizophrenia, for example, which promote the view of mental illness as 'an illness like any other', can actually *increase* prejudice, fear and a desire for distance from the afflicted individual (Read et al. 2006), increase harsh behaviour towards sufferers (Mehta and Farina 1997), and increase the perceived 'dangerousness' of afflicted individuals (Corrigan and Watson 2004). In contrast, Read et al. found strong evidence to suggest that viewing psychiatric symptoms as 'understandable psychological or emotional reactions to life events' can reduce fear, discrimination, and the desire for distance from afflicted individuals (2006, 313). In fact, it seems that in a number of Western and non-Western communities, overall, lay people often prefer 'psychosocial' explanations for schizophrenia, and this was found to be particularly the case in India and China, where Read et al. found an overall preference for psychosocial over biogenetic causative explanations (2006, 306–11). Indeed, it seems that the majority of people place emphasis on 'adverse life events' and other psychosocial explanations rather than on genetics or brain abnormalities (Read and Bentall 2012, 90; see also Read et al. 2006; Read et al. 2008). Perhaps psychosocial explanations can help us make sense of conditions—whose symptoms can be frightening and unpredictable—for both sufferers and those around them, in a way which 'biological' explanations cannot necessarily.

If we turn to examine the views of patients themselves, Williams and Healy have described the often fluid ways in which patients attempt to make sense of their initial experience of mental illness, delineating 'external', 'internal' and 'direct' causes (2001). They propose the idea of 'exploratory maps'—a 'map of possibilities'—whereby patients move between a 'varied and complex set of beliefs' in order to provide a 'framework for the ongoing process of making sense and seeking meaning' (2001, 473). Indeed, conducting qualitative research with a small sample (thirteen participants) of his clinical psychology patients suffering

---

11. A good example of this perhaps the perception of schizophrenia as describing a 'split personality' (Kruszelnicki 2004), or in unrealistic media portrayals of individuals with psychiatric illnesses as 'threatening, irrational and unpredictable' (Beresford and Wallcraft 1997, 73).

from psychosis in New Zealand, Geekie found them 'untroubled' by multifactorial—and often contradictory—explanations (2004, 154). In addition, religious and/or spiritual concepts may be prevalent in patients' explanatory frameworks (Borras et al. 2007), forming a significant part of their condition (for example, in the form of religious 'delusions'[12]), or simply included to a greater or lesser extent in patients' worldviews. Moreover, for many experiencing mental health problems, religious professionals may well be the first 'port of call' (Dein 2004, 292). However, patients' religious perspectives on their illness can sometimes cause conflict between themselves and their psychiatrist (Dein 2004), and in some cases can influence adherence to treatment (Borras et al. 2007; Mitchell and Romans 2003). Perhaps in response to this, patients' religious and spiritual beliefs are increasingly being taken into account in medical care in some Western spheres,[13] leading to questions of how this situation is navigated in places such as Darjeeling, where religious concepts are often evident in explanations of causation and treatment, and traditional notions of health and illness sit alongside more recently-imported biomedical ones.

Benedict, Mancini and Grodin argue that successful treatment adequately responds to the patient's *own* interpretation of illness in addition to biomedical categories, enabling the patient's active participation in healing (2009, 486). Indeed, Burns suggests that 'psychiatrists who do not take their patients' own wishes into consideration will achieve poor results' (2013, 27). Unfortunately however, patients sometimes find their own perspective(s) brushed aside (Geekie 2004)—the very perspectives which can contribute significantly to our understanding of mental illness. Geekie argues that this 'undermining' or 'overlooking' of the patient's perspective may also serve to invalidate her experience (2004), where it is her experience of illness which not only informs coping and health-seeking behaviour(s), but also often her relationship with the wider community and environment. (This issue of course becomes particularly pertinent in different cultural contexts, where patients' explanatory models of mental illness often include fundamental notions of the involvements of spirits and/or deities in daily life, as we saw in the previous chapter.)

---

12. The prevalence of religious delusions is debated, and has been reported as occurring in between fourteen and forty-five per cent of patients diagnosed with schizophrenia in the UK, for example (Dein 2004, 290).

13. In the UK for example, due to the prevalence of 'religious and spiritual needs' amongst patients with acute and chronic mental illness, hospital chaplains—who have generally had some training in mental health—are 'increasingly becoming a part of the multidisciplinary team', often involved throughout the different stages of a patient's illness, providing religious or spiritual support or counselling (Dein 2004, 292).

Thus we find the picture of mental illness and its treatment in the contemporary West one of a pragmatic (if uneasy) co-existence of multiple explanatory models, with biomedicine at the forefront. Within this system, medical practitioners', lay people's and patients' perceptions of mental illness encompass a broad range of diverse and often conflicting notions of causation and treatment. Here, different explanations and treatment methods may be invoked by patients and their psychiatrists—particularly in the initial stages of illness— as patients navigate a path through their illness experience via 'exploratory maps'. Meanwhile, critique of the biomedical approach and its reliance on pharmacological interventions continues amongst patients, psychologists and a number of psychiatrists themselves, as we have seen. These questions are only magnified when we apply the biomedical model of mental illness in cross-cultural contexts, as we shall see in the next section.

Biomedical Psychiatry in Cross-Cultural Context

If, as I have described here, approaches to mental illness in the West are often highly plural with a plethora of diverse voices, and the practice of mental health care is often based on multiple factors (such as affordability and availability), this raises a number of questions about how these systems might play out in diverse cultural contexts. The most obvious question, perhaps, is about the often diverse range of resources in different cultural settings, but questions of the supposed cross-cultural validity of the perspectives underpinning biomedicine are equally pertinent. As we have seen, biomedical psychiatry follows cultural trends: psychiatric categories appear, evolve and disappear as a reflection of broader social and cultural trends in the West, as much as trends in medical thinking (Summerfield 2008, 992). There are a number of interesting illustrations of this, such as the reinvention of madness as a 'disease' in the early 1800s (Rissmiller and Rissmiller 2006, 863), or the more recent and oft-cited example of the changing status of 'homosexuality' in the Western biomedical sphere and its inclusion and exclusion in the different editions of the DSM and ICD.[14] And yet, programmes such as the WHO's *mhGAP for Low- and Middle-*

---

14. This was included in the ICD and DSM psychiatric diagnostic systems until relatively recently, having been removed from the ICD-10 only in 1992 (Smith, Bartlett and King 2004, 429). More contemporary contested diagnoses include Attention Deficit Hyperactivity Disorder (ADHD), Post-Traumatic Stress Disorder (PTSD) and Dissociative Identity Disorder (DID, formerly Multiple Personality Disorder, or MPD), as I noted in the previous chapter.

Income Countries arise from assumptions of a *universality* of Western biomedical approaches, that is, the premise that the same conditions occur across time and space, that the same causal factors are involved and the same treatments will work across different cultural contexts. If, as Burns suggests, one of the reasons that mental illness is 'different' from physical illness is that it exists 'between people' (2013, xiii), how do we define 'illness' where social relationships and interactions often vary cross-culturally? Furthermore, how do we draw boundary lines between 'normality' and 'abnormality'—surely the main job of the medical specialist in order to determine who needs treatment and who does not—when 'norms' vary significantly across cultures, and concepts of the person and the relationship between the mind and body often differ widely? In this section I will examine the practice of biomedical psychiatry in some non-Western contexts and the questions of cross-cultural validity it provokes, where even definitions of 'efficacy' can vary significantly in different contexts.

In addition to its dominance in Western spheres then, the biomedical model of mental illness—with its focus often on pharmacological intervention—predominates in many governmental and non-governmental health planning and intervention projects in non-Western contexts. Guides such as Patel's *Where There Is No Psychiatrist: A Mental Health Care Manual* (2002) illustrate this, with medications recommended for: 'severe mental disorders, including schizophrenia, manic-depressive illness and acute psychoses'; 'common mental disorders' and 'acute stress situations, such as excitement and restlessness following the death of a close relative' (2002, 29). Similarly, Read argues that psychotropic medication 'continues to dominate psychiatric treatment, particularly for psychosis' in both high- and low-income countries (2012, 451). A glance at the WHO's policy guidelines for LAMIC clearly illustrates this. Their mhGAP (set up in 2008) states its aim to 'facilitate mhGAP-related delivery of evidence-based interventions in non-specialized health-care settings' (WHO 2010b, 1), and the *mhGAP Intervention Guide for Mental, Neurological and Substance Use Disorders in Non-Specialized Health Settings: Version 1.0 Health and Development* (WHO 2010b) focuses on the purported 'treatment gap' between the numbers of individuals suffering from 'mental, neurological, and substance abuse disorders' and the limited mental health services available to them, with a number of researchers describing the 'scarce' mental health resources in LAMIC (Patel 2007, 92). The *mhGAP* states,

> About four out of five people in low- and middle-income countries who need services for mental, neurological and substance use conditions do not receive them. Even when available, the interventions often are neither evidence-based nor of high quality (WHO 2010b, 1).

Similarly, Kleinman describes the common lack of treatment for those in China who suffer from severe mental illness, commenting on the lack of efficacy of 'folk healers' who are often consulted instead, but 'have little to offer that has been shown to be helpful' (2009, 603). In the same article, Kleinman describes the horrific treatment he has seen levelled against those with psychiatric illnesses in 'east and southeast Asian towns', painting a very distressing picture (2009, 603). These examples are no doubt upsetting, but of course they are not the whole picture of 'global mental health'. In many cultural contexts there may also exist a plethora of highly-valued indigenous healing traditions and local knowledge which have not necessarily been included in the research on cross-cultural psychiatry. In comparison to such local healing traditions, Calabrese argues that some Euro-American psychotherapeutic interventions may be 'irrelevant and useless, if not harmful' in other cultural contexts (2008, 349). Furthermore, Read argues that whilst pharmacological treatments clearly bring significant benefits to some patients, critiques of biomedicine are often brushed aside in low-income countries, with criticisms of drug treatments by both patients and practitioners in the West 'barely acknowledged' in the development discourse of global psychiatry (Read 2012, 439). In Ghana, for example, Read argues that in 'the push to scale up mental health services', considerations regarding the limitations of psychotropic treatments and the 'ambivalent attitudes they provoke in those who take them' are often 'sidelined' (2012, 439–51).

Furthermore, documents such as the *mhGAP Intervention Guide for Mental, Neurological and Substance Use Disorders in Non-Specialized Health Settings: Version 1.0* do not give us a clear picture of how biomedical treatment approaches actually play out on the ground in different cultural contexts, where there may be a 'tension' evident between global policies and local realities (Kleinman 2010, 1518). As I discussed above, within Western contexts such as in the UK and USA there are multiple influences on the practice of psychiatry; similarly in non-Western contexts, influences and constraints on the utilisation of biomedicine may be financial, practical (in terms of doctors' time and facilities), or ideological (in terms of what is promoted by governmental policies or native or non-native health-planners, Non-Governmental Organisations (NGOs), or charities involved in the implementation of health services). Saraceno et al. describe some 'barriers' to the improvement of mental health services in LAMIC including a dearth of mental health care workers and resistance to the decentralisation of mental health services (2007). The resultant diversity of diagnostic and treatment methods in different contexts can be significant, with global health programmes often taking on 'culturally distinctive significance' in different contexts (Kleinman 2010, 1518). Moreover, in the 1980s, Hepburn argued that ineffective treatment (sometimes due to poorly equipped clinics where minimal treatment was often given) served to undermine faith in the treatment's ability to cure and wasted resources (1988, 69–70). More than two decades later, it seems that, in many places, this situation has not changed significantly. Writing in 2009, Tomlinson et al. noted that around the world, health systems were still faced with a 'scarcity of financial resources and qualified staff', a situation often compounded by a 'lack of commitment from public health policy makers' and 'inefficient use of resources' in LAMIC (2009, 438). Indeed, the WHO states that, '[w]orldwide more than 50% of all medicines are prescribed, dispensed, or sold inappropriately, while 50% of patients fail to take them correctly' (WHO 2002, 1).[15]

Even where there are adequate resources and training for biomedical specialists, questions remain over the cross-cultural validity of Western-derived biomedical categorisations of mental illness. Many have critiqued historical European and North American understandings of 'modernisation' and 'development' which are seen to underlie these assumptions of cross-cultural validity, echoed in many of these discourses about the West's 'responsibility' to provide biomedical psychiatric care to those (low- and middle-income countries) deemed to be lacking it, as we saw above.[16] Whilst such health interventions are often borne out of the best intentions, they tend to still prioritise Western over local approaches, when the psychiatrist Derek Summerfield has suggested that it would, in fact, be 'extraordinary' if these Western-derived biomedical classification systems 'made sense' across diverse societies and situations (2008, 992).

Cross-cultural research published in the 1970s and '80s sought to investigate this very question, with a number of studies exploring the occurrence of particular ICD-categorised disorders across different cultural contexts.[17] Whilst many of these claimed findings of cross-cultural similarity of symptom profiles

---

15. This document describes common problems as including the 'failure to prescribe in accordance with clinical guidelines' and 'inappropriate self-medication, often of prescription-only medicines' (WHO 2002, 1).

16. As Walker argues, these assumptions about the 'inevitable' transition from 'traditional' to 'modern' (that is, 'capitalist, industrial, urban, individualist, bureaucratized, secular and scientifically-organized') society also held a 'significant role' in legitimising imperialism. Furthermore, such notions of 'modernisation' were also part of broader notions of race, class and gender, where 'inferior groups', such as women and 'primitives' were set apart from the educated Western male (2005, 25–6).

17. See, for example, the WHO's International Pilot Study of Schizophrenia (IPSS) (WHO 1974, 1975; also the 1974 report by Sartorius, Shapiro and Jablensky), which was carried out across nine different countries, and its five-year follow-up study (Leff et al. 1992) and the Determinants of Outcome of Severe Mental Disorders study (DOSMeD) (Sartorius

and cross-cultural validity of diagnoses,[18] others have argued that the very design of the research projects—research carried out by psychiatrists, using 'standardised' (that is, 'standardised' in the West) diagnostic categories—suggests that researchers were looking for similarities rather than differences (Kleinman 1991, 19–22).[19] More recently, a number of researchers have taken a different view. For example, following a review of cross-cultural research conducted between 2009 and 2011, Myers argues that variation in the cross-cultural experience of schizophrenia is so significant that 'the use of the term schizophrenia may not adequately account for the variety (and local specificity) of symptoms, experiences, explanatory models, and outcomes described here' (2011, 309). Back in the 1990s, Thakker and Ward had questioned how the search for schizophrenia could be undertaken in other cultures when the 'uncertainty about the nature and boundaries of schizophrenic symptoms' continues (1998, 512). Nearly twenty years later, this question still awaits a coherent answer.

In fact, what we are actually asking here are two different questions: firstly, whether similar symptoms occur across diverse social and cultural contexts (and if this in itself reflects a common underlying cause or condition); secondly, whether the boundaries of 'madness' and 'sanity', 'health' and 'ill-health' are drawn in the same places cross-culturally. For while it might be true, as Kleinman concludes, that schizophrenia's core symptoms are found in 'a wide variety of societies' (1991, 35), this does not necessarily indicate that such symptoms are universally-recognised as a condition requiring some kind of (medical) treatment, or that they are thus indicators of some universal disorder (Bentall 2004, 120–21). In the emergent 'global mental health' field, division is often evident between psychiatric and medical anthropological approaches to these questions. For example, Summerfield argues that numerous ethnographic studies conducted since the 1970s have shown that the 'presentation, attribution,

---

et al. 1986); also Singer's research on 'depressive disorders', which concluded that the cross-cultural similarities he encountered considerably outweighed any differences (1975, 297).

18. The 1975 summary report from the IPSS claimed evidence of cross-cultural validity, concluding that symptom profiles were similar between patients diagnosed with 'schizophrenia' (ICD category 295) across the different centres and describing 'a high degree of similarity among the centres with regard to the psychopathology of individual schizophrenic subgroups' (WHO 1975, 141). It concluded that, 'schizophrenia, mania, and depressive psychoses' could be found in a series of patients across the nine centres (WHO 1975, 144).

19. Indeed, the WHO 1975 report itself stated that, '[o]ur techniques have mainly been designed to discover common characteristics, and these are undoubtedly present' (1975, 145), and explained that '[s]chizophrenia was chosen for this study because of its apparent universality' (1975, 16).

classification, prevalence, and prognosis' of psychiatric conditions vary greatly between cultures. Whilst these are reported in social science journals,[20] such studies, he says, are 'under-represented' in mainstream psychiatric literature, where Summerfield argues that cross-cultural similarities are overemphasised, and differences minimised (2008, 993).[21]

For many psychiatrists, for the main part, biomedical diagnostic categories—especially those related to depressive disorders—are valid cross-culturally; it is only their *manifestation* which differs. Following research in China and Taiwan for example, Kleinman argued that the underlying 'disease' of 'depression' is the same cross-culturally; it is only the *illness* which differs (1977, 9). This perspective references the concept of an assumed greater somatisation of mental illness in non-Western cultures in its explanation. Here, patients' greater emphasis on somatic—as opposed to psychological—symptoms is often interpreted as a result of the stigmatisation of mental illness or cultural norms of expression which do not, for example, permit demonstrations of emotion. In Taiwan, Kleinman described the patients he encountered:

> 10 of 25 patients (40%) exhibited all the signs and symptoms of the depressive syndrome, and seven of those (28%) responded completely to specific treatment for depression, but none of them reported depressive affect or would accept the medical diagnoses that they were suffering from depression or mental illness. They looked upon their physical complaints as their "real" sickness, a physical sickness (1977, 5).

Similarly, in the Tibetan context, both Jacobson (2002, 2007) and Millard (2007) have described how physical or somatic—rather than psychological—symptoms were often emphasised by patients suffering from *rlung* disorders, which Jacobson equated variously with depression, GAD and panic disorder (2000, 2002, 2007). However, as saw in Chapter Three, these Tibetan categories in fact include a number of both physical *and* psychological symptoms, which appear to hold equal weight in diagnosis. Here then, I would argue that it is not that physical symptoms are necessarily somatic; rather, that in these

---

20. See, for example, *Social Science and Medicine, Transcultural Psychiatry, Anthropology and Medicine* and *Culture, Medicine and Psychiatry.*

21. Indeed, these two diverse fields are often approaching the question from different positions, with psychiatrists (broadly speaking) attempting to use biomedical concepts to explain illness across different cultures, and anthropologists exploring cross-cultural concepts of normality and abnormality (Bentall 2004, 121). There are, of course, some notable exceptions to this, with some researchers, such as Arthur Kleinman and Roland Littlewood, spanning both fields (Bentall 2004, 121).

different understandings of health and illness, there is less of a division between physical and mental illnesses, and illness categories more usually contain both physical and psychological symptomatology (a point which will become clearer when we examine some case studies in Part Three).

One of the much-debated issues of the biomedical diagnostic systems refers to their management of diverse cultural 'norms' of experience and illness. One way in which the DSM and ICD have evolved markedly with each edition is in their accessions to cultural differences via the inclusion of 'culture-bound disorders' or 'syndromes'—categories which have consistently caused debate amongst mental health professionals. Viewed by Western psychiatry as conditions 'that do not fit easily into psychiatric classifications' (Fernando 2002, 41), these were originally named 'peculiar psychiatric disorders' (Tseng 2006), and were included in the DSM for the first time in an appendix to the DSM-IV (APA 1994).[22] Similarly, the ICD-10 (WHO 1993) listed 'culture-specific disorders' in an 'annex to its criteria for research' (Fernando 2002, 43). Several years and one edition later, Alarcón et al. suggested that most of those listed in the 'culture-bound' category in the revised version of the DSM-IV (DSM-IV-TR, APA 2000) were *not* actually 'culture-bound syndromes' at all—rather they were 'causal explanations' which could be applied to a broad range of conditions which occur in 'closely analogous forms' across diverse settings (2002, 244–45).

Fernando argues that racist connotations are inherent in these concepts, where Western notions of 'modernisation' and 'development' are evident in their assumptions of the cultural neutrality of Western classifications, juxtaposed with conditions demarcated as 'culture-bound' if they could not be subsumed within Western categories (2002, 42–43). If, as we have seen, *all* mental illness—'and indeed the definition of mental health'—is in fact 'culture-bound' (Fernando 2002, 43), then such a category is by definition, invalid. The most recent edition of the DSM seems to agree: the term 'culture-bound syndrome' has been removed from the DSM-5 (APA 2013). The text now includes the statement that, '[t]he current formulation acknowledges that *all* forms of distress are locally shaped, including the DSM disorders' (2013, 758).

---

22. Littlewood has written an elucidating description of the 1991 NIMH-sponsored meeting of psychiatrists and anthropologists in Pittsburgh which aimed to 'enhance the cultural suitability of the DSM-IV'. In attendance were only two (out of a total of fifty) participants from outside North America, and Littlewood describes the tensions which arose between the anthropologists, who acted as 'representatives for non-Western societies' and the North American psychiatrists from 'minority groups', who discussed racism and the relevance of psychiatric diagnoses on different minority populations within North America (1992, 258–59).

'Cultural' issues are now included in *Section III: Emerging Measures and Models*—under the heading of 'cultural formulation' (2013, 749–59), and 'culture-related diagnostic issues' are (briefly) discussed for many of the diagnostic categories. However, the authors' position becomes clearer when they explain: 'Across groups there remain culturally patterned differences in symptoms, ways of talking about distress, and locally perceived causes, which are in turn associated with coping strategies and patterns of help seeking' (2013, 758). Again there is the suggestion that the underlying diagnostic categories are universally valid—it is only their *manifestation* (in terms of symptoms), their naming and 'perceived' causation which differs.

Thus, despite an increasing awareness of differences in cross-cultural norms with each new incarnation of the DSM, there remains, as Thakker and Ward suggest, an 'implicit assumption that the diagnostic categories represent universal disorders' (1998, 502). Indeed, whilst many within the biomedical system are critical of such an approach, the very existence of classification systems such as the DSM and ICD requires a certain standardisation which will, by definition, struggle to accommodate cultural differences. These issues lead to questions about how this 'cultural formulation' might play out in Tibetan communities, and whether we can situate the Tibetan diagnoses of *rlung*, *smyo nad* and others somewhere in the biomedical model of mental illness, as has been suggested by Jacobson and Millard.

Finally, there are also questions about cross-cultural differences in notions of 'recovery' and 'efficacy' in the treatment of mental illness. Shah and Mountain state that patients are more interested in 'what helps and what harms' than they are about any 'ideological background' of a treatment (2007, 375). However, I would argue that the situation is often more complex than this perhaps suggests. A patient (and her family) might in fact have different motivations in different contexts and at different stages of her illness. An acute episode of psychosis, for example, may demand an emergency treatment of medication (perhaps in order to prevent the afflicted individual from harming herself or others). However, once this 'emergency' situation has calmed down and the patient and her family adjust to their new life within this new context, she may wish to investigate factors such as what might have precipitated this episode, where it fits into her life, what this means for her future and her place in the world, and what these diverse explanations of her experience mean in a broader sense. Such questions may play out quite differently in different cultural contexts.

Burns suggests that, ultimately, 'it is what works that matters' (2013, xvi), but, as Holloway asks, 'what do we mean by "work"' (2008, 246)? Holloway delineates two very different approaches to recovery from mental illness: 're-covery-as-getting-better' and the more contemporary conceptualisation of 'recovery as a journey of the heart', a much more individual process related to 'finding personal meaning even in the face of ongoing illness and disability' (2008, 245). Concepts of 'help', 'harm', 'efficacy' and 'recovery' can differ significantly between different patients and between patients and their doctors, and may demonstrate significant cross-cultural differences. For example, Bentall argues that people with psychosis may well value their experiences and appraise their treatments differently from 'second hand' observers such as friends, family or health professionals (2004, 510–11). Doctors and patients may in fact be seeking different results from any proposed treatment(s). For example, an individual with manic depression may not be aiming to get rid of his condition, but rather to manage it, without the necessity of life-long medications (which they may have experienced as having severe or unpleasant side effects). His clinician, on the other hand, may wish for a calm patient who is not a danger to himself or others, and who complies with the prescribed treatment. Where cross-cultural differences in concepts of 'normal' and 'abnormal' are brought into this equation, there may well be an amplification of such differences. For example, Adams has described the difficulties of defining 'efficacy' in a contemporary Tibetan context—even in cases of physical illness—when it is being concurrently measured by two different medical systems (in this case, via biomedical computerised tomography (CT) scans and Tibetan medical pulse and urine diagnostic methods) (2011). Clearly, notions of 'efficacy' and 'recovery' can vary significantly within, as well as between, cultures, and these different perspectives will likely impact on patients' and their families' views on different types of treatment, and their expectations from them.

Biomedicine in Tibetan Contexts: History and Contemporary Practice

So what do we know so far about how these multiple factors play out in Tibetan communities? If we examine the use of biomedicine in ethnically Tibetan contexts, it seems that, as Kleinman suggested, biomedical practice is often significantly different to its practice in the West, and may also show distinct variation between urban and rural areas. In addition, various political factors have influenced the introduction and spread of biomedicine in the Tibetan context—particularly in the early days in Central Tibet. Moreover, biomedicine's interaction with Sowa Rigpa has influenced how it is viewed in many Tibetan communities, often seen as particularly good for treating 'acute' or 'emergency' conditions, with Sowa Rigpa, in contrast, relegated to managing chronic conditions, as we shall see here.

In Tibet itself, biomedicine was initially introduced through the British imperial medical services and missionary medical practices in the early twentieth century, and later (since the 1950s), via India and China (McKay 2011, 33). Initially, with Christian missionaries' medical activities confined to the border areas of Tibet, biomedicine was introduced into Tibet proper primarily through the British Government of India and its British Indian invading forces, who used it as a political tool through which to gain the goodwill of the Tibetan population and, they hoped, political support. Free biomedicines were offered to all, and a number of biomedical dispensaries were set up. Keen to 'sell' biomedicine to the local Tibetan population, the British made a number of adaptations to their biomedical practice during the 1930s and 1940s in an effort to increase its uptake. These included letting Tibetan patients determine (elective) surgery days through consultation with religious specialists, and also some alterations to the hospital environment in accordance with Tibetan traditions (McKay 2011). However, in reality, such medical services were mainly confined to the Indo-Tibetan trade route between Bengal and Lhasa, and the vast majority of Tibetans in fact had little or no experience of biomedicine until the Chinese intervention in the 1950s (McKay 2011, 34–35).

However, this 'integrative' approach taken by the British helped to establish biomedicine in Tibet over a century ago—and I found a similar approach being taken in contemporary biomedical practice in a Tibetan exile community when I interviewed Dr. Tsetan Dorji Sadutshang, Chief Medical Officer of the biomedical Delek Hospital in Dharamsala, India.[23] Dr Sadutshang, a first-generation exile from east Tibet, explained that he felt it important to take an 'integrative' approach to treatment at his hospital. He noted that his 'Indian training'—i.e. biomedical training in India—seemed to extol the view that, as he said, 'everything Western is the full answer', causing Tibetans to neglect their own medical traditions. And, whilst he stood by his biomedical training, he gave some examples of the kinds of integration he encouraged at his hospital, explaining that while people were hospitalised, they could leave the hospital to do *pūjā* (religious rituals)[24] if they wished, and that in the event of a patient's death, monks were welcome to come to the hospital to conduct traditional Tibetan Buddhist death rituals.

---

23. Interview with Dr. Tsetan Dorji Sadutshang conducted at the Delek Hospital, Dharamsala, by the author, 28th July 2012.

24. This Hindi/Nepali term was commonly used by Tibetans in Darjeeling to refer to a variety of Tibetan, Nepali and/or Indian rituals.

For Tibetans arriving in India following the Chinese intervention in the 1950s, they of course encountered a well-established biomedical tradition stretching back to the days of colonial rule. However, in both Tibet and India, the contemporary practice of biomedicine may be significantly different from its practice in the West. McKay has examined the 'indigenisation' of biomedicine in both Tibet and Sikkim (2005, 2011), and more recently, Adams and Li described the 'little resemblance' between the biomedicine that they saw practised in the TAR and across China and that practised in the West (2008, 106). Indeed, pragmatic problems such as linguistic barriers—particularly in more rural areas—can contribute to significant difficulties in the administration and reception of biomedicine. For example, in Spiti in northwest India, Besch described some of the problems of utilising biomedicines when neither patients nor local amchi are clear either on what they might be or be prescribed for, and nor are they able to read the packaging or instructions. He witnessed patients frequently taking prescribed medicines home from the (biomedical) hospital on discharge, only to leave them unused or used incorrectly (2006, 7). Similarly, in Dharamsala, Wangda found that patients were often left confused by the 'specialized nature' of biomedicine (1996, 132), and in rural areas of the TAR, Hofer found biomedical drugs often stocked by amchi and administered at the patient's request, where patients held a strong preference for medicines delivered by intravenous (IV) drip (often containing saline solution and/or antibiotics) or injection to orally-administered pills (2011, 216–20).

Within the context of such 'integration', in Darjeeling I sometimes found Sowa Rigpa and biomedicine clearly delineated into different spheres: Sowa Rigpa described as good for dealing with 'chronic' conditions and 'cutting the roots of disease'; biomedicine as best for the treatment of 'acute' or 'emergency' conditions. Thus, as has been reported by others (see, for example, Samuel in Dalhousie 2009; Wangda 1996), biomedicine was viewed by many Tibetans in Darjeeling as a fast-acting treatment for conditions such as colds and coughs, sleeping problems and medical emergencies—but a system which often only treated the *symptoms* of an underlying condition. In comparison, Sowa Rigpa was often described as a slower-acting, longer-term treatment, with many people explaining to me that it treats the *cause* of an illness. Indeed, when I interviewed Tenzin (26), a second-generation exile, in July 2012, while he was on holiday from his medical studies in the US, he argued that whilst it was important to keep an open mind and respect the different medical traditions (in fact, his grandfather had been a Tibetan amchi), from his perspective, 'Tibetan medicine is great but lacking'. In the past, he said, he had taken both Tibetan medicines and biomedicines, but he felt that Sowa Rigpa was less good at treating 'modern diseases'. Similarly, Samten (42), also a second-generation exile living in Darjeeling, explained, 'For emergency, I take allopathic medicine; for non-emergency, definitely take Tibetan medicine—Tibetan medicine is especially good for old diseases ... chronic diseases'.

On the question of how such practices and perspectives play out in the sphere of *mental* illness and its treatment through biomedicine in Tibetan communities, there has been very little research to date, with the work so far mainly limited to the specific context of Tibetan torture survivors in Dharamsala (see for example, work by Benedict, Mancini and Grodin 2009; Keller et al. 2006; Lewis 2013; Mercer, Ager and Ruwanpura 2004; Ruwanpura et al. 2006; Sachs et al. 2008; Terheggen, Stroebe and Kleber 2001). Here, interventions have tended to be based around Western-style counselling, meaning that we do not yet have a clear picture of biomedical interventions in the broader sphere of mental illness in the Tibetan context.

For Tibetan exiles residing in India, the availability of mental health treatments and facilities often differs greatly in different areas across the country, and the practice of biomedical psychiatry may be significantly different from its practice in the West. Facilities for mental illness often demonstrate a vast diversity of available care in different places, and may be of poor quality and oversubscribed in some areas. In 2010, a WHO report on 'mental health and development' stated,

> An investigation by the National Institute of Mental Health and Neurosciences in Bangalore, India found that in 16 of the 37 hospitals examined residents were forced to live together in overcrowded single-person cells. Many hospitals placed people in cells without water facilities, toilets, or beds, and residents were forced to urinate and defecate in them. In addition, residents received inadequate treatment and care. Less than half of hospitals had clinical psychologists and psychiatric social workers. Comprehensive medical and psychosocial treatments were almost nonexistent in one third of the hospitals (WHO 2010c, 12).

This reflects what I witnessed in Darjeeling, where facilities (and even beds) were severely limited, as we saw in Chapter Two, and comprehensive mental health services were only available in larger cities, several hours' drive away.

However, in February 2014, the *British Medical Journal* reported that the Indian government was set to table a new mental health bill ('The Mental Health Care Bill 2013') seeking to 'protect, promote, and fulfil the rights of people with mental illness and ensure the availability of high quality services', 'including the provision of acute mental health services for outpatient and inpatient care' (Chaudhuri 2014). In addition, as Chaudhuri noted, the new bill promised 'halfway houses and sheltered or supported accommodation' and 'mental health services for patients' families' (2014). Of course, such changes will take time to implement, and are likely to be employed perhaps more successfully in India's larger cities, where there are greater resources and perhaps more reliable infrastructure than in smaller towns. Chaudhuri also noted that 'leading psychiatrists in government hospitals' had clearly stated a need for stronger clinical psychology services 'across the country in all institutions' (2014)—a sentiment echoed by Dr. Ghosh at the government hospital in Darjeeling who, as I have already described, expressed his regret that it was impossible to offer psychotherapy to his patients. Such services were available in Gangtok, but were often hard to access, depending on a patient's financial and/or practical circumstances.

Realities such as this illustrate how the diversity in the practice of psychiatry and psychology in the West which I described above often does not filter through into the diverse communities within which biomedicine is practised. For example, psychological treatments often do not 'travel' to other contexts alongside the biomedical model. In countries such as India, while 'talking therapies' such as counselling and CBT are recommended by the WHO (2010b) and available in a number of larger cities across the country, financial and practical constraints mean that this is simply not the reality in smaller towns such as Darjeeling, as we have seen. Unsurprisingly perhaps, limited resources (be they government, individual, charity or NGO) often translate into limited options for patients. Thus, an individual diagnosed with 'schizophrenia' in the UK might (depending on his luck and/or financial situation) receive a broad range of treatments which fall under not only the 'biological' category of treatment (for example, anti-psychotic medication, electro-convulsive therapy), but also perhaps treatments such as psychotherapy, psychodynamic therapy, CBT or family therapy (and perhaps they might also be able to access other, more creative, therapeutic interventions such as art or drama therapy). In contrast, someone given the same diagnosis in Darjeeling is likely to have significantly fewer options, often limited to pharmacological intervention(s). The WHO *World Health Care Report: 2001: Mental Health: New Understanding, New Hope* (WHO 2001) tells us that '[t]he management of mental and behavioural disorders—perhaps more particularly than that of other medical conditions—calls for the balanced combination of three fundamental ingredients: medication (or pharmacotherapy); psychotherapy; and psychosocial rehabilitation' (2001, 59). However, in reality, this is often not possible, as we saw in the government hospital in Darjeeling. Furthermore, even where the facilities, funds and infrastructure do exist to implement these three approaches to psychiatric illness, questions around cross-cultural validity and utility remain. Indeed, ideas about the utility of 'psychotherapy' may be quite culture-specific, with 'talking therapies' viewed as more harmful than helpful in some cultural contexts. In Dharamsala, for example, one ex-political prisoner who received Western-style counselling as part of a now-defunct integrated health project likened the counselling sessions to 'interrogation' (Mercer, Ager and Ruwanpura 2004, 182–85). It is very clear that we have so far only limited knowledge about how such Western-derived services, and the explanatory frameworks which underlie them, are viewed and used by Tibetans.

* * *

What I have attempted to make clear in this chapter is that whilst the particular 'biomedical' approach to mental illness has come to dominate much psychiatric research and practice in the West and also globally, the practice of biomedicine often differs greatly across different cultural contexts. This is a result of multiple influences in both Western and non-Western communities—often driven by financial, practical, political and/or ideological factors. Thus whilst in Western contexts such as the UK and USA, mental health treatment may allow for an array of available psychological treatments alongside pharmacological ones, in many non-Western contexts such as Darjeeling, this is simply not the case, and drug interventions are often the only treatment available. The particular availability and practice of biomedicine in Darjeeling, and the medically-pluralistic context within which it is situated, likely influence people's views on 'Western medicine'—or 'Indian medicine', as it was often referred to by Tibetans—in terms of expectations of availability, appropriateness and efficacy. Furthermore, if we return to the subjective and culturally-determined endeavour which is the drawing of 'boundaries' between 'sane' and 'insane', mental 'health' and 'illness', we are left with the question of how to approach those designated to be in need of treatment according to one system, and not in another. How do Tibetans in Darjeeling themselves make sense of and manage their experience where they are simultaneously diagnosed as 'well' and 'ill'? Do they, as Williams and Healy suggest, combine multiple explanations simultaneously in 'exploratory maps', or instead employ more defined explanatory frameworks to their experience? These questions, and the broader picture of mental health and illness in a contemporary Tibetan community, will be examined in Part Three where I explore lay perspectives on mental health, illness and healing through a series of case studies and a broad spectrum of interview material from Darjeeling.

PART THREE
THE CASE STUDIES

CHAPTER SIX

LOBSANG:
rLung AND DEPRESSION

Of course there's no denying that the principal cause of all mental problems is rlung ... rlung *is always there—*rlung *is the main factor which disturbs the person's sanity.* (Amchi Sonam Dolma, Dharamsala, August 2012)

Lobsang's Story

When I asked a Tibetan friend, Gyaltsen (28), what he knew about any local mental health facilities, he suggested that he knew someone—'Lobsang'—with 'mental depression' that I could talk to. My attempts to meet Lobsang proved to be rather protracted however; the result not of *Lobsang's* reticence, but the reluctance of my friend. Gyaltsen initially mentioned Lobsang and his illness in September 2011, and in early October, confirmed that he had spoken to Lobsang, who had been told about my research, and was happy to meet me. However, as he did not own a mobile telephone, we would have to wait until Gyaltsen bumped into him in town—which he assured me he often did. As time went on, and I repeatedly asked Gyaltsen about meeting Lobsang again, I started to wonder if he was procrastinating. Each time he confirmed that Lobsang was happy to talk to me, but had some reason why we could not meet him. Finally, Gyaltsen explained that although Lobsang had agreed to meet me, he (Gyaltsen) felt that talking to me about his condition would make Lobsang feel worse. Contrary to the Western conception of the 'cathartic' function of talking about one's problems, Gyaltsen was echoing a view that I heard from several other informants; that talking about one's difficulties makes one feel worse, and that talking about other things as a 'distraction' is generally preferable.

127

When Gyaltsen finally agreed to introduce me to Lobsang, the encounter proved interesting. Gyaltsen knew roughly where Lobsang lived, so we walked down the street as he tried to determine exactly which building it was, asking neighbours along the way. He referred to Lobsang as 'the man with *sems ma bde ba* [uneasy mind]', and in response, several people clarified using an English term: 'the man with mental problems?' Before we found his home, several neighbours told us Lobsang was most likely sitting on one of the benches nearby some of the local shops, where they said he often spent time during the day.

Indeed, we found Lobsang there, and he led us over to another, quieter bench, where we sat down and I explained my research again to him, reconfirming that he was happy to talk about his experience. The interview was a slightly strange encounter for me too—perched on a bench in the light rain, with a number of locals watching this foreigner talk to a local man, well-known in the area for his 'mental problems', I was concerned that Lobsang might feel uncomfortable with this situation. He, however, did not seem perturbed. He answered all my questions willingly, and appeared comfortable discussing his experience of illness and the different healing methods which he had tried.

Lobsang (50) had been born in the area, his parents having fled Tibet for India before he was born. He lived with his elderly mother, and his two sisters lived locally. Lobsang was quiet and polite, answering questions and explaining when he could, and describing his illness:

> My health condition is not bad—compared to [the] early time.... Before I felt pressure on my chest—like someone holding me from behind.... I was thinking continuously—strange things, no control over it. Now I'm really better than before—because of medicine.... I take Indian medicine [biomedicine] ... 'Paxidep' [i.e. paroxetine, one of the class of medicines known as selective serotonin reuptake inhibitors (SSRI), generally used to treat anxiety and depression], and two others [he was not sure of their names].

Lobsang explained that this medicine was prescribed by a 'neuro doctor' in Siliguri, who had been prescribing this medication for him for around six years—after the problem began around seven years previously—and whom he continued to visit for 'check-ups'.

Lobsang described how, when he first began to experience symptoms, he had visited a monk he knew of in Nepal. The monk had blessed him, and held a *rdo rje* ("dorje", Skt.: *vajra*)[1] to the top of his head. However, as he did

---

1. Translated as 'thunderbolt' or 'diamond', this ritual object was originally associated with the Vedic god Indra and symbolises strength and power (Samuel 2012, 50), and is commonly used for Tibetan Buddhist ritualistic purposes.

so, Lobsang had had the strong desire to run away. Next, the monk tried to give him a *srung nga* ("soonga", protective amulet), but as Lobsang held out his hand to receive it, he felt as if someone was pulling his hand away. He described how the monk had grabbed the collar of his T-shirt so that he could not move, and placed the *srung nga* into his hand. Lobsang related how as he took the *srung nga*, 'I felt as if someone was leaving my body'. I asked if this treatment had helped, and he explained that it helped a 'little bit', describing how he had felt 'relaxed for a few days ... a little bit cured from this'. He went a few times to this monk for blessings, but unfortunately some of his symptoms persisted.

Lobsang's description of the events on visiting the monastery hints at the suggestion of a spirit or possession of some kind. However, even with the presence apparently removed, some symptoms continued, leading him to consult other practitioners in addition to this. Lobsang had tried 'Tibetan Medicine', but found that it did not help and, believing that other herbal medicines such as Ayurvedic medicine would not help either, he tried biomedicine instead, initially consulting a local Indian biomedical doctor who was popular with the Tibetan community in Darjeeling. The doctor suggested he visit a psychiatrist, and the initial psychiatrist, on being unable to help, recommended a second psychiatrist, who Lobsang continued to consult. It was this doctor who prescribed his medicine.

Gyaltsen translated as Lobsang described the symptoms he experienced:

> Sometimes I feel the earth is coming towards my face. When feeling pressure [he indicated his chest], I have no problem breathing, but feeling fear and pressure on the back of my neck ... I have many thoughts ... [which I] can't control ... I feel threatened.

Lobsang explained that before he had started taking the medicine, he had also had trouble sleeping. He said that he was now much better, but the symptoms had not totally gone. For example, although he no longer had trouble sleeping, he explained that, when sleeping, 'I do not fully relax'. He felt that 'medicines are best, but also support and encouragement from others helps.... The doctor says it will take time, but it will be cured'.

Discussing the possible cause(s) of the illness, Lobsang explained that he had experienced a lot of 'pressure' in a previous job. Gyaltsen translated: 'He had been designing carpets.... He was deeply thinking about designing all the time ... [his] brain got a lot of pressure', explaining that the concentration and 'pressure' of the job had been involved here. More recently, in 2011, Lobsang had been to work in a tea factory in Bhutan for eight months. He explained that he had been appointed as a low-level leader, but unfortunately he had experienced some difficulties, and he had found it very 'stressful'. This had exacerbated his illness, and consequently he had resigned and returned to Darjeeling where, unable to work, he usually spent his days in town, talking to others and looking after his elderly mother at home. I enquired about his diagnosis, and Lobsang and Gyaltsen discussed this briefly in Tibetan—both seemingly unable to recall the English word—Gyaltsen finally saying, 'Depression—that's it'. I asked if the doctor had also mentioned 'anxiety', but Lobsang said no—only 'depression'. Asked how he referred to his illness in Tibetan, he used the terms *sems nad* and *srog rlung*.

In many ways this is an unremarkable story: a man with a fairly common case of depression, exacerbated by stress, which was responding to some degree to fairly standard and commonly-prescribed biomedical antidepressant medication. However, it is also a good example of some of the ways in which the Tibetan notion of *rlung* has been linked to contemporary discourses on 'stress' and 'pressure' in relation to 'modern life'. Named *srog rlung*, *rlung* and 'mental depression' by others, and diagnosed as 'depression' by his psychiatrist, Lobsang viewed his illness as caused by 'stress', 'mental pressure' and 'concentration'. In this chapter I will examine the concepts of *rlung* and *srog rlung* and their relation to mental health and illness from the perspectives of amchi and lay Tibetans; and contemporary Tibetan notions of 'stress', 'pressure' and 'depression', as well as the politicisation of the *rlung* diagnosis.

Non-Textual Concepts of *rLung* and *Srog rLung* in Darjeeling and Beyond

In Darjeeling, I discussed these *rlung*-related disorders with several amchi. At the CTMI clinic, for example, Amchi Teinlay described the symptoms of *srog rlung*, which echo Lobsang's description of his experience:

> The patients [with *srog rlung*] will have ... high and low mood, and ... sometimes, some of them get a blocked feeling in the chest region ... [also] sometimes, in a closed room, they feel ... they think that they are getting suffocated ... [also] sometimes they'll have disturbed sleep ... [also] if you press their *rlung* points ... they will be very sensitive and tender.

Similarly, at the Darjeeling MTK clinic, Amchi Lobsang Thubten described some of the symptoms of *srog rlung*, explaining that each patient will have a selection of symptoms:

[The patient might be] very sad, restless, unable to stay in one place, not hungry, tearful, laughing for no reason, afraid when alone or in a crowd, [they] can't concentrate, can't remember things … doubting [others]…. staring at one particular spot without blinking for a long time, breathing heavily … [the] person feels better for stretching or yawning … They want to be with close friends…. Talking or doing their usual hobbies and things that make them feel better…. Also maybe suicidal, fainting, asking the same question again and again … The *rlung* increases, the *rlung* is mobile—not stable, so therefore [the patient] forgets things…. Sometimes [the patient is] aggressive, talking to themselves.

Others have described a large number of physical symptoms of *rlung* disturbance. Epstein and Topgay list symptoms including a dry, red and rough tongue, 'erratic and diffuse pains', tinnitus, a 'sensation of broken bones', 'sensation of eyes and other organs bulging out', an excess of saliva and mucus and 'looseness' of limbs (1982, 74). Drungtso describes symptoms including 'dark complexion', dehydration, rough skin, numbness, spasms and paralysis (2004, 222–23). How then do lay perspectives compare to these specialists' understandings? In his research in Darjeeling, Jacobson found that most lay Tibetans held 'simplified cognates' of the *rGyud bZhi*'s terminology and theory, transmitted via amchi's 'provision of truncated bits of the classical model when patients request an explanation for their illnesses' (2007, 231–32). He found, however, that in relation to *srog rlung*, patients often demonstrated an understanding of a broader range of symptoms than those listed in the *rGyud bZhi* (2007, 233). In addition, other researchers have found that the lay discourse on *rlung* often encompasses perspectives as diverse as exile and identity politics, the encroachment of 'modernity' and 'Westernisation', and the perceived 'emotional' causes[2] of *rlung*.

In Darjeeling, a number of Tibetan informants described the symptoms of *rlung* and *srog rlung* in a similar manner to those given by the amchi above.[3] Furthermore, some of my Tibetan informants who had a good knowledge of English or a significant amount of contact with Westerners likened some individuals' *rlung* disorders to biomedical diagnoses of 'anxiety' or 'depression'.

---

2. I follow Ekman's 1999 definition of 'emotion' here, which encompasses seventeen states including anger, contentment, fear, pride, sadness, and sensory pleasure (1999, 45–60).

3. For some of the Tibetans I spoke to, the terms *rlung* and *srog rlung* were interchangeable; for others, they delineated slightly different disorders. However, they were never described to me as divergent enough to definitively separate them out. Sometimes, when I asked about *srog rlung*, my informant would answer referring only to *rlung* and vice versa. Because of this, I have indicated each time which term the individual used.

For example, Metok (63), a former nurse who had received her training in the UK many years before, explained that *srog rlung* is 'maybe like depression'. However, she added, '*Khrag rlung* [blood pressure] also is like depression—high blood pressure ... [it is] related to nerves'. When I asked one informant, Dolma (31), about the symptoms of *srog rlung*, she referred to it in English as 'anxiety disease', and proceeded to call a friend in another town who she told me suffered from this condition, to ask him about it. She related some of his symptoms as he listed them in a mixture of Tibetan and English on the other end of the telephone line, for example, 'panic ... especially in a crowded place, or when he goes in a car or jeep', explaining that the symptoms come and go. He said that he does not take any medicine, after his (biomedical) doctor told him that it was better to manage without medicine if possible. In his experience, he said, 'the best treatment is meditation'. Discussing his illness over the telephone in Tibetan, they both referred to it as 'anxiety *na tsha*' ('anxiety sickness'). After hanging up the telephone, Dolma explained to me that this kind of illness is caused by 'loneliness', 'too much thinking' and a 'competitive mind'. In terms of its symptomatology, Metok explained that individuals with this kind of condition 'want to be alone in dark place, talking to oneself', often making repetitive movements with their hands or talking nonsense, but rarely violent.

Jacobson concludes that there is a 'significant overlap' between Tibetan categories of *rlung* illness and 'biomedical constructions of depression, anxiety and somatization', suggesting that *srog rlung* is 'most similar' to 'major depressive and anxiety disorders' (2000, 529). However, despite these equivalences being drawn by some Tibetan doctors and lay individuals, I would argue that the differences are simply too great to view *rlung* disorders as equivalents of biomedical diagnoses related to depression and anxiety. This is perhaps particularly the case for *srog rlung*, which has been variously equated with a number of biomedical categories as diverse as PTSD (Benedict et al. 2009) and psychosis (Millard 2007). During my fieldwork, both Amchi Teinlay (who had a very good knowledge of English and experience of treating foreign patients in the West) and Amchi Sonam Dolma named 'depression' and 'schizophrenia' (two significantly different biomedical categories) as different kinds of *srog rlung*. Similarly, in his research at a Tibetan medicine clinic in Scotland (UK), Millard had similar findings, describing five case studies, all diagnosed with *srog rlung* to varying degrees of severity, who related their symptoms/illnesses in Western terms of 'stress', 'anxiety', 'panic attack', 'depression' and 'psychosis' (2007, 253–58).

Lay Tibetan informants in Darjeeling often had much broader understandings of *rlung* and *srog rlung* disorders than simple equivalents of depression and anxiety, which will be examined in more detail below. I would suggest that these diversities make it impossible to equate the different kinds of *rlung* disorder with biomedical categories. The symptom clusters are too divergent, and the somatic symptoms too significant for any kind of easy or uneasy comparison. Furthermore, *rlung* is not the only *nyes pa* to be related to symptoms such as those discussed here. Various symptoms of *sems nad* which would be classified in biomedicine as 'depressive' symptoms can also be related to *other nyes pa*. For example, in my interview with Amchi Sonam Dolma, she described some of the symptoms related to a disturbance in the *nyes pa* of *bad kan*:

> The patients who are more associated with *bad kan* would just reclude themselves like the depressed, depressive people.... *Bad kan smyo nad* ['phlegm madness'] ... [refers to] people who have very very very depressive state, who don't want to engage with people, always try to exclude—reclude—themselves, and exclude themselves from the company of others.... [Also] they always like to eat too much cold food, heavy food.... What we see in the West, like depression-related over-eating, these are more related with *bad kan*.

It becomes clear not only that the different *rlung* diagnoses do not match easily with biomedical categories of 'depression' or 'anxiety', but also that a number of other Tibetan diagnostic categories share similarities in symptomatology with these same biomedical categories. Furthermore, the notion of *rlung* has also taken on broader meanings in the context of cultural and political changes for contemporary Tibetans. The first of these is perhaps the political discourse of *rlung* in both Chinese-controlled Tibet and exile Tibet. Moreover, related to this concept of unhappiness and political tension, in exile Tibet, *rlung* has also become a way to describe purported negative aspects of modernity, such as 'stress', 'competition' (for example, for jobs, or in school/university exams) and 'pressure'—this English term was often used by Tibetans in Darjeeling to denote high blood pressure, often indicating 'stress'—and it is to these concepts of *rlung* which I turn next.

Politicisation of the *rLung* Diagnosis

Several researchers have documented the notion of *rlung* as political discourse in both Chinese-controlled Tibet and exile Tibet (mainly in Dharamsala, India). In Lhasa, for example, Adams described the broader meaning given to *rlung* to refer to social, cultural, and political forces, and as an idiom through which to express suffering amongst Tibetans (1998, 83). Similarly, Janes suggests that in the politically-charged arena of Tibet, where religious practice has been increasingly controlled by the Chinese government, 'medicine may remain the only institution in which Tibetans can articulate, through the language of the body, dissatisfactions over modern life that are not interpreted as signs of nationalism' (1999a, 407), and it is often the notion of *rlung* which is at the forefront here. Janes found that some of his Tibetan informants in the TAR quite directly linked *rlung* with political issues, including one doctor, who explained,

> Rlung [is] more common nowadays because Tibet is no longer free. The Chinese government is the government of rlung. The Chinese government makes people unhappy, and so rlung must be more common…. Tibetans have rlung because they are not free (Janes 1995, 31).

It is evident that in the TAR, *rlung* is not only an idiom through which to express dissatisfaction with the status quo, but also a means through which Tibetan identity can be expressed 'safely' (Janes 1999a, 407). In fact, I would argue that the notion of *rlung* is fundamental to Tibetan identity—intimately related to consciousness, it is tied to mental and physical health—and is therefore integral to a Tibetan understanding of the mind and body, and thus, also to the surrounding environment. *rLung*, in fact, is a way of describing, mediating, and making sense of the world. This is not to say that *rlung* is not also a condition in its own right, divorced from its politicised aspects; but it makes sense that this condition has become strongly linked to the very real distress and illness caused by events occurring within Tibetan communities. In fact, if *rlung* disturbance can be caused by—amongst other factors—psychological stress or negative mental states, from a Tibetan medical perspective, it is entirely unsurprising that Tibetans in both Chinese-controlled Tibet and exile Tibet would suffer from *rlung*-related illnesses.

In India, newly-arrived refugees from Tibet—many of them former political prisoners—frequently have high levels of *rlung* disorders (Prost 2006). Prost argues that here, *rlung* is often linked to the 'trauma of exile', and felt to be exacerbated by unfamiliar environmental conditions, such as the hot weather (which the majority of the newcomers are not acclimatised to) (2006, 123). In Darjeeling and Gangtok, Jacobson noted that several of his case studies diagnosed with *srog rlung* 'had experienced a brutal military occupation in which the violent death or forced separation of family members, friends and neighbours were consequences' (2007, 241). Furthermore, if Tibetans have traditionally constructed their identity through a relationship with their *pha yul* ("payul", fatherland, hometown), encompassing the local landscape of mountains, valleys, lakes and rivers and their resident deities, as well as local dialects (Lopez 1999, 197), how then do exile Tibetans construct an identity in the absence of these things—where their dialect is constructed from the diverse Tibetan spoken in different regions, and where the land which is not their own does not contain their history or their deities? In Dharamsala, as we have seen, an identity is often constructed via the Tibetan political movement, and there, the fundamental concept of *rlung* is often used to articulate personal and societal distress. However, the manifestation of *rlung* is not solely political— sometimes, as in Lobsang's case, it is simply an illness to be managed and treated. In Darjeeling this was more often the case. There, with no new arrivals from Tibet, and few Tibetans even arriving from other areas in India, the Tibetan political discourse—whilst not entirely absent—was rather drowned out by the local political discussion. As a result, I never heard informants in Darjeeling discuss *rlung* in relation to Tibetan politics. Instead, *rlung* was solely described in relation to notions of mental health and illness, from mild cases of *rlung* disturbance to incidences of *smyo nad* related to *rlung*. In this context, comparisons were often made between *rlung* disturbance and Western notions of stress, as we shall see next.

The *rLung* of Modern Life: 'Stress', 'Pressure' and 'Depression'

We have seen how *rlung* can be an idiom of 'distress' in the Tibetan political context. However, the notion of *rlung* is also utilised as a symbol of distress in other, diverse contexts. In this section I will examine the notion of *rlung* as a symbol of 'stress' and 'pressure' in the Tibetan discourse on 'modern life' and 'Westernisation'.

For many Tibetans, the notion of *rlung* is part of lay discourse, with a similar meaning to the English term 'stress' in the West. Leaving aside the fact that the concept of 'stress' has a fairly recent history in the Western world, the term has become a common translation of *rlung* amongst many lay Tibetans with knowledge of English, some of whom also relate it to high blood pressure. This equating of the Tibetan *rlung* with the English 'stress' is not without basis. For example, disturbance in the *snying rlung* (heart wind) can lead to blood pressure variation, and is related to symptoms synonymous with Western concepts of 'stress', such as palpitations and rapid heartbeat (Janes 1999a, 394), with both systems describing a mix of psychological and somatic symptoms. Moreover, in Darjeeling, I found that many of the Tibetans I spoke to were familiar with the Western discourse on 'stress', and equated it easily with *rlung*. One informant, Phurpu (50), who engaged in frequent contact with Westerners through his work, explained in English that both *rlung* and *srog rlung* refer to 'stress', 'tension' or 'depression'. As we discussed these Tibetan terms, he asked me what kind of problems 'stress' causes in the West. I offered some suggestions: high blood pressure, digestive problems, anxiety, worry and insomnia. He responded definitively, 'Yes—*rlung* is like this'. I asked him what causes *rlung*, to which he responded, 'What do you say causes this [i.e. stress] in the West?' I suggested: family problems; divorce; long-term illness. He concurred, 'Yes, it's the same—like this'. Another informant, Nyima (35), agreed, telling me that *srog rlung* is 'tension ... stress', caused by 'not keeping the mind calm'. On another occasion, he described it in relation to blood pressure, explaining that *srog rlung* can be caused by 'high [blood] pressure ... anger ... heritage and sugar', and Metok explained, '*Srog rlung* and *khrag rlung* ... are like depression ... high blood pressure'. This was evident in Lobsang's narrative too, where his condition was understood as a result of the 'stress' and 'pressure' of his job.

In Dharamsala, financial worries have often been cited as the main cause of *rlung*, with 'worry, anxiety and sadness' also frequently mentioned (Prost 2006, 121). And in Lhasa, Janes noted that the factors most frequently cited as causes of *rlung* were 'rapid social change', financial or employment problems, 'anger and frustration over the current political situation', 'disappointments with children and other family members' and arguments within the family (1999a, 400). Janes has suggested that the 'polysemantic quality' of *rlung* renders it an 'effective means to respond to and articulate the impacts of modernity of the Chinese variety' (1999a, 396). However, it is not only *Chinese* modernity that is rejected here, I would suggest that the discussion of *rlung* as 'stress' also encompasses a rejection of certain facets of 'Westernisation'. Here, the equating of *rlung* with Western notions of 'stress' is relevant not only in the political discourse of the Tibetan independence movement, but also in the arena of exile identity politics.

As might be expected amongst a community whose culture and very identity are under immense pressure—not only from Chinese government policies, but also from the Western appropriation of their suffering and vision for their future (Adams 1996; Janes 1999a)—some of the Tibetans I spoke to in Darjeeling appeared keen to paint a particularly positive portrait of Tibetan culture. Such a depiction requires a corresponding counter position, and this sometimes came in the form of the denigration of certain aspects of 'Western culture' or 'modern life', as informants often referred to it. In Dharamsala, Prost found that *rlung* disturbance manifesting in high blood pressure could be used to denote 'Westernisation' as a positive symbol of modernity. Here, a *rlung* illness conferred status, indicating the busy life of an important person (2006, 124–25). In contrast, in Darjeeling, I came across *rlung* disorders discussed as a consequence of some of the *negative* aspects of modern life. When I asked about *rlung*, several informants responded by mentioning the notion of 'competition' in the West—in terms of competition for jobs, school places, exam marks and such like. In this way, the 'difficult' life in the West and the larger cities in India, were denigrated as causing *rlung* illness, in contrast to a traditionally 'relaxed' Tibetan lifestyle. I would suggest that this discourse is wrapped up with the presentation of an idealised Tibet that many Tibet-born Tibetan exiles remember, and Indian-born Tibetans have heard mythologised by older relatives and others within the community. In Darjeeling, for example, several informants described the 'clean air' and 'happy-go-lucky' people of Tibet, contrasting this with the dirty streets, polluted air, and 'stressed' individuals with 'no time for family or friends' in both India and the West.

When I discussed *rlung* with Samten (42), who had a lot of contact with Westerners through her work, she told me definitively, 'You don't find depression in Tibetans'. When I explained that I had heard several stories of 'depression' from Tibetan interviewees, she qualified the cases as 'very less'—that is, less than in other cultures. Her position became clearer as she discussed Tibetan Buddhist practices in depth, and explained that certain practices could both prevent and cure various kinds of *sems nad* or *smyo nad*. Confirming this, when I interviewed him in Delhi, Amchi Pema Dorjee explained that whilst 'mind-related diseases' do occur amongst Tibetans, he felt that they are more common in the West. He also felt that Tibetans were helped to deal with such illnesses by their understanding of karma—leading them to be more 'accepting' of a given situation, compared to Westerners, who do not hold this belief. Similarly, Amchi Lobsang Thubten explained, in 'more advanced, developed' countries, 'there is more competition', and therefore a higher suicide rate, concluding definitively (but erroneously), 'There's no suicide in villages'. Not having visited the West, he was still confident to tell me, 'In Western countries people have no-one to talk to.... They are not close to their family, and do not have friends as they are too busy'. He explained that this causes mental illness. In this discourse, Western culture and 'modern life' are the roots of 'stress', and contributors to mental (and physical) illness in the form of *rlung* disturbance. In Lhasa, Janes describes that for many Tibetans, what is often desired is the equal right to 'participate in China's rapid economic modernization' (Janes 1999a, 402). In contrast, for many Tibetans in India, it seems that such modernisation can be a symbol of everything that is not 'Tibetan', and as such, is to be rejected.

A number of Tibetan informants described the Tibetan medical system as superior to Western medicine for dealing with such conditions. In Dharamsala, Amchi Sonam Dolma explained in English,

> In much of the cases—particularly in the West—people have too few people to speak to, so just speaking to them, to some extent helps a lot … and particularly, when you come across patients with a mental problem, because of *how* Tibetan doctors entertain patients is entirely different to Western medicine…. Of course I don't say [that] all the Western doctors are insensitive, but normally, the very atmosphere is like that—you are always attended through a help of instrument or [something] like that…. But in Tibetan medicine, when they come to a Tibetan doctor, it's a person-to-person contact, so this—to some extent—helps a lot—*because* they need somebody to speak to—they are very lonely…. [Some people,] maybe they will say "Tibetan medicine [is] not *so* effective like Prozac" and all those things—so not so strong like that. Of course even we have to accept that. But Tibetan medicine—when we take care of the patient, we deal with the *rlung*. And *rlung* is the main factor which disturbs the person's sanity. So, there's no denying the effect…. It's not *only* the medicine that's helping in Tibetan medicine—[also] the doctor counselling the patient.

This perspective is interesting, as it contradicts the view I heard from a number of lay informants—for example, Gyaltsen's thoughts of speaking to Lobsang, mentioned above—that talking about problems leads the individual to feel worse, again highlighting some of the different perspectives of lay Tibetans and amchi.

Keeping the Mind Calm: Causes of, and Treatments for, *rLung*

If there's balance in your mind, whatever happens … you don't need to take medicines…. Once the mind is in balance, everything else also balances. (Dawa, 51)

In addition to the notion of *rlung* as 'stress' and 'tension' in the context of Tibetan discourses on politics and modernity, similarly to Lobsang's case, I found that explanations of others' 'depressive' or 'anxiety' states through the concept of *rlung* were common in Darjeeling. Here, the term *rlung* was frequently used to denote numerous emotional states of shorter or longer duration, such as grief, sadness or anger. For example, in the days following a significant—and very frightening—earthquake in the area in September 2011,[4] some of the *momo-la* at the TRSHC were not in the workshop as usual, and when I asked after them, the others explained that they had *rlung*—discussing that they had been especially upset and afraid as a result of the earthquake. Similarly Lhamo (45), a biomedical nurse, explained, '*srog rlung* means that you have [experienced] some trauma', and Metok (63) described the symptoms of *srog rlung*: '[People with *rlung*] get emotional very fast, get depression very fast ... [they] hurt so badly over little things.... If [there is] no cure for *rlung*, then [that person] can go into depression'.

As discussed in Chapter Three, the flow of *rlung* can vary over the course of one's life and from person to person, and it is also possible to 'inherit' 'dysfunctioning winds' from a previous life (Adams 1998, 84). In addition, *rlung* currents can be intentionally (or unintentionally) manipulated as part of certain Tantric practices.[5] Moreover, the flow of *rlung* can be disrupted by multiple environmental, behavioural and psychological factors, from the ingestion of different foods to particular mental states. For example, behaviours such as 'over-thinking' or 'constant worry about the future' can cause a disturbance in the *rlung* (Dorjee 2005, 139), and certain mental or emotional states are considered to be as important as dietary or climatic factors in affecting *rlung* (Adams 1998, 83). Indeed, when I interviewed him in Delhi, Amchi Pema Dorjee described how the mind can affect the *rlung*, and vice versa, explaining that when *rlung* increases,

> ... it overwhelms the mind. So [usually], the mind controls the wind, but now, *rlung* controls the mind ... If one of the channels becomes blocked [by illness, or by an increase in one of the other *nyes pa*] ... now the *yid* [mind, thought[6]] cannot go inside there and [so] it goes in the wrong way, and this is the stage when people become completely mad ... their mind is now overwhelmed by *rlung*, and then [*rlung*] goes in the wrong direction.

---

4. This earthquake (magnitude 6.9) on 18th September 2011, had its epicentre north of Darjeeling in Sikkim, causing landslides and power cuts across the region. Whilst a number of people were killed in India, Nepal and Tibet, Darjeeling was, thankfully, surprisingly unscathed (http://www.bbc.co.uk/news/world-south-asia-14965598).

5. Here, of course, we are talking about the Indian-derived Tantric practices which deal with *prāṇa*, rather than the Ayurvedic *doṣa* of *vāta*.

6. According to Millard's research, '*sems* signifies the mind that consists of constantly shifting thoughts; *yid* is a deeper layer of mind in which the thoughts circulate' (2007, 268).

Psychological states then, can be both a cause and effect of *rlung* disturbance, and in Darjeeling, I found that it was emotional and psychological factors which often predominated in discussions of *rlung*.

We saw in Chapter Three that from a Tibetan Buddhist perspective, the three root *nyon mongs* of desire, hatred, and ignorance are said to give rise to the three *nyes pa* (Epstein and Topgay 1982, 71). Wangyal explains a more direct cause and effect relationship between some of these *nyon mongs* and the *nyes pa* of *rlung* in particular, relating the different *rlung* currents to different emotions and mental states. He describes for example how the *srog rlung* 'manifests negatively as anger and hatred; positively as strong will, happiness, joy, and the development of wisdom' (2002, 79).

I discussed the nature of *rlung* with Dawa (51), a local monk. He was an interesting and knowledgeable man: having studied commerce at university, he had come to monasticism slightly later in life, joining a monastery at the age of twenty-one. He explained,

> I think *rlung* is dependent on your emotions ... if you have anger it affects your body.... Because of our negative emotions, we create negative karma, and this becomes sickness.... Karma manifests as illness.... *Sems nad* is a physical and mental illness, it also indirectly depends on your emotions, the five poisons, [and] the karma which created that.

It is clear then, that from a Tibetan perspective, mental illness can manifest as a result of numerous factors, including one's thoughts and emotions. This highlights some of the similarities between certain *rlung* disturbances and biomedical categories of 'depression', where Lutz argues that depression is 'fundamentally emotional in nature' in terms of both state and syndrome (1985, 64). However, it is important to note some of the significant differences between Western and Buddhist notions of 'emotion'. Ekman et al. explain:

> In contrast to Aristotelian ethics, [Indo-Tibetan] Buddhism rejects the notion that all emotions are healthy as long as they are not excessive or inappropriate to the time and place. Rather, Buddhism maintains that some mental states are afflictive regardless of their degree or the context in which they arise. (2005, 60[7])

---

7. Ekman, of course, is a proponent of the theory of 'basic emotions', arguing that research demonstrates the existence of distinctive patterns of autonomic nervous system activity for a number of specific emotions (1999).

In addition, there are some quite different perspectives in Western and Tibetan approaches to *specific* emotions. Shweder et al. use a comparison of Western and Tibetan approaches to anger to emphasise some of these. The Tibetan term *rlung langs* ("loong lang") is similar in conception to the English term 'anger', and translates literally as 'rising wind'. Yet there are significant differences—Shweder et al. note, for example, the difference between Tibetans' appraisal of *rlung langs* as 'morally bad', assimilating it with the *nyon mongs* 'hatred', and Americans' views of anger as morally ambivalent—a neutral process, which can even have some positive aspects (1993). However, this appraisal ignores the fact that anger has often been linked to illnesses including cancer in the West (see, for example, research by Thomas et al. 2000), and the concept that 'repressing' anger can be unhealthy—a concept also mentioned by informants in Darjeeling. In fact, the notion of 'anger' was mentioned by several informants in Darjeeling in the discourse on *rlung*. Some interviewees suggested that a person's inability to deal with their anger—for example by holding it in and not expressing it—could lead to *srog rlung*. Lhamo (45), explained, '*Srog rlung* is if you are very angry, you know ... something will get inside you ... and you cannot control [it] ... If you cannot control your anger, you get *srog rlung*'. Some of these ideas were summed up quite succinctly by one interviewee, Tsering (59), who explained, 'If you can't control your mind, you'll become mad. If you can control your mind, you'll never become mad'.

As we can see then, from a Tibetan perspective, certain thoughts and emotions are often implicated in the causation of various types of mental illness. These perceptions are frequently reflected in health-seeking behaviour, and a number of behavioural treatments were sometimes described too. Thus Metok, for example, explained,

> Depressed people shouldn't drink alcohol—it makes you violent.... [They] should go for a long walk, be with someone cheerful, who makes them laugh, do yoga.... Yoga is very good—[it] calms you down.... Go for a walk, don't go into depression, think positive, don't be worrying, take it easy, relax.... Be positive, think positive.... If you can't, then you become *smyo nad*.

Sometimes Tibetan medicine was discussed as a treatment for *rlung* disorders. Dawa, for example, stated that 'the main thing to treat this is to keep busy ... but [also] I think Tibetan medicine is good for this'. Several informants mentioned the *rlung* incense that was sold at both the MTK and CTMI clinics, and was—I was told by Amchi Lobsang Thubten—'very popular with Westerners'. Others discussed 'powdered nutmeg', which I was told could be either sprinkled into burning incense, or mixed with butter and applied to certain *rlung* points on the body. Indeed, Dorjee explains that *rlung* disturbances can be 'controlled by both medicine and meditation' (2005, 167). In addition, treatment for *rlung* disorders can include dietary guidelines such as a high protein intake (from sources such as meat, bone soup and dairy) as well as behavioural guidelines including 'a congenial, warm … environment … the company of congenial, amiable friends; and a comfortable room and bed in which to induce undisturbed sleep', in addition to a number of herbal medical compounds (Epstein and Topgay 1982, 76).

However, it was the psychological factors that Tibetan informants in Darjeeling discussed most frequently in relation to *rlung* disorders. Dorjee explains that 'it is the mind that is the key to healing our worries' (2005, 139), and in Darjeeling, several informants related stories of particular emotions such as sadness or loneliness having directly caused an episode of *sems nad*. Consequently, 'control of the mind' in terms of controlling one's emotions or thoughts was often discussed as an effective treatment. For example, when I asked Dolkar about *rlung*, she gave an example: 'If I am worrying about my son in Delhi [in the past he had been very ill with TB], if I am worrying about his health, and what will happen to him, I will get *rlung*…. If you can control [your worry, your mind], then it's ok'. Other informants demonstrated similar views. Nyima (35) explained that as *srog rlung* is caused by an inability to control one's anger, a calm mind will cure it. Several other interviewees also stated that a 'calm mind' will cure variant kinds of *sems nad*. Again, we find that 'controlling the mind' often seems to refer to controlling the thoughts and emotions, and this is emphasised by the suggestions that the way to help a depressed person is to 'distract' them away from their sadness or grief, or relate to them a story of someone in a far worse situation than them, which will make them feel better. As Dolkar (55) explained: 'the Tibetan doctor will tell you — if you have *rlung*, don't think too much'.

Gyaltsen summed up many interviewees' comments when he stated emphatically that such illnesses 'caused by the mind, can only be cured by the mind'. In fact, prior to meeting Lobsang, I asked Gyaltsen if he knew if Lobsang was taking any medication for his illness. He replied that there is no medicine for this, and it needed to be fixed 'from the mind's side only'. Lutz suggests that from a Western perspective, 'emotional' behaviour is 'not fully intentional' — thus, depression could be viewed as something that 'happens' to someone, leaving the afflicted individual absolved of any responsibility for it (1985, 79–80). However, Lutz's 'ordinary discourse' metaphors do in fact suggest some apportioning of responsibility: talk of 'getting a grip' on oneself or emotions 'getting the best of' someone (1985, 79) suggest that a certain amount of control might be possible here too. And, from the Tibetan perspectives depicted here, the condition of *rlung* only 'happens' to someone unable to 'control' their mind.

∗ ∗ ∗

In Chapter Three I discussed the role of *rlung* in Tibetan understandings of mental health, illness and consciousness. In this chapter, I have illustrated some of these perspectives through Lobsang's—and others'—narratives of *rlung* and the mental health conditions which can be a consequence of its disturbance. As we have seen, in addition to its role in mediating the Tibetan political discourse, *rlung* is also a fundamental Tibetan concept which can allow for explanations of health, illness and healing in a multitude of ways. In Darjeeling, lay Tibetans had much broader conceptions of *rlung* than was sometimes explained by amchi. In addition, as in other Tibetan communities, *rlung* had taken on a meaning similar to the English term 'stress', in a position to articulate some of the difficulties of 'modern' life. Here, *rlung* might be viewed as somewhat comparable to biomedical categories of depression and/or anxiety. Certainly, Lobsang's condition appeared to demonstrate similarities between the categories of 'depression' and '*rlung*', and he seemed to have no problem holding both of these diagnoses simultaneously, and consulting a number of different medical and healing specialists in his attempt to make sense of and treat his condition. Despite the brief reference of a possible spirit in his narrative of the visit to the monastery, in his case, Lobsang was clear that his illness had been caused by 'stress' and 'worry'. Perhaps for Lobsang, in this case *rlung* and depression were simply analogous—Tibetan and English terms for one condition, where his explanatory framework seemed quite singular in essence. In Lobsang's case then, his 'exploratory map' mainly took in notions of stress, pressure and depression which appeared to be equally well-explained by the two different systems. However, when we situate *rlung* in the broader context of Tibetan ideas about health and illness, a number of differences start to become apparent. Where *rlung* disturbance can become *smyo nad*, where *srog rlung* has been equated variously with biomedical categories of bipolar disorder, depression and schizophrenia, and where physical symptoms of *rlung* disturbance seem to hold equal weight with psychological ones, I would suggest that in *rlung* we are looking at quite a different category from depression or anxiety—although, as we saw, it may encompass some of these symptoms. Furthermore, the *rlung* currents in the body may be disturbed not only by other currents of *rlung* or other *nyes pa*, but also by *gdon*. This can produce very severe symptoms, and this topic will be examined further in Chapter Nine. Despite the central role that *rlung* appears to have in mental health and illness in some cases, such as Lobsang's, in other cases, it may not even be mentioned. In the next chapter, I will examine a more severe narrative of *sems nad*, where *rlung* was not discussed at all, and where the sufferer and his family were also viewed by many to be responsible for his condition.

CHAPTER SEVEN

JIGME: MADNESS AND ITS CAUSES

If you're sick, you can take medicine, but if you're smyo nad, *there's nothing to do. You can read* pecha[1] — *this is the best thing to do.* (Dekyi, 75)

Jigme's Story

When I asked a Tibetan friend, Nyima (35), some questions about *smyo nad* (madness), he suggested I meet Jigme, a neighbour of his and a former monk, whom he described as a *smyon pa* (madman). When we went to meet Jigme, he was alone in his very small room, half dressed, with an overgrown beard and dishevelled hair, lying on the wooden floor with pieces of a broken bed strewn about him and talking quietly to himself. My companion explained that Jigme did not wash, and rarely changed his clothes. Nyima spoke to Jigme a little— asking how he was, if he had eaten lunch, and introducing me. They chatted briefly and Jigme greeted me, mainly giving one-word answers to Nyima's questions. All the while he continued quietly chuckling to himself, and seemed unperturbed by our presence: calm and quite cheerful in his demeanour.

As we left, I felt quite shocked by the situation I had witnessed. Nyima explained that Jigme had been *smyo nad* for many years, and older members of the community later concurred, saying that he had been 'like this' for at least twenty to twenty-five years. They described how Jigme had often been

---

1. Whilst 'pecha' (Tib.: *dpe cha*) literally translates as 'book' or 'script', referring to the Tibetan religious texts, it is also used as a shorthand for the conducting of other Buddhist rituals.

aggressive or violent towards others, throwing stones at people, or shouting at or hitting them in the past. However, these days he was calm and did not disturb anyone, as long as no-one aggravated him. Nyima told me that people in the community took him three meals every day, and a *momo-la* later told me that she and a friend helped him to change his clothes every few months, enticing him to be calm with sweets.

Later, I met Lhamo (45), a biomedical nurse, who explained that although Jigme had not received any treatment for a long time, many years ago, she used to visit him with a local biomedical doctor to administer a monthly injection of biomedicine, as well as some biomedical pills. She said that these had helped to some extent—at that time Jigme had often been violent or aggressive, and the injection had tended to calm him down for a while, with the effect usually 'wearing off' near the end of the month when the next injection was due. Lhamo was not entirely sure when the treatment had ceased, but felt it was likely related to the fact that his father, on becoming ill, had been unable to help, and the administration of medication had required his practical help in physically restraining his son. However, it is important to point out that neighbours reported that even when he was receiving this treatment, Jigme had remained incapacitated to a significant degree. From speaking to people in the community, it seemed clear that the medications he had received had served only to keep him calm; he had not been able to work, marry or conduct any of the other activities of 'normal' Tibetan life. Others remembered vaguely that his family had initially conducted *pūjā* (religious rituals) for him and he had received blessings from a lama, but these activities had not helped significantly.

Within the community, the most common explanation for Jigme's illness was that it was some form of (this-life) 'karma' resulting from his father's poor behaviour. I was told by a number of informants that Jigme's father had taken some religious artefacts from a monastery many years ago, in order to save them during the destruction and looting of monasteries in Tibet during the Cultural Revolution. Having subsequently fled Tibet, his father should rightly have 'returned' the artefacts to a Tibetan Buddhist monastery in India. However, it was said that because these objects were worth a lot of money, Jigme's father had not wanted to let them go. Another neighbour, Sonam (21), a second-generation exile and student at a local college, explained, 'People say that his father had this gold thing, and monks told him he should give it to the *gonpa* (monastery), but he didn't want to as it was worth a lot.' This 'greed' or 'attachment' to the valuable objects was understood to have caused Jigme's illness. Jigme would subsequently continue to be *smyo nad* until his father returned the objects. Unfortunately, as a few people explained, this was unlikely to happen, as his father was now very elderly and suffering from ill-health, living at a home for the elderly at a monastery just outside the town. Therefore, I was told, there was likely to be no resolution to this situation. Lhamo suggested that—even after all these years—'if his father would repent and ask forgiveness, it would bring things back to normal'. But she explained that because his father is also 'half-mad' (described by two nurses who knew him as likely suffering from some form of dementia), he was not able to do this. She stated, 'It's true—if you take things like that from a *gonpa*, it can haunt you ... it's true'.

When I discussed this case with Amchi Lobsang at the local MTK clinic, he stated that this explanation was nonsense, telling me that the effects of karma cannot pass from one person to another like this. But many of the lay Tibetans I spoke to did view this as a possibility, even if they were unaware of this particular case. Nonetheless, not everyone I spoke to was convinced by such explanations involving theft of religious artefacts: as Gyaltsen, a 28-year old man from Lhasa who had fled Tibet as a teenager, wryly commented, 'Taking things from the monastery can't be the cause—the Chinese took many things [during the Cultural Revolution], and had no bad results!'. Phurpu (50) took an equally cynical view, explaining,

> There is a traditional belief among Tibetan people of this—that you can have problems if you take religious things from the monastery. But I think this was just said by the monks to make people afraid— to stop them taking things.

I discussed this case with Tsering (59), a senior member of the community and first-generation exile from Lhasa who had left Tibet as a child with his family. He had a different understanding of Jigme's illness: agreeing theoretically that such conditions *can* occur if someone steals from a monastery, in this case, he did not believe that this had been the cause. He felt instead that Jigme had conducted some Tantric Buddhist practice using a human bone incorrectly, and this had caused his illness. He explained that whilst human shin bones and the top part of a human skull are often used in Tantric Buddhist rituals, 'only some Tantric lamas' should use such objects, and explained that there was a particular way to 'purify' them, first burying them in the earth, and then boiling them for many hours. He said that Jigme had 'found' a human shin bone and, instead of conducting the correct purification ritual, he had simply put the bone into a fire in order to clean and purify it. Tsering explained that this incorrect practice had harmed nearby spirits, whose subsequent anger had caused his *smyo nad*. There is another suggestion here too—that Jigme had been attempting a Buddhist practice which was too advanced for him, which can be dangerous in itself. We will see a similar explanation in Chapter

Nine, through the narrative of a young lama who apparently died as a result of attempting to deal with spirits which—due to his insufficient experience— he was unable to handle, and this narrative of the 'danger' of advanced Tantric practices was not uncommon in Darjeeling. Finally, a few other informants who either knew—or knew of—Jigme held different views on the cause(s) of his condition, with a couple of people suggesting that there might be some kind of *gdon* or *'dre* possession involved, and one interviewee postulating that perhaps his state of mind had been negatively affected by too much monastic study—another fairly common explanation for mental illness which I encountered several times in Darjeeling.

Within the local community then, there were a number of diverse explanatory models of Jigme's illness, and informants who knew him sometimes discussed a number of these simultaneously, suggesting multiple contributory causes in a reflection of Williams and Healy's notion of exploratory maps. Others, however, saw a clear line between the cause (Jigme's father's behaviour) and the result (Jigme's *smyo nad*). That is not to say, however, that they had not also perhaps considered a number of explanatory frameworks during the initial phase of Jigme's illness, as they tried to ascertain what might be going on in the situation, but in this case, with so much time passed, it was just not clear. In terms of local perceptions of possible treatment(s) for Jigme, it was interesting to note that even where people felt that the illness was caused directly by his father taking something from a monastery, suggested treatments were often unrelated to this perceived cause. Sonam (21), for example—who thought that Jigme's illness was most likely caused by his father taking a 'gold thing' from a monastery—explained that he felt that the best way to treat this kind of *smyo nad* was to go to a 'psychiatrist'. Others suggested that it was now too late to help him, asserting that such illnesses need to be treated early on: Dekyi (75), for example, a first-generation exile *momo-la* at the TRSHC, explained, '*Thab shi mi 'dug—dus tshod ring po song*': 'There is no way [to treat him]—a long time has passed'. However, the majority of people who knew Jigme explained that in his case, if his father would only overcome his 'greed' and return the objects he stole, he would recover completely.

So what did all this mean for Jigme and his father? Different perceptions on the causes of mental illness can bring with them the stigmatisation of the afflicted individual, or, as we see in this case, their family. For many in the community, the blame for Jigme's illness rested squarely with his father, seen to have caused this situation for his son through his own greed. Consequently, the possibility of a 'cure' was also perceived to rest in his hands. In this way, in the majority of explanations proffered by those in the community, whilst Jigme's father was stigmatised, Jigme himself was viewed essentially as blameless. Neighbours thus felt sad and sorry for him—their compassion was evident in the way they not only discussed his case, but also through their continued provision of food and help for him—but essentially helpless, viewing themselves as unable to rectify his situation in any way. In this narrative, there was no way for anyone else to 'fix' the situation (in other words, cure Jigme)—his father had the power to resolve this situation, but has chosen not to—leaving Jigme's illness impossible to cure, and thus no efforts were now made to treat him. Nonetheless, despite this rather sad situation, Jigme—at that time at least—did not appear to be in any distress or pain, and was not bothering others, making this an improvement on his situation in the past.

This case illustrates some complex Tibetan perceptions on the causation and treatment of 'madness'. As I noted in the Introduction, ethnographic research on mental illness within Tibetan communities has to date mostly focused on *rlung* illnesses, leaving conceptions of *smyo nad* unrelated to *rlung* disturbances broadly unexamined. As such this case is rather interesting. There was no mention of *rlung* in discussions around causation here; instead, there was a focus on particular behaviours thought to have caused this illness. Furthermore, in Darjeeling, informants' descriptions of *smyo nad* and its symptoms (whether in terms of individuals they knew or knew of with this illness, or in more general terms) also generally focused on behavioural as opposed to cognitive aspects of symptomatology. Only one or two informants mentioned that an afflicted individual might 'see or hear things that are not there' (and 'hallucinations' were given as a symptom only by Lhamo, a nurse who had trained and worked in a biomedical clinic), whereas everyone was in agreement that *smyo nad* manifests in 'strange' or aggressive behaviour. Thus these narratives surrounding Jigme's illness can highlight for us some of the complexities of dealing with severe mental disturbance. Some of these—such as the community's feeling of helplessness, or the limited efficacy provided by the prescribed medication—may be familiar across cultures. Other aspects of this story—for example, notions of causation—only serve to illustrate some of the cross-cultural differences in understandings of conditions such as this. Furthermore, whilst similarities have been noted between *smyo nad* and Western understandings of 'psychosis', for example by Millard (2007) and the Tibetan amchi, Pasang Y. Arya, who divides 'insanity' into '[d]emonic possessions (possessions and schizophrenia)' and 'madness',[2] in fact the drawing of such equivalences is rather complex, not least because of the aforementioned overlap between the Tibetan diagnoses of *smyo nad* and *srog rlung*, only highlighting the diffi-

---

2. http://www.tibetanmedicine-edu.org/index.php/psychology-and-psychotherapy.

culties of attempting to analogise diagnostic categories from these two very different systems. Without being able to talk to Jigme more fully, it was difficult to get an understanding of his symptoms. However, as we saw, Millard has compared *smyo nad* with psychosis, and in Darjeeling, Lhamo, perhaps as a result of her biomedical knowledge, also used the term psychosis—alongside the Tibetan term *smyon pa*—to describe Jigme's condition. In the next chapter I will examine another case of 'madness', which highlights some of the difficulties of drawing comparisons between the Tibetan and biomedical categories, but first I will examine in more depth some of the different understandings of *smyo nad* that I encountered in Darjeeling, and what these mean in terms of health-seeking behaviour.

Madness and Its Causation in the Tibetan Context

'Madness', 'Insanity' and 'Psychosis': Examining the Tibetan Notion of sMyo Nad

In Chapters Three and Four I described some Tibetan perspectives on *smyo nad*, including those found in the Tibetan texts and discussed by amchi. Speaking to Tibetan amchi in both Darjeeling and Dharamsala, I received fairly homogenous answers to questions regarding English translations of *smyo nad*, all of them translating it as 'madness', 'insanity' or 'crazy' [sic]. In addition, some amchi discussed other Tibetan terms which they explained held similar meanings. These included *sems rnyog khra* ("sem nyokdra", complicated/troubled/confused mind), described by Amchi Lobsang Thubten in Darjeeling as indicating that an afflicted individual's personality as 'changeable—unstable' and prone to 'extreme moods', a term also observed by Millard in his work in Nepal (2007, 247–48); and *sems ma bde ba* ("sem ma déwa", uncomfortable mind). Epstein and Topgay describe several types of 'madness' listed in the *rGyud bZhi*: madness primarily attributed to a disturbance in one or more of the *nyes pa*; madness 'primarily categorized by depression (psychotic depression)'; madness primarily related to 'toxic causes', such as internal or external poisons; and madness caused by spirits (1982, 77).

At the Darjeeling MTK clinic, Amchi Lobsang Thubten explained that such states of mind can be the result of some kind of shock, family problems, spirit possession, or 'attachment' to something which fails to come to fruition. He described how *smyo nad* often manifests as strange behaviour, giving examples of someone 'eating from a dustbin', behaving in an 'opposite manner to normal', or 'having no inhibitions'. During his research in Darjeeling in the 1990s, Ja-cobson found that the term *smyo pa* was used as a 'generic term for conditions marked by obvious hallucinations, delusions, and disruptive speech and be-haviour' (2002, 261). However, in Tibet there is also a tradition of *bla ma smyon pa* (saintly madmen): 'visionary' or high-level tantric practitioners who may appear *smyo nad* or be described as *smyo(n) pa*, but are not 'mad' in this sense, instead understood to be operating at a level incomprehensible to less spiritually-advanced individuals.[3] In addition, in Darjeeling, the term *smyo nad* was also often used in lay parlance in a similar manner to the English words 'crazy' or 'mad'—to denote someone doing something odd or inexplicable (but not necessarily pathological). During fieldwork I too found lay under-standings of *smyo nad* to be mostly quite consistent amongst Tibetan inform-ants, with the majority of those with some knowledge of English translating it as 'crazy', 'mad', 'insanity', or occasionally 'psycho'. In addition, the majority of interviewees listed similar symptoms: aggressive or violent behaviour towards others; strange behaviour not consistent with the individuals' usual behaviour; a lack of inhibitions (often manifesting in 'running around naked' in public); laughing for no reason, or talking to oneself. Some of these were summed up by Phurpu's (50) description of his twenty-year old neighbour, who had ap-parently suddenly 'become *smyo nad*' a few years ago: '*Gang byung mang byung byed pa red*—She would do just anything!'.

In fact, many interviewees related stories of individuals with *smyo nad* that they either knew directly (family members or neighbours) or were aware of within their community, and all reported some or all of the symptoms listed above. Where they differed, however, was in their perceptions of the causes of *smyo nad*. Some of these notions reflected concepts covered in the *rGyud bZhi*, such as *rlung* disturbance or *gdon* possession, whilst others included much broader notions of mental health and illness than delineated in the texts, and which often reflected wider Tibetan notions of the person and the world. For example, as we saw in the previous chapter, many informants explained that various thoughts and emotions such as sadness or anger could directly cause psychiatric problems, describing an explicit causal relationship between the two, and in discussing *smyo nad*, lay Tibetans often explained the condition via concrete links to activities and emotions in direct 'cause and effect' terms, such as we saw in discussions of Jigme's condition. In addition, perceptions of 'correct' and 'incorrect' behaviour wove in and out of the interviews—mainly

---

3. See for example Stefan Larsson's work on Tsangnyön Heruka, where he describes this fifteenth century figure's transformation into a 'mad yogin', and his activities following this transformation (2012), and DiValerio's 2015 work on the topic.

in terms of religious practice, but also in terms of social behaviours. From stealing religious artefacts to 'spending too much time alone', 'studying too much' (either monastic or scholastic study) or talking to oneself, the individuals I interviewed had clear ideas of what might lead someone to become *smyo nad*. In the following sections I shall examine these concepts in more detail, and then consider how these perceptions of causation are reflected in health-seeking behaviour and attempted preventions against *smyo nad*.

Lay Perspectives: Religious Causes of Madness

Earlier I discussed some aspects of the relationship between religion and mental health in the Tibetan context, and a number of these concepts were evident in Tibetan informants' perspectives on 'madness' in Darjeeling. Certainly, diverse strands of the relationship between religion and mental illness were clearly demonstrated by both the common local explanation regarding the actions of Jigme's father and Tsering's description of offence caused to local spirits through Tantric practice. Other causes of *smyo nad* which referenced religious notions encompassed cognitive and behavioural elements, such as a monk's inability to follow monastic rules, or the frequently mentioned example of foreigners (particularly non-Buddhists) 'jumping too quickly' into the study of Buddhist philosophy with too little preparation.

In the explanation regarding Jigme's father's actions, we see the referencing of 'karma' (Tib.: *las*), in this case, as a result of actions not only carried out in *this*—rather than a previous—life, but also carried out by a person other than the one most affected by its results. In fact in Darjeeling, karma was often mentioned as an underlying factor in everything from various types of misfortune to illness, with Dawa, a monk, responding to my questions about *smyo nad*: 'Maybe he or she has to be mad throughout their life—it's not based on the mind itself—it depends on karma.... Maybe he will have to be mad in every life!' Karma, then, can be an underlying cause (Tib.: *rgyu*) of illness, as opposed to a more immediate 'condition' (Tib.: *rkyen*), such as spiritual or seasonal influences, 'luck' (Tib.: *rlung rta*) or some of the causes discussed in relation to Jigme's illness, such as incorrect religious practices and spirit possession. In explanations of cases such as Jigme's, some perceptions of the cause of *smyo nad* involved significant 'wrongdoing' on the part of the individual who subsequently became afflicted: not only such misdemeanours as offending local spirits through 'incorrect' Tantric practice, but also factors such as a monk finding himself unable to follow monastic rules, or an individual starting meditation before they are ready or without proper instruction. A number of informants discussed this last point in relation to Westerners' Buddhist practice—

thought to be particularly risky when undertaken with insufficient preparation or guidance. Gyaltsen explained, 'They [foreigners new to Buddhism] jump suddenly into [the philosophical notion of] emptiness', but with little background knowledge or preparation, 'they go crazy'. Norbu (35) agreed, 'If Westerners grow up Christian, and try to become Buddhist … thinking deeply about hell [from] reading Buddhist texts—they go in deep and become *smyon pa*'. He laughed, 'They are more deep than us! [As a result] they will be crazy forever I think'.

In Dharamsala, Amchi Sonam Dolma agreed, noting that the manipulation of *rlung* through Tantric practice could especially cause problems for Westerners:

> Many people in the West, they do Dzogchen[4] practice without initiation.… I know somebody in Germany who has this problem—[a] breakdown, because everybody wants to have instant Nirvana, and then they over-exert themself, and then, they are not able to … adjust their inner channel.… [The condition known as] *srog rlung* is nothing but disturbance of the inner channel. This is possible—very possible.

This reference to the *srog rlung* channel is a reflection of such concepts in the *rGyud bZhi*, and evidences the above-mentioned overlap between notions of *srog rlung* and *smyo nad*. Rapgay explains a particular form of *srog rlung* disorder caused by improper meditation practice:

> A specific kind of sok-rlung disorder is said to be associated with meditation: it is a complication of improper meditation practice and is widely referred to simply as "*sok-rlung*." It is more likely to arise in meditators who are improperly instructed in methods designed to concentrate the mind. If the meditation object is not suitable for the individual, if the developed concentration is tarnished by negative states of mind or not balanced with sufficient mindfulness, or especially if the mind is not concentrated with proper effortlessness, *sok-rlung* may develop (Rapgay 1985, 44).

He goes on to explain that this leads to the mind becoming restless, emotional, anxious, and 'insensitive to the guidance of teachers' (1985, 45). This phenomenon is also mentioned by Epstein and Lieff, who note that it is 'specifically defined as an obsessive-compulsive-like complication of meditation' in Tibetan medical theory (1981, 143). Moreover, it is not only ostensibly Buddhist prac-

---

4. Dzogchen (Tib.: *rDzogs chen*)—'Great Perfection'—refers to the highest level Tantric teachings of the Nyingma and Bon traditions.

tices which can cause *rlung*-related illnesses which may result in *smyo nad* amongst other, less severe symptoms: Amchi Teinley explained that incorrect meditation practice, or other practices such as yoga or t'ai chi which manipulate the 'winds' inside the body can cause *rlung* imbalance, sometimes leading to *smyo nad*.

If some explanations regarding the causes of mental illness were clearly related to Buddhist notions of karma and/or Tantric concepts of *rlung*, or derived from Buddhist perceptions of 'correct' or 'incorrect' practice and behaviour, others were more clearly aligned with what might be termed 'folk-religious' practices and concepts, such as explanations of *gdon*-caused *smyo nad*. In addition, other explanations of *smyo nad* spanned diverse religious concepts (as Tibetans' reasoning about many events often does). However, as we have seen, there is significant overlap here, where spirits and deities have been incorporated into Buddhism through their subjugation by Padmasambhava in the eighth century. This is evident, for example, in Tsering's explanation of Jigme's offence of local spirits through 'incorrect' Tantric practice. Moreover, in Darjeeling, other explanatory notions of *smyo nad* were less focused on religious concepts, and more related to cognitive and/or behavioural factors, and it is to these perceptions which I turn next.

Lay Perspectives: Non-Religious Causes of Madness

As I discussed in the previous chapter, a number of Tibetan informants in Darjeeling explained that various emotions such as sadness or anger could directly cause mental disturbances—including *smyo nad*—sometimes mediated by *rlung*. For example, Metok explained: 'If [there is] no cure for *rlung*, then [the afflicted individual] can go into depression.... If you don't look after yourself and control your mind then *rlung na tsha* [*rlung* sickness] can lead to *smyo nad*'. A number of other informants echoed this view, explaining that *sems nad*, or some kind of depression may come first which, if not successfully treated, can lead to *smyo nad*. As Samten (42) described, 'First you are *sems nad*, then you become *smyo nad*'. Similarly, when I asked Tenzin (28) what causes *smyo nad*, he responded that it comes 'mainly from depression'.

Other causes of *smyo nad* discussed in Darjeeling referenced more 'social' concepts of 'correct' and 'incorrect' behaviour, such as spending too much time alone or talking to oneself. Dorje (49), for example, described how his brother-in-law had become 'mad' with a 'mental illness' around one year previously, suddenly becoming aggressive, violent and verbally and physically abusive towards others for no reason. Dorje explained that his illness was caused by 'thinking too much, sitting quietly alone watching TV'. Similarly, Sonam (21) explained, 'Thinking too much … intrapersonal communication [talking to yourself]—this is the main cause. That's why I don't like to sit alone at home'. Finally, 'too much study' was frequently mentioned as a cause of *smyo nad*—either monastic or scholastic study—often discussed in relation to 'competition' and 'stress', as we saw in the previous chapter. Working in Dharamsala, Prost found that '*rlung* illnesses are common in religious studies, where intellectual overexertion is common' (2006, 125). Similarly in Darjeeling, Norbu (35) described witnessing this in a man in the Tibetan community in which he had lived in Nepal in the previous few years. In addition, he noted that, 'these things happened in our school'—especially, he explained, to people studying complex subjects such as science and physics.

Other causal explanations of *smyo nad* seemed to straddle both religious and cultural concepts, sometimes related to emotions and/or thoughts. Many interviewees explained that *sems nad* and *smyo nad* were caused by an individual's inability to control their mind, concentrating all the time on things that they cannot have (for example, more money, a bigger house or an expensive car), or an inability to deal effectively with emotions about life events. Phurpu (50), for example, told me about a woman in town, who had suffered from *smyo nad* which 'comes and goes' for approximately ten years, with episodes lasting two to three weeks at a time. He explained that this had been caused by her frustration and sadness over her husband's affair with another woman; and Dolma (31) explained that *smyo nad* can result from worry over family or business problems. In a similar manner, several informants argued that a person's inability to deal with their anger—holding it in and not expressing it—could lead to *srog rlung*, and Samten (42) explained, 'If you are very much unsatisfied by everything…. If your mind is thinking too much … being angry, or asking again and again why you're sick, you'll become *smyo nad*'. Gyaltsen stated that *smyo nad* is caused by 'not keeping your mind clear, thinking about things like wanting to be a millionaire, always thinking about this. This kind of desire can cause hallucinations'. Again, we return to the notion that not 'controlling the mind' can lead to mental illness of various kinds.

Treating and Preventing Madness in Darjeeling

Some of these comments on the treatment of *smyo nad* also suggest the possibility of *prevention*—not only in terms of avoiding religious or social 'wrongdoing', but also in relation to the ability to 'control the mind', as we saw in the previous chapter. For example, when I discussed *sems nad* and *smyo nad* with Metok (63), a former biomedical nurse, she explained, 'It also depends on how

strong you are from the heart. Some people are not affected by bad things....
These people are very lucky—they can really take things so easily'.

In Darjeeling, Tibetan informants' health-seeking behaviour and notions
of treatment for *smyo nad* often reflected these multiple explanations of its
causation. Thus, as I noted previously, whilst Sowa Rigpa describes a number
of herbal medicines for use in the treatment of *smyo nad* (particularly those
for reducing *rlung* or the other humours involved), few of the Tibetans I spoke
to discussed this as an option, instead favouring religious practices. For
example, echoing the comments of many informants, Norbu told me that the
best way to treat *smyo nad* was through 'religious blessings from a high lama....
[and] do *pūjā*'. In Jigme's case, Lhamo stated—as did several others—that if
his father was able to 'repent' and ask forgiveness for his 'bad' behaviour
(through stealing the religious artefacts), 'it would bring things back to normal'.
Indeed, in cases where there was felt to be a certain amount of responsibility
for the illness by either the individual himself, or someone in his family, the
'cure' was often also felt to be in his hands, or in those of his family members.
'Treatment' thus often involved the rectification of the causal circumstances,
for example through the appeasement or subjugation of the spirits which had
been involved.

In addition, a number of religious activities were often said to be helpful in
treating many kinds of illness, including mental illness. For example, Nyima
explained that the recitation of a particular prayer could cure any kind of madness, asserting that even reading it only once would help to some extent. Other
Buddhist practices were discussed too, and often particular prayers or ritual
activities were thought to be effective in treating *smyo nad*. For example, Penpa
(44), a first-generation exile who had arrived in India aged nineteen,
mentioned *gcod* practice, a particular form of Tantric meditative practice involving the practitioner visualising the cutting up of his own body and the in-
vitation to spirits to feast on his corpse, often conducted in graveyards or
charnel grounds. This could be conducted, he said, by the afflicted individual
himself, or on his behalf by someone else. He explained that this practice was
'very effective'—able to cure any kind of madness, no matter the cause, adding,
'I have seen this [be successful]—especially for mental illness and demons'.
Jacobson found this ritual mentioned in Darjeeling too, described by one informant as effective in providing temporary relief for symptoms of her *rlung*
condition (2000, 508).

I discussed such treatments with Phurpu, who related the story of a Tibetan
neighbour of his who, a few years ago, at the age of around thirty-five, 'all of
a sudden' went 'crazy'. He explained that 'there was no clear reason' for this
smyo nad, as his family, business and financial situation were good. At that

time, he had become very violent, throwing stones at people, shouting very rude things at them, and Phurpu described how his two brothers had walked alongside him holding sticks—'this is how serious it was'—in an effort to control him. After one week his brothers took him to a local diviner, who instructed them to read some particular prayers and, he said, 'in one week he was cured'. Here, Phurpu emphasised the importance of 'belief' in the treatment, explaining, 'If you strongly believe, it will cure'. In addition, blessings from high lamas and the making of offerings at monasteries were often felt to be generally helpful in cases of mental illness.

Finally, whilst a handful of informants discussed the possibility of consulting a biomedical psychiatrist, others felt that such practitioners were unable to help in cases of *smyo nad*. For example, Norbu was clear that 'there's no Western medicine for this', discussing instead the use of Tibetan medicine and *rin chen ril bu* (empowered substances) and the importance of compassionate care for patients. He related the story of a Tibetan neighbour in Nepal who had become *smyo nad* 'six or seven years ago', describing how, aged around forty-two, the woman had left her home and children and 'wandered everywhere', for two or three days at a time. This had recurred for around two years, and on one occasion she was found by her neighbours sleeping outside, inside dense thorn bushes, inexplicably, he said, without a scratch on her. Today she is 'completely ok' and running a restaurant, and Norbu explained that her recovery was due not only to the *pūjā* she conducted, but also to the community's support. He stressed the importance of the fact that, 'we didn't consider her crazy', instead they looked after her, making sure that she always had food and water. Norbu concluded that when dealing with someone with *smyo nad*, 'Most important is love and care ... family and community support'.

* * *

The narrative of Jigme's illness raises a number of interesting issues regarding Tibetan perspectives on the causation and treatment of *smyo nad*. Despite the lack of any formal treatment at that time, Jigme was provided with food daily, helped to change his clothes occasionally and generally not treated poorly by others. At that time, this lack of treatment seemed to 'suit' him—when I met him, whilst not in a good state of health or hygiene, he appeared not to be in any distress, and neighbours told me that he was much calmer than in the past. However, as we saw, Jigme's father had been stigmatised and held responsible for his son's illness—characterised as 'greedy' for his apparent prioritisation of wealth over his son's health, leaving Jigme untreated and in a poor mental state long term. There may have been little intervention for Jigme but, whether his mental health would be improved with any kind of treatment is impossible to say. In the absence of any treatment, Jigme also seemed to be in a better condition than he had apparently been in the past. Bearing in mind the fact that his past treatments appeared to have provided only limited help, perhaps this is the best outcome one might hope for in this situation.

Jigme's case was fairly representative of the broader lay Tibetan perspectives that I encountered in Darjeeling on the causation and treatment of *smyo nad*, where the focus was often on religious causes and treatment, and both biomedical intervention and Sowa Rigpa were understood to be able to offer little in the way of treatment. I was not able to ascertain, of course, how Jigme viewed his own condition, but for those around him, there were often a number of causal and contributory factors which were discussed. These narratives around his illness highlight some of the similarities and differences between Tibetan and biomedical perspectives on *smyo nad*, 'madness' and 'psychosis'. Here, listed symptoms appear to overlap significantly in both systems, but causative explanations and treatments are often significantly different, with a focus on religious concepts as well as a number of more 'social' norms in the Tibetan context. In the next chapter I will examine a contrasting case of short-term 'madness', understood to have been caused by sadness and worry. Whilst biomedical intervention was similarly of limited effectiveness, in that case, as we shall see, treatment through religious means was highly successful.

CHAPTER EIGHT

WANGMO:
'BELIEF', 'FAITH' AND HEALING

Yid ches la nus pa yod red—in my *opinion, there is power in belief.*
(Phurpu, 50)

Wangmo's Story

In September 2011 I was introduced to Pema (50), a second-generation Tibetan exile who had grown up in Darjeeling, and had a background in biomedical nursing. Pema spoke fluent English, and was keen to discuss her work and other issues related to health and illness, including a story about her own mother's episode of 'madness', as she described it, which had been cured through the blessings of a rinpoche (Tib.: *rin po che*).[1]

Pema had been born in Darjeeling, not long after her parents had left Tibet in 1959. After attending a convent school in the area, she had trained and worked with a local biomedical doctor for a number of years. Pema discussed her experiences of treating local Tibetan, Nepali and Indian patients, and when I explained my interest in 'mental illness', *smyo nad* and *sems nad*, she was keen to narrate the story of her mother Wangmo's brief period of illness many years previously. Pema described how, not long after she (an only child) had moved away to Sikkim with her new husband around thirty years ago, her mother, at that time aged around fifty-two, 'went a little crazy', as she explained in English. She returned from Sikkim at her father's request to find her mother acting very

---

1. Literally translated as 'precious one', this is usually used—as in this case—to refer to an incarnate lama.

strangely: talking nonsense; experiencing hallucinations; and unable to recognise either her or her father. Naming it in turn as 'madness', 'craziness', *sems nad* and *smyo nad*, Pema explained that she thought that perhaps her mother had been 'lonely' and 'worried' following her move away from home, and described how she and her father had initially taken Wangmo to a local biomedical doctor, whom they knew well:

> I was the only daughter. I got married—in Sikkim—and maybe … we have been together for a long time, you know … the break must have deeply hurt her … Maybe because of that … she worried a lot— what was happening to her daughter … maybe the worry might have caused her bad thing [condition], you know.
>
> All of a sudden … she had this some sort of insomnia … she couldn't sleep, and she went to the hospital, but even the sedatives [were] not working. At night she used to say that she tried to close her eyes, you know? If I can remember, the doctor gave her 25mg Diazepam five times a day—you know, Valium tablets—but still the medicine was not working … She tried to close her eyes but she said, 'I can't sleep—I can see things … people talking around [me], shouting in my ears' and all these kinds of things … She wouldn't sleep, [and] because of that she started getting very weak too. She was saying she didn't want to eat also … She was very weak at that time, yes … [and] just talking to herself. And when we tried to, you know, like talk to her, she doesn't recognise you…. So she was talking nonsense and all.

Pema described how, after approximately twenty days of being 'crazy … *sems nad*', in the midst of her confusion, Wangmo asked for one of her prayer books (Tib: *dpe cha*). On being handed this, she had flicked through it, coming across a picture of the second reincarnation of Domo Geshe Rinpoche (Jigme Chökyi Wangchuk) slotted inside, and proclaimed that she must visit him. Pema explained to me that this well-known rinpoche was often in USA, but at that time he happened to be at his monastery—Gaden Tharpa Choling Gonpa—in Kalimpong, approximately two and a half hours' drive away:

> So she used to believe [in] him … so she said 'I want to meet him'. At that time we were lucky because he was in Kalimpong, and my auntie had a car, so we took her to Kalimpong. But before entering the lama's room we had to prepare everything, you know, [explain] what caused the insomnia; and auntie and me were discussing how to open the topic of her sickness and all. But then she went inside, she bowed three times,

and she started relating her thing—her problems—to that lama directly, you know? Even we were surprised because suddenly she seemed completely normal! Before she was talking nonsense … like sometimes slightly mentally retarded, you know … and then the lama gave her some kind of a blessing—using all the five fingers, like this [she indicated her hand with the fingers and thumb spread out wide, being placed on the top of the head] … we call it *bka' sgo* ["kargo", command, instruction] … this … all the evils … he imprisons all the things like evil deeds … that sort of method … She was there maybe for nearly an hour—yes, maybe one hour—and after she came back she seemed really quite normal, like before, you know—we were all surprised! All surprised. He sprinkled her with *chu gsos* [blessed water] … and blessed her every morning for three or four days.… Then from that time until up to now she's quite normal.

Pema described how following the blessing, her mother had slept well for the first time in three weeks, and then quite quickly recovered. There had been no previous episodes like this, and had been none since. Pema concluded: 'My mother's faith in the lama saved her'. In addition, Pema emphasised the importance of her mother's 'connection' (Tib.: *'brel ba*[2]) to this particular rinpoche, explaining that her parents had known well his previous incarnation, who had been from the same area in Tibet as them.[3] She described a meeting many years later with the most recent reincarnation, Jigme Ngak-gi Wangchuk (born in 2003):

He [the initial Domo Geshe Rinpoche, Ngawang Kalsang] used to be a lama for our forefathers—we used to worship this lama.… The last time Domo Geshe Rinpoche [the third reincarnation, Jigme Ngak-gi Wangchuk] came to Kalimpong, we had a special audience, because my parents used to know him—from the previous birth [the second Domo Geshe Rinpoche, Jigme Chökyi Wangchuk]. As soon as he saw my mother—my mother wanted to see his reincarnation before she died—as soon as she saw him she said, 'This is our rinpoche', because the features—they were quite similar, and Rinpoche also held her hand, and wouldn't let her go. When we were leaving he gave a *khatak* [Tib.: *kha btags*: ceremonial scarf] to my mumma—it was *amazing*—amazing.

---

2. This Tibetan term is translated into English as both 'connection' and 'relation(ship)'.

3. The life story of the previous incarnation of the rinpoche, Ngawang Kelsang, has been related by Anagarika Govinda—who was a student of his—in his autobiography (1974, 7–11, 116–22).

Several features of this illness narrative are quite striking, such as Pema's description of 'sadness' and 'worry' as the main causative factors in Wangmo's condition, and the role of Buddhism in rapidly curing Wangmo of what perhaps sounds—from a biomedical perspective—like a severe psychotic episode, from the moment that she requested a prayer book to receiving the blessings and purified water from the rinpoche and returning to 'normal'. We saw that Pema and her family had initially tried an alternative method of treatment for her mother—consulting a biomedical psychiatrist and taking the prescribed medicine—to no avail. Interestingly, Pema told me that whilst her and her family had utilised Tibetan medicine and consulted local *jhānkri* on other occasions for other illnesses, they had not done so in this case. Here, the role of Buddhism and her family's 'connection' to the rinpoche were instead paramount. In addition, as we shall see below, concepts of 'belief' (Tib.: *yid ches*, "yiché") and 'faith' (Tib.: *dad pa*: "dé pa") also played an important role in the success of her treatment by the rinpoche. Furthermore, whilst I have discussed the role which emotions and thoughts can play in the causation of *sems nad* and *smyo nad*, and the role that *rlung* often plays in such explanations, in this narrative, Pema never mentioned *rlung*, focusing instead on the rinpoche's power to heal her mother, in comparison to the failure of the biomedical intervention. Another aspect of this case which struck me was the fact that, despite her biomedical training and work, Pema never used any biomedical categories to describe her mother's condition (some of which she mentioned in discussions we had about other cases). In fact, the possible causes and categorisations of her mother's illness were rather secondary to her narrative. When I initially met Pema and explained my interest in *sems nad*, *smyo nad* and 'mental illness'—she introduced the topic of her mother's illness by saying, 'Sometimes this can be cured by lamas—have you heard about this?' In addition, we can also observe that the perceived causation ('sadness' and 'worry') was unrelated to the treatments sought: sleeping pills (which addressed one of the symptoms, but in this case were not found to help) and the rinpoche's blessings. In the discussion around her and her family's health-seeking behaviour, the focus was instead on her mother's 'belief' and 'faith' in the religious practitioner, and the importance of this in the efficacy of the treatment. In the next sections I will examine these Tibetan notions of *'brel ba*, *yid ches* and *dad pa*; and how they may interact with a number of other Tibetan concepts often mentioned by informants, such as karma, *rlung rta* and *dbang thang*, in discussions surrounding mental health, illness and healing.

The Power of 'Belief':
Connections, Faith and Healing

I noted above how, during Pema's narrative of her mother's illness, she emphasised the importance of her mother's 'faith' (Tib.: *dad pa*) in the rinpoche, and her family's 'connection' (Tib.: *'brel ba*) to him. These two concepts were discussed by a number of informants in Darjeeling, with several interviewees describing the importance of a 'connection' to the consulting medical or religious practitioner and its effect on treatment efficacy. As Dawa (51), suggested, 'Maybe if you have some connection with the doctor, medicine works well'. These concepts were also discussed in explanations around the causation of illness, as well as other types of misfortune. Here, individuals often discussed 'belief' (Tib.: *yid ches*) or 'faith' in a particular deity, and how this might facilitate that deity's 'power' to affect you.

Pema described the 'blessings' (Tib.: *byin rlabs*, "chinlab") that her mother received from Domo Geshe Rinpoche in Kalimpong over several days, similar to the 'blessing' described here by the Tibetan amchi, Lobsang Dolma Khangkar, which she calls an 'empowerment of the hand':

> It is not an actual, complete empowerment, but when the hand of the lama touches the head of the patient, of any person, since the lama is always in meditation and has a realization of his true being, then just by physical contact a great number of diseases and harmful influences are cleared (Khangkar 2009, 61).

Clearly, this is quite different from the Western (or Christian) use of the English term 'blessing'. Gerke notes that the notion of *byin rlabs* is understood as 'the blessing-power inherent in sacred sites, objects, landscapes, and deities, which can be exploited through a ritual engagement by a lama'. This power can be 'absorbed into the body through a substance, through touch, or across distance psychically' (2012a, 232). This notion of the conferring of blessing or healing 'power' from religious specialist to lay individual reflects Tibetan notions of the stratified relationships between different entities—from spirits and humans through to Tantric deities— that we saw in Chapter Four. Here, this holding of differential levels of 'spiritual power' (Tib.: *dbang thang*) creates a hierarchical relationship, ultimately based upon the supremacy of Buddhist 'power' over non-Buddhist forces, where religious specialists' practice (particularly the higher levels of Tantric practice which relate to enlightened Tantric deities) gives them access to 'spiritual power' superior to that held by lay Buddhists and local worldly (in other words, unenlightened) deities.

Of course, as Kleinman has noted, power differentials are inherent in all practitioner-lay relationships—whether the practitioner is religious, medical or both—and interpretations of illness experience are communicated and negotiated within them (1991, 7). Such relationships are perhaps particularly interesting in the Tibetan context, with its interrelationships between medicine and religion and the fact that religious leaders have also historically held political power in Tibetan society which, I would suggest, continues to contribute to their high status for Tibetans, and the esteem in which they are held in the Tibetan context. Hepburn has noted that in non-Western societies, traditional healers are often viewed as 'active and trusted members of a lineage or community, sometimes with religious authority' (1988, 65). As we saw, this was particularly evident here, where Pema stressed the family's connection to the rinpoche's previous incarnation, who hailed from the same area of Tibet as Wangmo and her husband. In a place as vast and under-populated as Tibet, where regional dialects can be mutually unintelligible, such relationships are perhaps particularly significant. Similarly, relationships can be cultivated between the members of a community and their local area gods (Tib.: *yul lha*), who may be able to afford some protection against low-level malevolent spirits such as *gdon* or *'dre*, who possess much weaker *dbang thang*. Dawa, a local monk from the Nyingma tradition, described this 'connection' in terms of the Buddhist notion of karma, suggesting that 'there can be some karmic connection between you and that spiritual being'. This notion of a 'connection' or 'relationship' between individuals was often coupled with the twin notions of *yid ches* and *dad pa*. Thus, as she narrated the story of her mother's illness and healing to me, Pema described not only the importance of her mother's *relationship* to the rinpoche, but also her 'faith' in his ability to treat her:

> The important thing was [that] my mother believed that she had been cured by him … her faith in him was amazing, you know? Amazing.…
> The most important [thing] is … you should have faith that he can cure you.… My mother had *strong* faith … there was some strong relationship between the lama and my mumma.

These notions of 'belief' and 'faith' in relation to the treatment of illness were discussed by many in Darjeeling. For example, Tenzin (28) emphasised: 'In Tibetan culture we believe that faith is very important—if you believe that the lama's blessing will cure you, then it will'. Similarly, when I discussed Tibetan Buddhist treatments for illness described by others, such as reading particular *dpe cha*,[4] with Phurpu (50), he explained: 'The main thing is be-lief—*yid ches*—if you strongly believe, it will cure'. Similarly, a *lack* of *yid ches* or *dad pa* can be thought to affect treatment efficacy. Indeed, in Amdo, Schrempf quoted a *sngags pa* bemoaning the lack of 'faith in religion' that pa-tients demonstrate these days, leading to a decline in the efficacy of what he referred to as Tibet's 'spiritual medicine' (2011, 169).

These notions of *yid ches*, *dad pa* and '*brel ba*, and their significance in mental health and illness, also came up in relation to the *causes* of illness in Darjeeling, where a 'connection' to, or 'relationship' with a deity or spirit was often described as facilitating its ability to cause harm. This was particularly the case in conditions thought to have been caused by the action of local deities such as *btsan* and *rgyal po*, two classes of worldly deities characterised by arrogance and pride. I will discuss the role of spirits in mental illness in more detail in the fol-lowing chapter, but here I will delineate the particular role that *yid ches* and *dad pa* can play in deities' capacity to cause harm. For example, when I discussed entities such as these with Phurpu, he explained, 'If you have no connection to local gods, then they won't harm you. But if you have a connection, they may'. He continued to note the importance of 'belief' here, explaining that if people believe that some harm will come to them, it will; but if they believe that every-thing will be ok, it will be. He concluded in a mix of Tibetan and English: '*Yid ches la nus pa yod red*—in *my* opinion, there is power in belief'. Here then, the power of spirits or practitioners to affect you can be facilitated by your *yid ches*—'belief'—in them, and/or by your '*brel ba*—'connection'—to them. Thus, through the same network of relationships between people and the panoply of spirits and deities that reside in the environment which enable deities and prac-titioners to help individuals, it is also possible to be harmed by them.

How then should we understand this Tibetan concept of *yid ches*? Why should one's 'belief' in something affect its efficacy? Perhaps a problem lies in our translation: Good has explored some of the problems of the English term 'belief' and its translation from other languages. To illustrate, he describes Steedly's research in Sumatra, where she was asked by her informants, 'Do you believe in spirits?'. Only later did she realise that what she was actually being asked was, 'Do you *trust* spirits? Do you believe what they say? Do you maintain a relationship with them?' (Good 1994, 15). This is very different from the contemporary English meaning of 'belief' as an acceptance of some-thing's very existence. In fact, in the English language too there have also been

---

4. As I noted in the previous chapter, whilst literally translated this means 'book' or 'scripture', it is often used to refer to any ritual Buddhist activity. Here, it was used to refer to a particular prayer.

significant changes in the meaning of the word 'belief' over time. Good points to Cantwell Smith's assertion that the notion of 'belief' in God historically held the meaning of 'a loyal pledging of oneself to God' (Good 1994, 15).[5] 'Belief' here then, is an *action*, rather than a state of mind, as we might understand it now (Smith 1977, 42), the former perhaps more similar to the Tibetan notion of *yid ches*. Following her research in Tibet's capital, Lhasa, Adams explained *yid ches* thus:

> To make the mind go in a certain direction is not only to have faith but also to create its existence in the mind and in the world. The generative effect is to make something greater than the mind, to produce effects that are tangible beyond the mind.... The believer participates in the world that is created in the wake of his/her actions.... Belief was a principle of knowing, not a way of arbitrating between knowledge and what we might call a "figment" of the mind. The believing mind understands that it has an effect in, a role in, producing reality (2005, 98).

So what does all this mean in terms of the treatment of illness? In Lhasa, Adams found that in consulting lamas, Tibetans she spoke to used the term *dad pa* in a similar manner to the term *yid ches*, as a connotation of 'faith' or 'devotion', rather than an 'index of credibility': 'One believes in the power of lamas to change the universe in the same way that one expresses one's devotion to them' (Adams 2005, 97). Here, 'belief' and 'devotion' are not analogous, 'rather, they are alike because they are both affective forces that produce tangible outcomes' (Adams 2005, 97–98). Here then, 'belief' or 'faith' in the practitioner and his healing can enable the individual to travel from illness back to health. Furthermore, in terms of illness caused by spirits or deities, the afflicted individual (or their family) can either attempt to improve the relationship or connection with the deity—by making offerings or repenting for any offence caused to it—or they can break their 'connection' with the deity, thus bringing an end to the deity's power to harm them. If the individual is afraid to do this, he can call on Buddhist monks for help, whose superior spiritual power (Tib.: *dbang thang*) is of course stronger than that held by the lowly unenlightened local spirits and deities. Such practitioners are thus able to subjugate the deities in question through Buddhist ritual, essentially pushing them back into the background environment, unable to cause harm.

---

5. See also Southwold's discussion on the variant meanings of both 'belief' and 'truth', and his note that 'to believe' can mean either 'to hold as factually true' or 'to hold as symbolically true', where he suggests that it is 'quite impractical' to try to restrict the sense of this term to the former (1979).

Karma, *rLung rTa* and *dBang Thang*: 'Causes' and 'Conditions' of Illness and Healing

In fact, there are multiple interrelated factors which may be involved in the causation and treatment of mental illness in the Tibetan tradition, some of which have already been mentioned here. I have described already the notion of *dbang thang* (perhaps best-described as 'spiritual power') and the notion that Buddhist specialists such as lamas and rinpoches—due to their practices related to enlightened Tantric deities—have access to superior *dbang thang* than 'ordinary' lay individuals and unenlightened deities. This concept of *dbang thang* is often interwoven with the related notions of 'luck' (Tib.: *rlung rta*), 'merit' (Tib.: *bsod nams*) and karma in explanations of mental illness. These overlapping concepts can be hard to disentangle—particularly as the this-world results of these different factors often look the same (Lichter and Epstein 1983, 241)—and they can all be involved in the causation of illness (or misfortune), working together in numerous ways as *rgyu* ("gyu", Skt.: *hetu*) and *rkyen* ("kyen", Skt.: *pratyaya*). Often translated as 'cause(s)' and 'condition(s)' respectively, Tsarong translates these two concepts as 'distant' and 'proximate' causes, delineating them in Buddhist terms, with the 'general' distant cause as ignorance (Tib.: *ma rig pa*), and the 'specific' distant causes as the three poisons (Tib.: *dug gsum*) of greed/desire (Tib.: *dod chags*), hatred/anger (Tib.: *zhe sdang*) and ignorance/delusion (Tib.: *gti mug*). He names *rlung, mkhris pa*, and *bad kan* as 'proximate' causes, in addition to the five elements of earth, air, fire, water and space, which may also be involved (1991, 44). However, in reality these concepts are quite situational—often invoked in a variety of ways in different contexts. Thus whilst Gerke translates them as 'material'/'primary' cause and 'cooperating'/'secondary' cause respectively, she argues that in fact there is most likely 'no pan-Tibetan view' on these two notions. Instead, the division between them is sometimes made in relation to the likely effectiveness of rituals dealing with particular *rgyu* and *rkyen* (rather than as an interpretation of the likely causes of the problem in question) (2012a, 172–73). Thus karma, the *nyes pa* and ignorance could all be delineated as *rgyu* under different circumstances and in different situations, interacting with numerous *rkyen* in the causation of illness or misfortune.

Clifford noted the listing of 'karma' as one of the five causes of *smyo nad* in the *rGyud bZhi* (1989, 137), and in Darjeeling, karma was sometimes named quite directly by informants as a causative factor in illness, for example as we saw in explanations of Jigme's illness in the previous chapter. In fact, the notion of karma is fundamental in Tibetans' appraisals of the world around them: Prost describes it (along with *rlung*) as a 'cognitive and narrative

vector' which helps individuals to make sense of their life, by instilling significance into traumatic events (2006, 26).[6] However, in Darjeeling I found
'karma' invoked with differing levels of conviction by different people. For
example, during fieldwork, I found that sometimes 'karma' was referenced in
situations in much the same way that a person in the UK might respond to
an unfortunate incident or unexpected illness with a shrug of their shoulders
and a comment of, 'That's life'. Here, the notion is not necessarily felt or examined in any depth, instead it is perhaps more of a placation to oneself and/
or others, or even a gloss for more complex explanations which we may be
unable—or unwilling—to articulate. As Amchi Pema Dorjee explained when
I interviewed him in Delhi, some patients 'accept [that] this is karma, so this
relaxes the mind very much'.

However, the notion of 'karma' was also often more than simply a 'placation',
and a number of informants in Darjeeling discussed this explanatory concept
in more depth. For example, Gyaltsen explained that when he saw how people
behaved and how they sometimes got away with being dishonest, 'I wonder if
karma is really true'.[7] Moreover, karma is only one of a number of explanatory
factors invoked in cases of (mental) illness: as Lichter and Epstein suggest, 'the
woes of the world are not to be explained entirely by fatalistically invoking
karma' (1983, 238), instead, *rgyu* and *rkyen* are often invoked simultaneously
to explain an episode of illness.

These different causative factors often interrelate in perhaps unexpected
ways. For example, our karmic 'fruit' can be improved: through Buddhist practice, 'merit' can be increased, favourably influencing future rebirths. In
addition, *dbang thang* can also be influenced by merit, and is also related—at
least in part—to behaviour in previous lives (Calkowski 1993, 32). However,
whilst *bsod nams* only relates to merit accrued from a previous life, *dbang thang*,
as Calkowski explains, may be accrued in this life through various methods:

> [I]t may be obtained through application to Buddhist meditational
> deities, contagiously acquired through the touch of a high lama,
> achieved through religious initiations actualised by lamas who them-
> selves possess it, or, according to the logic of exorcism, through the
> defeat of one's enemies (whether they be demons or lamas).... *dBang-*

---

6. See also Lichter and Epstein (1983) for an examination of the notion of karma and
how it interweaves with the notions of *dge ba* (virtue) and *sdig pa* (sin), as well as its limitations as an explanatory concept.

7. Of course, karma can in fact manifest in this life or another, and we do not know
what fate awaits anyone in future lives.

thang can supersede karmic considerations by extending an individual's lifespan (1993, 32–33).

For example, when I arrived back in Darjeeling in February 2012, Nyima (35) described how he and his father had recently convened a ritual to increase their *dbang thang*. The fact that it was low had been evidenced by several members of their family having suffered from serious illness and dying young: his only brother had died in his twenties from epilepsy; his mother had died in her fifties from high blood pressure; and his uncle had recently passed away suddenly, killed by a *sri* ("see", a kind of malevolent spirit).

However, whilst only Buddhist practices have the ability to increase an individual's *dbang thang*, it is possible to elevate one's *rlung rta*—another causative factor not only in illness, but also in its healing—through good relations with local deities, and rituals to improve them. Lichter and Epstein describe *rlung rta* as 'the state of a person's worldly luck', which can be either 'high' or 'low', and can even mediate the effects of karma in this life (1983, 240–41). For example, one day I discussed a local biomedical doctor with Phurpu (50). He told me that in the past he and his family had consulted this doctor on numerous occasions, but that he no longer consulted him, explaining: 'He was very good in the past—when luck favoured him.' However, now, he said, this doctor's luck had 'broken' (Tib.: *chag*), and he was therefore no longer a good doctor. In fact, he argued, there is a natural fluctuation of *rlung rta* throughout one's life, explaining via an 'English saying' he knew:

> Don't you say, "Everything that rises must fall"? It's like this—it's like this for all doctors: when luck favours them, they are very good....
> It's true ... it's karma—there is nothing you can do about this.

Again, we find the notion of *rlung rta* interwoven with the concept of karma. To illustrate, he explained that this doctor had recently 'made some very serious errors', including apparently leaving scissors inside one patient during an operation, and not long ago treating Phurpu's wife with 'incorrect medication', leading to 'swelling up' of her body. Again he referenced 'karma', explaining that whether a particular doctor or medicine 'suits you' or not is down to your and the doctor's karma.

However, unlike karma, *rlung rta* is exclusively related to this life: Calkowski explains that *rlung rta* is 'synonymous with unpredictable good fortune' such as 'the victory of the underdog in a sports competition, winning a lottery, absolution in the event of unwitting moral transgression, and so forth' (1993, 32). She suggests that it 'flows unilineally from gods to humans', and is 'transmitted asymmetrically' as the deities 'confer it at their discretion' (1993, 32).

In Darjeeling, Phurpu confirmed this, describing how '*rlung rta* can be improved by invoking the *yul lha* [local deities]'. Moreover, he explained that it is when a person's *rlung rta* has 'run out' or 'broken' that he is able to see spirits and ghosts. Similarly, Dolma (31) explained that it is when someone's luck has broken, and their *bla* ("la", life force) is weak that *gdon* will attack. In such an event, the affected individual needs to conduct a *sku rim* ("ku rim"), a particular type of ritual which aims to 'recover' the *bla*.[8] Thus, whilst *bsod nams* is cumulative and linear, *rlung rta* fluctuates naturally and may undergo cyclical alterations throughout one's life (Lichter and Epstein 1983, 240).

Examining these notions of karma, *dbang thang*, *rlung rta* and *bsod nams*, we start to build up a complex picture of the multiple levels of causation in mental ill-health in the Tibetan context, perhaps reflecting Williams and Healy's notion of 'exploratory maps'. Here, however, the different explanatory frameworks which are often invoked simultaneously need not be contradictory, and we can see how, from a Tibetan perspective, they can interact in a number of different ways in different situations to explain a single experience of illness. It starts to become clear why, in the event of illness, afflicted individuals and their families frequently consult multiple healing practitioners concurrently, in response to this multitude of causative factors. Interestingly, when I discussed these concepts with a clinical psychologist back in the UK, she commented how 'functional' many of them were from her perspective on Western psychology. In a similar manner to the Tibetan importance of the 'connection' between a patient and her practitioner, this relationship is also viewed by many as crucial in Western psychotherapy and psychiatry. The importance of this has been demonstrated, for example, by the higher treatment compliance demonstrated where patient and doctor share a similar world view (Hepburn 1988, 64). In addition, we might suggest that whether a practitioner's previous treatment success evidences his *rlung rta* and *dbang thang*, or his skill and expertise (or both), it is doubtless an important consideration for prospective patients. Finally, these concepts are also used to explain a lack of treatment ef-

---

8. See Day (1989) and Lichter and Epstein (1983) for detailed descriptions of this ritual. In addition, Cassaniti and Luhrmann describe a Thai concept that is perhaps similar to the Tibetan notion of *bla*, explaining, '[w]hen one is not mindful—when, as people say, the mind is scattered around—all sorts of problems occur'. Here, the supernatural 'is created and experienced by the uncontrolled mind' and '[t]he uncontrolled mind is permeable' leaving it open to 'energy' crossing into it (2011, 41). They describe one informant recalling an encounter with the supernatural: 'I didn't have any energy [of my own] when I saw it, I was tired' (2011, 42). Other times when the mind is more 'permeable' than usual include the time between wakefulness and sleep, or when an individual is preoccupied by a difficult issue or is ill (2011, 44).

ficacy for patients. For example, where a medical and/or religious intervention fails to achieve the desired outcome, it can be explained through the patient's or practitioner's *rlung rta* or *dbang thang*, which, on this occasion, simply was not strong enough.

Making Sense of 'Madness'

As we saw, Pema and her father initially consulted a biomedical doctor in their attempt to treat her mother. He prescribed Diazepam, one of a class of drugs known as benzodiazepines, often prescribed for anxiety and/or insomnia. Interestingly, despite her biomedical background, Pema did not use any bio-medical terms to describe her mother's illness, even though her description of her mother's symptoms was very similar to biomedical perspectives on 'psychosis'. Such conditions fall under one of the six sub-types of the ICD-10's F.23: 'acute and transient psychotic disorders' (which all come under the broader category of 'schizophrenia, schizotypal and delusional disorders') (WHO 2010a) or the DSM-5's 298.8: 'brief psychotic disorder' (APA 2013), a category included under 'schizophrenia spectrum and other disorders'. Both of these systems de-lineate brief episodes of psychosis characterised by a sudden, acute onset and complete recovery, and the ICD-10 describes this F.23 group of disorders thus:

> A heterogeneous group of disorders characterized by the acute onset of psychotic symptoms such as delusions, hallucinations, and perceptual disturbances, and by the severe disruption of ordinary be-haviour. Acute onset is defined as a crescendo development of a clearly abnormal clinical picture in about two weeks or less. For these disorders there is no evidence of organic causation.... Complete recovery usually occurs within a few months, often within a few weeks or even days. If the disorder persists, a change in classification will be necessary. The disorder may or may not be associated with acute stress, defined as un-usually stressful events preceding the onset by one to two weeks.[9]

As we saw, Wangmo recovered within approximately three to four weeks, meaning that her condition might perhaps be classified as an incident of 'brief

---

9. http://apps.who.int/classifications/icd10/browse/2010/en#/F20-F29. Interestingly, the ICD and DSM have quite different notions of what constitutes a 'brief' episode, with the ICD describing recovery as occurring within days, weeks or months, as described above, and the current fifth edition of the DSM stipulating that the episode last less than one month (APA 2013).

reactive psychosis', a sub-type of the ICD's F.23: 'acute and transient psychotic disorders' in the biomedical system (WHO 2010a[10]) (or indeed, the DSM-5's 'brief psychotic disorder'). This case then, which did not include any reference to *rlung*, can lend weight to Millard's comparison of *smyo nad* and psychosis.

I do not mean to suggest here that Wangmo's illness of *sems nad* or *smyo nad* was no more than an episode of this biomedically-recognised diagnosis. What this biomedical category consists of, in fact, is essentially a descriptive list of symptoms, possibly triggered by 'stress', a description that easily matches Pema's portrayal of events. However, when we situate Wangmo's experience in the context of some of the broader Tibetan notions of mental health and illness that I discussed in earlier chapters, we can see that this narrative of 'madness' fits into conceptions of causation and healing which differ significantly from biomedical perspectives. Here, for example, 'sadness' and 'worry' can lead to a severe episode of *smyo nad*, and this can be cured by the intervention of the religious practitioner and the patient's belief or faith in the religious practitioner and his ability to heal her. Wangmo and her family seemingly had no trouble in moving easily from one treatment system to another when initial attempts at treatment showed no results, and this rather pragmatic health-seeking behaviour was fairly typical of mental illness narratives I encountered in Darjeeling, where diverse treatments were often utilised concurrently apparently with little or no conflict.

* * *

Pema's narrative about her mother's brief episode of 'madness' illustrates a number of concepts of health, illness and healing which recurred throughout this research project. The role of Buddhist rituals and blessings in the treatment of mental disorders was discussed by numerous informants, whether they formed part of a broader picture of health-seeking behaviour, or were sought without the accompaniment of any other treatments. In Wangmo's case, we saw that her and her family consulted only two specialists—a biomedical doctor and a rinpoche—both of whom they already knew quite well, highlighting the importance of a 'connection' to the healing practitioner. Furthermore, whilst Wangmo's illness was thought by her daughter to have been caused by 'sadness' and 'worry', this was not addressed by the treatment which was eventually successful: the blessings of the rinpoche. Here instead, the focus was on the roles Tibetan notions of *dbang thang*, *rlung rta*, *dad pa* and *yid ches*. These concepts are of particular significance in relation to mental disorders caused by spirits, a topic which will be examined in more detail in the following

---

10. http://apps.who.int/classifications/icd10/browse/2010/en#/F20-F29.

chapter. In addition, cases such as Wangmo's can illustrate the complex task of constructing meaning in the event of illness in a medically-pluralistic context such as this, where multiple explanatory models—with their attendant treatment options—compete for space and custom. As we have seen here, even when local and biomedical diagnostic categories overlap to a greater or lesser extent, the broader explanatory models in which they are situated, and their attendant treatment methods often differ significantly. In the next chapter, I will examine a case of spirit/deity affliction, and the role of spirits in mental illness, which illustrates this point even further.

CHAPTER NINE

DECHEN: POSSESSION AND MEDIUMSHIP

Actually in Tibet it is a common case ... Many people say 'I saw this, I saw that'—especially in the evening ... But I think it's some psychological problem ... the mind becomes disordered and you see things that aren't there. (Urgyen, 39)

Dechen's Story

When I went to interview Dechen, a Tibetan *lha bzhugs mkhan* (spirit-medium[1]), in June 2012, it felt more like a social outing than an interview. A Tibetan friend, Gyaltsen, offered to introduce us, driving me out to her village about an hour from Darjeeling, and bringing along his wife Lhamo (25) and their baby, plus his friend Tenzin (28), who happened to be staying with them at the time. When we arrived at the house, Lhamo took the baby to join Dechen's mother and cousin in another room, while Dechen's father ushered us into the living room, calling for Dechen to join us. Over this initial two-hour visit and another meeting between only myself and Dechen a couple of weeks later, her narrative illustrated some of the ways in which spirit afflictions can either be related to, or show similarities with, some forms of mental illness in the Tibetan context.

---

1. Such individuals are also sometimes referred to as *lha bzhugs pa*, *lha pa* or *dpa' bo*. I will use the first two of these terms interchangeably here, as my Tibetan informants in Darjeeling did.

Dechen (38), a second-generation Tibetan exile and one of seven children, had grown up with her parents and siblings in Darjeeling, latterly residing in a small village around an hour's drive from the town. Her father described how Dechen had first become possessed by a *lha* at the age of three, at which time her family had taken her to a Tibetan *sngags pa*, who had been able to subdue the *lha* through ritual, blessing Dechen and giving her a *srung nga* (protective amulet) to wear, after which she recovered for a number of years. However, Dechen and her father then related how when Dechen was fifteen, this *sngags pa* had passed away, and the *lha*—no longer subdued—had started to possess her again. This possession manifested in numerous symptoms: Dechen described 'falling down' 'senseless' [unconscious] at school and then being confined to her bed, 'very weak' and vomiting, with many neighbours telling her that she 'must be dying'. She explained that at that time she had thought she was ill, perhaps even going mad. We discussed the case of a local Nepali *mata-ji*, who had described to me an initial sickness manifesting as crying and laughing 'for no reason', an inability to sleep for weeks at a time and the experience of 'people talking in my head', and Dechen described her experience as 'exactly the same' as this. When this happened, she explained, she had consulted several (biomedical) doctors—at one point even ending up an inpatient in a private hospital in Darjeeling—only to be told by all of them that there was nothing wrong with her.[2] In addition, Dechen visited several *jhānkri*, *mata-ji* and rinpoche who were also unable to help. Finally, Dechen and her father had travelled to Dharamsala, where they consulted a Tibetan female *lha bzhugs mkhan*, a medium for one of the *Tshe ring mChed lnga* ("Tsering Chenga", five long-life sisters, high level Buddhist protector) deities, who confirmed that she was affected by a *yul lha*—a local protector deity from her father's hometown in Tibet. The *lha bzhugs mkhan* gave them incense (*bsang*) blessed by the Dalai Lama, instructing them to burn it when the *lha* came to shorten the episodes as, she told them, it was not possible to prevent them. Following this visit to Dharamsala, the *lha* had not come again for three years. However, the episodes started again after this, and continued to this day. Dechen's father explained that when the *lha* came, he would burn a little of this incense, but, in Dechen's words, this 'sometimes helps, and sometimes it doesn't'.

---

2. It was suggested to me by the clinical psychologist Joseph Calabrese that Dechen's description of her condition matches the biomedical category of temporal lobe epilepsy. However, this does not appear to have been a possibility that was considered by the biomedical doctors who she consulted in Darjeeling (private communication, March 2015).

Dechen described her experience of the *lha* invading her consciousness: 'I see a lot of *lha* in front of my eyes … at that time I feel that the *lha* are my family … and when I look at my family, I don't know them or my home'. Her father explained that sometimes the *lha* spoke through her, either in Tibetan or *lha skad* ("lha ké", *lha* language), which her family were unable to understand. Dechen's father told us that the episodes lasted 'sometimes five minutes, sometimes one, two or three hours', and 'make her behave very strangely'. He noted, though, that the episodes were always 'peaceful', explaining that Dechen never became aggressive or violent in any way—unlike some of the stories I had heard in Darjeeling of *gdon* possession. Unusually for a *lha bzhugs mkhan*, Dechen sometimes remembered a little about the experience after it had ended. In addition, she explained that following an episode, 'I feel very sick for one week … very tired, [and] ache all over'. Sometimes during the possession, the *lha* would instruct Dechen to perform particular religious activities and, in addition, in her 'everyday' life, she also often experienced premonitory dreams, usually focused around predictions for her family (for example, impending sickness) or for Tibet itself (for example, predictions of self-immolations, which at that time were quite frequent in Tibet). These days, they told me, the *lha* was coming 'a few times', and was generally unpredictable, although Dechen noted that she sometimes vomited or experienced a feeling of déjà vu just prior to an episode of possession.[3]

The logistical problems caused by this situation for Dechen were evident— not knowing when the *lha* might come, she was reluctant to go out alone, and mainly stayed in the house and on the family's surrounding land. She explained that she would like to study or work, but this was simply not possible—whenever she had attempted this previously, the *lha* had come and told her to discontinue her plans, including, at one point, a decision she had made to take monastic vows. Thus, although Dechen's initial period of illness which preceded her recognition as a *lha bzhugs mkhan*—which was a fairly typical entry into mediumship—had long passed, she continued to experience symptoms of possession that were clearly very difficult to manage. In fact, this rather unusual narrative of spirit-mediumship highlights some interesting questions regarding 'possession' in the Tibetan context, and how it might be related to mental or physical illness. We saw in Chapter Four that there are certain spirits (Tib.: *gdon*) which cause madness, often dealt with by spirit-mediums.

---

3. I tried several times to ask how frequently this occurs, but unfortunately questions of time and detail were left mainly unanswered, making it hard to ascertain how often Dechen was experiencing these episodes.

However, Dechen clearly does not fit easily into of this category or that of a standard *lha bzhugs mkhan*. Possessed by a deity (rather than a malevolent spirit or ghost), but unable to control her possession, she could neither work as a *lha bzhugs mkhan* nor 'exorcise' her possessing entity, leaving her with uncontrollable symptoms. As we have seen, in the Tibetan tradition—as in many other societies—the initial stages of possession often appear as some form of 'madness'. Indeed, Day describes the predominance of such 'madness' above all other factors as an indicator of possession for new oracles in Ladakh (1989, 277; see also Rösing 2006). Day relates a number of diverse narratives of the initial stages of mediumship which include experiences that vary in severity, including 'unsettled minds', 'fits', prolonged periods of unconsciousness and extreme behaviours (1989, 273–77). She details one woman's description of the symptoms which preceded her recognition as an oracle in terms which show clear similarities with Dechen's narrative:

> I was very, very ill for a month. My body was so heavy that I could barely move. Yet, if I stayed at home I'd have a fit, that is, everything would go dark and I'd feel as if I were about to faint. Then, I'd come to with no recollection at all of what had happened. But, I didn't feel much better afterwards. I'd feel very weak and my head would hurt. I was ready to die, I was terrified (Day 1989, 273).

Some local biomedical practitioners clearly interpreted such cases as a form of mental illness; for example, when I discussed local spirit-mediums with Dr Sharma (one of the psychiatrists at Gangtok's STNM Hospital), his simple response was that 'many are psychotic'.[4] Similarly, on describing my initial meeting with Dechen to an American medical student friend living and working in the area, his immediate and only comment was, 'So, what do you think she has in terms of the DSM? Bipolar? Something else?'

This type of experience with *lha* is, of course, only one of a number of types of possession and spirit-mediumship delineated in the Tibetan tradition. Here, as Diemberger explains, a number of different kinds of divinities can enter the body through the energy channels (Tib.: *rtsa*), which can result in 'various problems, such as insanity' (2005, 132). In Chapter Four, I described a number of mental health conditions which can be caused by spirits and

---

4. In fact, on my first visit to the psychiatric department of his hospital, he introduced me to two local Nepali *mata-ji* sisters, who had just been admitted, and were in the process of being diagnosed—most likely, he explained, with some kind of psychosis—and medicated.

deities, such as the *smyo byed kyi gdon* (spirits that cause madness), delineated in the *rGyud bZhi*. However, lay Tibetan informants in Darjeeling had many—often quite diverse—perceptions of the numerous spirits and deities which might cause strange behaviour, confusion or 'madness' in afflicted individuals. Moreover, spirit 'afflictions' do not necessitate possession: some deities and spirits can cause harm—including illness—without invading a person's consciousness. These different understandings of spirit influence reflect broader Tibetan concepts of the fundamental role which such entities often play in everyday life—able to protect individuals as well as causing harm in numerous ways—and highlight the hierarchical relationships between them. Notions of spirit affliction also illustrate how a number of different Tibetan religious concepts (such as karma, *gdon* and *rlung rta,*) may interrelate in various ways, acting as *rgyu* and *rkyen* in a case of mental illness, as discussed in the previous chapter.

Almost all of the Tibetans I spoke to in Darjeeling related stories of encounters with spirits and deities: either stories of their own, or those of their relatives or friends. In the rest of this chapter I will examine the role that different types of deities and spirits can play in mental health and illness, and the management and healing of such spirit afflictions. In Darjeeling, these discussions mostly focused around a handful of entities: malevolent spirits such as *gdon* and *(shi) 'dre*, and certain types of *yul lha*, particularly the *bstan* and *rgyal po*. It is therefore these which I will focus on here.

Luck, Madness and Death: Spirits and Mental Health in the Tibetan Context

During my time with Dechen and her family, her father emphasised the fact that his daughter was affected by a *lha*, rather than a *gdon*.[5] This is a significant distinction: whilst both are types of 'worldly'—that is, unenlightened—entities, and therefore hold little spiritual power in comparison to enlightened deities, they are significantly different in nature. In general, possession by *gdon* or *'dre* is an undesirable state of affairs only likely to cause problems for afflicted individuals, and requires ritual intervention to 'exorcise' the spirit. Furthermore, as we have seen, it is often understood to be more likely to occur

---

5. I wondered whether perhaps this question had been raised within the community, although this was not made clear during the interview.

when a person's 'luck' has 'broken', or their life-force is weak—indeed, Calkowski describes two cases in Dharamsala: one in which a man's *rlung rta* was at its 'lowest ebb', leaving him 'extremely vulnerable' to attacks by spirits (1985, 71–72); and a case where the difference between two men's *rlung rta* is clearly illustrated by their differing responses to the wrath of *klu* (1985, 86–87). In contrast, I was told by several Tibetan informants that Dechen's experience of deity possession was considered 'lucky', and was more usually associated with spirit-mediums or oracles, who are often able to manage the possession to conduct divinations and/or heal others' illnesses or spirit afflictions. Nevertheless, as I have mentioned, the distinction between these different types of possession and mediumship is not always clear-cut, with the borderline between 'good' and 'bad' possession sometimes rather 'blurred' (Diemberger 2005, 132) and the symptoms often similar—at least initially—in both cases. In addition, sometimes an episode initially interpreted as a deity possession turns out, in fact, to be a 'normal' case of madness as an illness. Indeed, Pramila, a local (Buddhist) Nepali *mata-ji* in Darjeeling, explained to me that in some such cases, after a period of 'training' under the guidance of a more experienced medium, it eventually becomes clear that an afflicted individual is *not* in fact affected by a deity, and is therefore not a spirit-medium but rather a person experiencing what she called 'normal madness' (which may or may not respond to any given treatment). In the next two sections I will examine these different forms of possession and mediumship, and the diverse ways in which they can be related to mental illness in the Tibetan context.

Spirit-Mediumship

Despite the fact that, unusually for a *lha bzhugs mkhan*, Dechen remembered some of her trance events, a number of facets of her narrative echo those of other spirit-mediums in the Himalayan tradition, including the narratives of several Nepali *jhānkri* and *mata-ji* I interviewed in and around Darjeeling. Indeed, the period of unidentifiable illness followed by a recognition that this was in fact a possession by a deity which she described follows the familiar pattern of experiences of many spirit-mediums and shamans described by others such as Day (1989) and Rösing (2006) in Ladakh, Diemberger (2005) and Samuel (1993) in Tibet and Gutschow (2007) in Zangskar. In Tibet, Diemberger described a similar journey into spirit-mediumship, noting that when the energy channels—understood to be where the *lha* enters the body— are not 'purified', the medium may be unable to manage and control the possession, and may experience uncontrolled visions, voices, fainting and weakness (2005, 120). This echoes Dechen's narrative of her experience of uncontrollable possession, where she described seeing the *lha* in front of her and talking to her, as well as her description of the after-effects of possession, where she felt very weak and ached 'all over'.

Dechen described how the nature of her experience had finally been ascertained by the *lha bzhugs mkhan* whom she and her father had consulted in Dharamsala. In order to determine the nature of the possession, this spirit-medium had tossed *phyag nas* (barley grains) onto her: Dechen explained that if this action induces the entity to enter the afflicted's consciousness, then the possessing entity is known to be a *lha*. If, however, the afflicted individual 'falls down—unconscious' instead, then the possession is revealed as a *gdon*.

As in a number of other anthropological analyses of trance and possession (see for example Crook in Ladakh, 1997), Diemberger has discussed some of the social and political aspects of spirit-mediumship in the Tibetan context. She describes the form of female mediumship she encountered as the 'only available kind of empowerment' for many of the women concerned, where such conditions often 'reflect individual responses to social constraints', most likely to occur at particular points in a woman's life (2005, 120).[6] However, if this was some form of 'empowerment' for Dechen, it was really not clear in what form it might manifest. From what I could see, her situation appeared— certainly in terms of employment or marriage prospects—rather bleak. Unable to predict the *lha*'s intrusion, her life and movements were severely restricted— as she explained, 'I feel in my mind.... I think it's difficult. I feel like a prisoner in the home—I don't have any freedom'. Discussing this case later with Gyaltsen, he noticed my confusion at other Tibetan informants' comments that this form of possession was considered 'lucky', and explained that *lha* are understood to only come to very 'pure and clear-minded people'. He clarified: '*Lha* are a little better than us ... their life span is long, and they live a very luxurious—very happy, very good—lifestyle ... so they come into a very special human body'. Another informant, Nyima (35), echoed this, explaining, 'a god can only come to those who are very clean, kind and good'. This, of course, contrasts sharply with the notion that *gdon* are more likely to afflict individuals when, for example, their 'luck' is 'broken' and their 'life force' is weak. Thus, whilst Dechen's possession clearly presented significant difficulties for her, her situation remained quite different from that of possession by lower-

---

6. She found this to be more common in female oracles who did not belong to established lineages, perhaps similarly to Dechen's experience, who knew of no such history in her family.

level *gdon* or *shi 'dre*, or spirit afflictions caused by deities such as *btsan* or *rgyal po*, whom can be quite dangerous.

gDon *and* 'Dre *Affliction in Darjeeling*

Despite the numerous different classes of spirits and deities mentioned in some of the Tibetan medical and religious literature, Tibetans in Darjeeling— particularly lay Tibetans—discussed only a small handful of these with me, particularly in relation to mental illness. This reflects Samuel's suggestion that many of the spirits delineated in the *rGyud bZhi* do not necessarily correspond much with contemporary Tibetan lay notions (2007, 214). Entities discussed most frequently in Darjeeling were the *gdon*, *(shi)'dre*, *btsan* and *rgyal po*. In relation to illness caused by possession, the focus was usually on *gdon* and *'dre*. Similarly, in Ladakh, Day found that most cases of 'madness' were initially at- tributed to spirits such as *gson 'dre* (living demons), and in Nepal, Millard found all cases of diagnosed mental illness related to the action of 'harmful spirits' (here referred to as *gnod pa*) (2007, 259). In Darjeeling a number of informants narrated stories of *shi 'dre* possession, as well as tales of having seen (or heard) the activity of *shi 'dre* without possession (for example, things being moved around in a house by such spirits while no-one else was there). However, I also found that in Darjeeling the terms *(shi) 'dre* and *gdon* were often used interchangeably. For example, Tsering (59) talked of 'many different levels of *'dre*', explaining that 'some are very powerful' and may enter a person's consciousness. He explained, 'this makes them mad ... suicidal, violent to oth- ers ... The madness comes and goes ... you should go to a lama or *lha pa* for treatment', noting that a *lha pa* can usually ascertain who the *'dre* is and what they want, and should be able to subjugate it. When I discussed this with Champa (25), a young monk from Dali Gonpa, he described the symptoms of spirit possession: 'The main symptom is they're not feeling well, starting crying, weeping, and their hands become very strong, [they] gain double power'. He noted too that the spirit might start talking through the afflicted individual, and they may even start throwing things and/or behaving abnor- mally. Such recurring 'episodes', he explained, tend to be intermittent, usually lasting fifteen to thirty minutes, with the person affected having no memory of the episode afterwards.

Lhakpa

Some of the dangers of these types of possession were clearly illustrated by a story I was told by Lhamo (45). She related her experience of witnessing the possession of a close neighbour, Lhakpa, a young woman of around twenty-four who, approximately two years previously, had become possessed by a spirit not long after arriving in India from Tibet:

> This happened once, to a woman ... she came down to the toilet.... She felt giddiness ... and she fell outside the toilet, you know? Then everyone ... everyone helped her up [but] she was not herself, she was completely strange, you know.... Then all of a sudden she became conscious, and then she started speaking whatnot [nonsensical] things.... Maybe a spirit might have got her.... We kept her in the hospital—they said she might have ... um ... some problem with her brain and all, [but] medicine's not working.... Then we took her down to Siliguri. In the hospital the same thing, you know ... she became very violent and all. This was a *gdon* or something ... *shi 'dre* or something, yes.

This was perhaps fairly typical of other descriptions of *gdon* and *'dre* possession I had heard in Darjeeling, but Lhamo's narrative continued to explain how the woman's affliction had ultimately been cured, with tragic consequences for the close friend who had helped her. Lhakpa's friend, a young lama from a local Sakya monastery of around the same age, had conducted some rituals in an attempt to deal with the spirit. However, as a young, rather inexperienced lama, he had been unable to control it. Lhamo explained:

> When she was in hospital, this lama came, and did some *pūjā* and all.... There were lots of *pūjās* to do.... We have different lamas, you know ... the ordinary lama cannot do *all* the *pūjās*. You need special powers to do that ... But because his care for her was *so* strong, maybe he wanted to do it himself ... She got alright after a few days, but he died. He did some sacrifice ... the sacrifice was too strong for him maybe ... maybe the spirit was stronger than him [laughs, incredulously]. He died, you know. He died ... a young lama.... Suddenly ... all of a sudden, you know.... The devils [*gdon*] are more strong—more powerful ... he had to give up his life.

Lhamo noted ruefully that Lhakpa had struggled following this incident: 'People don't like her, because they say she's the cause of the lama's death, you know? People blame her'. Lhakpa's condition however, was now good, she told me: Lhamo noted that Lhakpa had experienced no further episodes, and now lived in Kathmandu, Nepal, 'doing very well'. This narrative further illustrates the concept of *dbang thang* that I discussed in the previous chapter, where interaction with spirits can be very dangerous for all but the most experienced of Tantric practitioners or spirit-mediums.

Migmar

Other cases of spirit affliction described by informants in Darjeeling did not involve 'possession' as such. One case of 'madness' caused by spirits was described to me by Sonam (21), a second-generation Tibetan exile and student at a local college, and Tsering (59), both of whom narrated the story of 19-year old Migmar, a neighbour of theirs. Described by Tsering in English as 'a little crazy', around two years previously Migmar had stopped sleeping, begun 'singing and crying' all day and night, and had started behaving very unlike himself, sometimes—uncharacteristically—arguing with his classmates and being verbally abusive. On occasion, I was told, he had even become violent, throwing crockery inside his house. In addition, Migmar had started to wear a very large number of strings of prayer beads around his neck, day and night. Sonam explained that after a while, every time Migmar had heard drumming, he would start dancing; and on 6th July 2010, at a local celebration for the Dalai Lama's birthday, he had suddenly started doing *'cham* (Tibetan masked religious dance, usually practised by monks). Migmar's family took him to a visiting biomedical psychiatrist who prescribed an unknown medication which, Sonam noted, 'really helped'. However, Migmar then followed a local *jhānkri*'s advice to stop taking the medicine, at which point he became 'bad' again. Migmar was then taken to a high-level lama in Kurseong (a few hours' drive away), from whom he received blessings and who conducted *pūjā*, and he became 'a little better'. However, a number of problems remained, and finally, Migmar's family had consulted another *jhānkri*, who conducted a ritual and was able to ascertain that this condition was caused by a particular spirit 'liking him'. The *jhānkri* performed the appropriate rituals and now, Sonam told me, Migmar was '90% better than last year'.

Migmar's story illustrates the interesting interplay between the different healing practitioners in the area and their diverse worldviews. Here, Migmar and his family navigated their way through a number of different explanatory models in their attempts to understand and treat his condition, in a demonstration of Williams and Healy's notions of 'exploratory maps'. This story serves to illustrate some of the difficulties of navigating different worldviews in an ethnically- and medically-pluralistic context such as this where, on occasion, one practitioner may advise against a treatment which appears to be working (at least to some degree), and patients and their families are caught in a web of sometimes conflicting explanatory models and their attendant treatment paths as they search for meaning and treatment.

Furthermore, this case highlights the fact that it was not only spirits and deities from the Tibetan tradition which were discussed in relation to health and illness by Tibetans in Darjeeling. Perhaps unsurprisingly in this ethnically pluralistic area, spirits from one of the local Nepali communities were also sometimes included in discussions around *smyo nad*. In particular, a handful of interviewees noted the fact that the Nepali Rai community—many of whom lived in the area—were known to bury their dead in the farmland, making it dangerous to walk in their fields. Nyima related the story of a Tibetan neighbour who 'became very quickly mad' and died within a few weeks, after inadvertently offending Rai ancestor spirits. He described how the ailing woman had been taken to a biomedical doctor but, not knowing this spirit cause, he had been unable to help her.

bTsan, rGyal Po *and the Dangers of Offending Local Deities*

In addition to spirits such as *gdon* and *'dre*, two types of *yul lha* (local deity), known as *btsan* and *rgyal po*, were often discussed by Tibetans in Darjeeling in the context of mental illness. Tibetan informants often talked of the importance of dealing very cautiously with worldly deities such as these who may help or harm, depending on their inclination. In fact, *btsan* has been translated as both 'god' and 'violent spirit', and they are often described as the 'spirits of erring monks of earlier times', with *rgyal po*—deities characterised by arrogance and pride—said to be the spirits of 'evil kings or high lamas who have broken their vows' (Cornu 1997, 250–52). Some *rgyal po*, such as Pehar (Tib.: *Pe har*), the Dharma protector of Samye Monastery in South Central Tibet, have been 'tamed' and bound by oath by Guru Rinpoche, consequently functioning as *srung ma* (protector deities). Local deities such as these are often able to afford some protection against harm from the less powerful *gdon* and *'dre*. Keeping on good relations with *yul lha* such as these is of paramount importance, and this is often achieved through the making of regular offerings. When happy, such deities will usually be benevolent towards humans; when offended or angry however, they may cause harm to humans quite directly, or they may neglect to afford protection against other harmful entities. Lhamo explained: 'They say if you don't worship your [local] deity in the proper way … you get possessed by these things, you know … *gdon*'.

In fact, I was told in Darjeeling that neglecting these *yul lha* can lead to numerous problems for people in the local community, such as misfortune of different kinds, illness or even madness. Tsering (59) explained that if someone stops honouring the local *btsan* or *rgyal po*, they may become 'sick' or 'crazy', the affliction depending on the deity involved. Tenzin (28) agreed, saying, 'if you stop worshiping *yul lha*, you can get *sems nad* or *smyon nad*—particularly in rural areas.... If you *start* worshiping you must continue'. Again we can see that the key here is the maintenance of good relations with such deities, a notion which links back to our discussion regarding the importance of individuals' 'connection' with such entities in the previous chapter. When I asked Phurpu (50) about this, he laughingly likened these deities to what he said he had heard about 'women in England': 'If you bring them flowers, they're happy and smiling, but if you then forget to bring flowers one day, or if you don't honour them, then they get angry, and they will harm you'. Examples of 'harm' he gave included the possibility that maybe 'things won't go smoothly ... many problems or bad dreams or sickness [may come] ... or one person in the family may go crazy'.

Moreover, one informant discussed how the recent political history of Tibet has contributed to problems like these: Tashi (53), a first-generation exile who had fled Tibet as a young child with his family, explained that in the past, people in every Tibetan village would make offerings to the local *btsan*. However, during the Cultural Revolution, when such practices were denigrated as 'superstition' (Tib.: *rmongs dad*) and actively discouraged or banned, much of the local knowledge regarding these practices was lost. As a result, Tashi said, today many Tibetans of the younger generation were ignorant of such things, leaving many of them unable to make the correct offerings (or in fact, any offerings at all). One result of this, he explained, was that they could get 'a kind of madness'—leading them to talk to themselves, or be aggressive towards others. This behaviour comes and goes, he said, but without any treatment, the symptoms will only escalate. 'Treatment' here takes the form of asking for forgiveness from the deities, resuming offerings, and consulting a lama who is able to subdue the deity through ritual. If these actions are carried out, said Tashi, the 'madness' will definitely be cured. In fact, I then came across a story in Darjeeling which particularly illustrated the dangers of dealing with deities such as these, which I will describe next.

Dorje Shugden

One particular deity, known as Dorje Shugden (Tib.: *rDo rje Shugs ldan*), was mentioned by several informants in this context. Viewed as a dangerous *rgyal po* by many Tibetans, the Dalai Lama has advised against practices related to this deity. However, there is an ongoing debate between him and the followers of Dorje Shugden, who argue that Shugden is in fact an *enlightened* god. By all accounts, this is a contentious subject, not least because the debate spilled over into violence and the death of three Tibetans in Dharamsala in 1997 (Clifton

1997).[7] Consequently, many Tibetans are reluctant to discuss this topic, although a number of informants in Darjeeling brought it up in interviews in the context of our dialogues on mental health and illness. One such informant was Urgyen (39), a first-generation exile, who had left Tibet as a teenager. He described the harm that can result from practices related to this deity:

> If you go and worship him, and then out of carelessness, you go to a monastery Shugden doesn't like, for example Nechung's [the monastery of one of the main protector deities of the Dalai Lama], then Shugden will get jealous and will harm you, or [cause you to] get crazy—I've seen this many times.... If you have no relations with him he has no power to harm you, he has no strength to do it. If you have relation with him he can.

Here again, it is through individuals' 'relation' to the deity that he is able to harm them, creating illness or misfortune. This is particularly significant here, where the propitiation of Shugden entails a 'life entrusting' (Tib.: *srog gtad*) ceremony, where followers 'swear fidelity' to the deity, who 'in exchange promises to serve him or her'—a 'solemn oath' Dreyfus likens to 'that of friends swearing life-long loyalty to each other' (Dreyfus 1998, 266).[8] Breaking this oath then, is likely to cause significant problems.

In the context of illness caused by this particular deity, there is a significant amount of stigma here, not only due to the Dalai Lama's advice against this practice, but also because—for those against this practice at least—this deity is particularly associated with the attainment of worldly goods. I have discussed some Tibetan notions of emotions and cognitions as causation in mental disorders, and here we find this concept again. However here, there is another layer of causation too, where the afflicted individual is also harmed as a result of the *deity's* emotions, through his hurt pride or anger. Due to non-practitioners' views of Dorje Shugden as a deity able to grant to his followers worldly goods such as 'money' or 'a nice car', in Darjeeling, Shugden practitioners were

---

7. It is important to note that there is also a political background to this debate—see Kay (1997) and Dreyfus (1998, 2005) for more on this. However, this should not subtract from the fact that for many Tibetan informants in Darjeeling, it was clearly something they were genuinely very concerned about, due to the perceived danger of conducting such practices, or even being associated with those who did. This was illustrated by the fact that there was in fact a local monastery not far from town, known locally to be a place where the monks honoured this deity, and consequently avoided by the majority of Tibetans in the area.

8. Dreyfus notes that this practice is not exclusive to the propitiation of Shugden, and does in fact exist for some other worldly gods too (1998, 266 [note 58]).

sometimes described as 'greedy' or overly concerned with material goods. Therefore, in cultivating a 'relationship' with Dorje Shugden, the practitioners themselves—through their desires—were seen to have created the problem, consequently leaving themselves open to the deity's whims of anger or jealousy. This perspective was voiced by some informants regarding a local family, with several people describing a woman and two of her sons as *smyo nad* ('psycho-type—mad ... *smyon nad*' as Sonam described it), with a third son apparently addicted to drugs, all as a result of this practice. Gyaltsen explained that it was said that, 'If you worship him, he'll give you anything you want, but he is a worldly god—if he gets slightly angry, he'll kill you.... You'll get sick—like vomiting blood—and then die'. Due to this strong relationship with the deity, abandoning practices related to Shugden was thought to be particularly risky in terms of the likelihood of causing offence, with one monk, Dawa, explaining that this would likely make Shugden angry and thus cause him to harm the practitioner. With regard to this particular family, a common explanation from Tibetans who spoke to me about this was that the deity had been inadvertently offended—most likely through the neglecting of regular offerings. Thus with worldly deities such as this, I was told, as long as individuals maintained their offerings to the deity, they were protected; but if such offerings were neglected (perhaps because the individual now had what she desired), they may arouse the deity's anger or jealousy, leading him to cause them harm. It is important to point out that this is *not* how the practitioners themselves view this situation, but from the outsiders' perspectives, it is the 'greed' or 'attachment' to such worldly goods which have led individuals to this practice, and it is this that has consequently opened them up to possible harm.

I have outlined here some of the complexities inherent in different forms of spirit affliction in the Tibetan context, where spirits and deities are often difficult to manage, and may be particularly dangerous to interact with. In the Tibetan context then, possession, mediumship and spirit affliction can take a variety of forms, some considered to be 'lucky', regardless of any difficulties they may entail, others more related to a low life-force or 'broken' luck. Despite such differences, they may manifest in similar ways, at least initially, particularly for individuals such as Dechen, whose experience falls somewhere between these different cate-gories of unwanted spirit possession and the traditional role of a *lha bzhugs mkhan*. As we have seen, these different relationships with non-human entities are often evidenced by periods of 'madness', as well as a number of other symptoms. In many cases, it is possible to either 'exorcise' a possessing entity, or bring it under control, but in others, this is not possible. In Darjeeling spirits and deities were often discussed by Tibetan informants in relation to mental illness, but there were sometimes disagreements over whether particular individuals were affected by spirits or deities, and occasionally, over the very notions of possession and mediumship, and it is these differing perspectives to which I turn next.

Spirit Affliction in Contemporary Tibetan Society: Uncertainties and Conflicts

For Dechen, her situation was clearly very difficult: told that there was nothing wrong with her by the biomedical doctors she had consulted and unable to control the *lha* through traditional means, she was unable to take part fully in daily life in the community. Whilst she told me that her community was generally supportive of her situation, she noted that 'Some [people] believe, some don't believe', illustrating the disagreements which sometimes arise within families or communities regarding the authenticity of local *lha bzhugs mkhan*. Indeed, Samuel related a case in Dalhousie where there was disagreement within the Tibetan exile community over whether a particular individual was a *lha bzhugs mkhan* or was simply suffering from some form of madness.[9] Moreover, in contemporary Darjeeling, disagreements over the very notion of spirits in general were sometimes evident. Here, a small handful of Tibetan informants expressed doubt about the existence of such entities, with some even suggesting that a belief in having seen spirits could simply be the result of a mental illness of some kind. For example, I discussed spirits with Urgyen (39), a first-generation exile from Central Tibet, who had arrived in India twenty years previously. He explained, 'Actually in Tibet it is a common case.... Many people say "I saw this, I saw that" — especially in the evening.... But I think it's some psychological problem ... the mind becomes disordered and you see things that aren't there'.

Dorje (49), a second-generation exile, hinted that this discussion over the reality of spirit intervention might in fact be related to some stigma attached to mental illness, suggesting, 'Maybe the person is ill or mentally ill, but their family and community say it's because they're possessed, and so then they too believe this is what it is'. Meanwhile, Gyaltsen was one of the few Tibetans who had told me clearly that he did not believe in 'spirits and all these things', declaring that he was sure they did not exist. Following our meeting with

---

9. Personal communication, July 2014.

Dechen then, I was curious to find out how he viewed her situation. He initially laughed off my question, exclaiming simply, 'I don't know!' However, a few days later, when we discussed her case again, he conceded that '*maybe*' Dechen was being possessed by a *lha*, noting after a pause that, 'It is very difficult to understand this process [of possession] ... Dechen leaves, and the *lha* comes', and wondering aloud how this might happen in terms of the biology of the brain. Similarly, after our discussion about the 'psychological problem' which he thought might cause people to think they have seen spirits, Urgyen laughingly told me, 'I used to believe, but I was Westernised by coming to India!', only to describe a few minutes later his view on the dangers of dealing with Dorje Shugden. Tenzin (26), a second-generation exile on holiday from studying medicine in the USA, told me that he did not believe in spirits at all, explaining that he thought that psychiatric illnesses were 'due to the mind only.... It's the condition of the brain ... the condition of the mind'. However, when I later asked his opinion on Dechen's case, he replied, 'That's something I don't have words for! [Laughing].... I myself, I look at it in a very ... with a critical eye ... I believe that maybe the god *is* in this person and *is* speaking. I keep an open mind'.

Such ambivalent views on spirits and their role in mental illness should not be surprising. As we have seen, patients everywhere often hold multiple, often contradictory, views on illness causation. Reflecting this, a handful of Tibetan informants answered my questions about spirits with a curious mixture of denial of their existence, coupled with a story about a spirit affliction which they could not quite discount. In contrast, others were definitive in their belief in the involvement of spirits and deities in day-to-day human life, health and sickness. Tenzin (28) summed up the majority of their responses when he stated simply that whilst he had never had any personal experience of spirit involvement, 'All these [deities and spirits] are very much true'.

Dealing with Spirits in Darjeeling: Treating and Preventing Spirit Afflictions

The relationship between human and non-human entities that I have described here suggests a rather porous boundary between individuals and their environment—including the spirits and deities which reside within it. I have discussed how a 'connection' to deities or a 'belief' in their power to harm can enable them to do so and, in addition, how this 'boundary' can also be manipulated to create a space for the healing of such illness, where 'faith' in practitioners and their power to heal is paramount. When dealing with cases of spirit affliction, there are a number of ways in which this 'boundary' between the person and spirits or deities can be 'strengthened'. These include personal religious activities such as repeating mantras, and the enlisting of ritual specialists, such as spirit-mediums, lamas or Tantric specialists such as *sngags pa*, who can often subjugate deities and stop them from causing further harm. Cases of spirit possession often require both personal Buddhist practices and ritual intervention. Moreover, as I have mentioned, whilst there are a number of Tibetan herbal medicines to treat spirit possession, in actuality, for Tibetans in Darjeeling, recourse to religious activities was almost always the first step in managing such a situation. As Amchi Teinlay explained,

> In such cases, the treatment from the spiritual side has to be done by the lamas. Then from the medical aspect, we the doctors can help the patient, but from the spiritual aspect, it is necessary for the lamas to treat … otherwise, it's difficult.... Medicines alone will not work on the patient.

Similarly, Amchi Lobsang Thubten explained—despite describing himself as 'not very religious'—that in cases of possession, 'you can go to a high lama with a lot of knowledge and power'. This echoes Besch's findings in Spiti, where he quotes an amchi thus: 'If someone has an evil spirit then what could an amchi do? With only medicine, the evil spirit will not leave' (2006, 162).

In Darjeeling, Amchi Teinlay described the contrast between the availability of different practitioners in pre-modern Tibet and modern times:

> Before, in the Himalayan regions, there was this custom of having these healers, *lha pas*—within the Buddhist community also. But nowadays it's decreasing I think slowly. Before, they used to say each and every village used to have many such *lha pa*, but nowadays it is decreasing, with the new generation.

Teinlay suggested that today—particularly with the availability of modern transport—it was much easier for people to visit a monastery for help in such cases, and explained that:

> In serious cases, we would recommend, if the patient is Tibetan, or Buddhist, I'd say to go to a lama—to a good lama—one that the patient has faith in, because again the patient may have faith in this lama, not that lama. So that person should go to that lama, and then take further advice, or further treatment, or whatever the lama suggests for this aspect, even if it's, like, diseases caused by evil spirits—or even if it's some diseases caused by *nāgas*, or whatever it is—then it's

best to follow their advice. And ... nowadays, like, in Tibetan communities, we don't see much of *lha pa* like before, no?

This certainly seemed to be the case in Darjeeling, where a number of informants reported that there were unfortunately no longer any working *lha pa* in the area. This contrasts notably with Diemberger's findings in the TAR, where she describes the 'numerous oracles' who continue to practise in both village and nomadic areas (2005, p. 116). In fact, despite the lack of such practitioners in Darjeeling, there was still a certain amount of demand for their services, and a number of Tibetans described to me occasions where they had travelled to other areas—such as Dharamsala or Ladakh—to consult a *lha pa* when they felt this would be the most effective action.

In some ethnically Tibetan areas, a few practitioners with specialist knowledge spanning spheres of both medicine and religion remain. In Spiti, Besch suggests that whilst the majority of amchi will need to refer such patients to *lha pa*, a few skilled amchi with particular religious knowledge are able to diagnose and treat such cases themselves, giving the example of the successful treatment of a case of possession by a *shi 'dre*, involving *pūjā* and *rdo me* ("do mé", stone fire) treatment[10] conducted by an amchi (2006, 164–65). However, when sufficient 'harm' has been caused by spirits as to result in illness, specialist ritual help is usually required and a number of informants discussed the important role that *lha pa* play here. As I mentioned in Chapter One, whilst there were no longer any Tibetan working *lha pa* in the Darjeeling area, there was a strong local tradition of male and female Nepali spirit-mediums who were sometimes consulted by Tibetans. For example, Migmar's family had consulted two different *jhānkri*, the second of whom had effected an at least partial cure, and a number of Tibetan informants explained that they had consulted local *jhānkri* and *mata-ji* in the absence of any local Tibetan ritual specialists such as this.

In addition of course, Darjeeling and its surrounding area have a number of different Tibetan Buddhist monasteries belonging to the four main Tibetan Buddhist schools, and the majority of those I spoke to felt that lamas were able to cure spirit possession: as Tenzin (28) said, 'I think it works every time'.

---

10. Also referred to as *me rgyab* ("mé gyup", putting fire), this treatment involves the very brief application of a heated iron/copper rod to particular points on the body in combination with the recitation of particular Buddhist mantras (see Besch 2006, 165). I was told that this had also been used by a visiting amchi in Darjeeling many years before to treat the brother of one informant, Nyima, who suffered from *gza'* (translated here by Nyima as 'epilepsy').

Illustration 12. *brGya bzhi* ritual for *shi 'dre* affliction,
Dali Gonpa, July 2012

Whilst I was in Darjeeling in July 2012, I attended a *brgya bzhi* ("gyub shi",
four hundred offering lamps) ritual[11] conducted at Dali Gonpa to deal with a
shi 'dre affliction affecting a local Nepali man from the Buddhist Tamang community, after his father had recently died.

Champa (25), one of the monks involved in the one-day ritual, explained
that this was a common ritual conducted for locals, who often commissioned
it by telephone if they did not live close by or were unable to attend the
monastery in person. He told me that there were a number of different such
rituals—more than twenty, he thought—each with a different 'suggested donation' (with the minimum around Rs.1–2,000: approximately £9–19). The
date for it, once commissioned, would be determined by the monastery's resident astrologer, who would perform a calculation to find the best date.

In addition to such ritual services available at the local monasteries, in Darjeeling—as in many other Tibetan Buddhist areas—there were also Tantric

---

11. See Eberhard Berg for a detailed description of a version of the *brgya bzhi* ritual in
a Sherpa community in Solu, Nepal (2008, 149ff).

**Illustration 13. Monks conducting a *brGya bzhi* ritual for
shi 'dre affliction, Dali Gonpa, July 2012**

ritual specialists such as *sngags pa* who could conduct various rituals to deal
with different kinds of spirits. In Darjeeling, Samten (58), a local *sngags pa*,
described some of the rituals he conducted to cure *shi 'dre* afflictions and other
types of spirit problems, and described how dangerous it can be to deal with
such spirits.[12] And, as we saw above, a handful of those affected by a spirit in
Darjeeling had initially consulted a biomedical doctor, with differing levels
of success.

A number of my Tibetan informants also discussed the prevention of problems related to spirits. For example, Phurpu (50) gave an account of an incident

12. In fact, he had recently conducted a ritual for a Tibetan friend, Nyima (33), after
his uncle had died suddenly, and it had been determined by a local astrologer that he had
been killed by a *sri*, a particular kind of spirit. Samten, a highly accomplished and skilled
Tantric practitioner recommended by the astrologer, explained that he had initially refused
Tsering's requests for him to conduct the ritual (known as a *sri gnon*), as it was too
dangerous. He eventually agreed, however, and was able to perform a successful ritual for
Nyima and his family. Nicolas Sihlé describes the sequence of this 'extremely violent
exorcism' in Baragaon, northern Nepal, in some detail (2002).

which happened to his father one day many years ago when walking to meet him from school. His father had described how he had encountered a *gdon* on the road and, seeing the black mass of the spirit moving towards him, terrified, he recited Buddhist prayers with his prayer beads (Tib.: *'phreng ba*) in his hand. Because of this, he said, the spirit swerved out of his way and around him, not causing him any harm. Such stories—indicating the strength of the dharma against the low spiritual power of local deities and spirits—were common amongst Tibetan informants in Darjeeling, and are an effective illustration of the notions of differential spiritual 'power' that I discussed in the previous chapter.

* * *

I have described here some of the variant ways in which spirits and deities can be involved in the causation of mental illness in humans in the Tibetan context. These illustrate Day's assertion that in many societies, 'possession' practices often 'straddle important local boundaries between sickness and health' (1989, 11). In Tibetan society, as we have seen, possession—where a spirit or deity is able to invade a person's consciousness—is not the only method through which such entities are able to cause harm and illness. As I have illustrated here, lay Tibetans' concepts of spirit affliction are often far broader than is expounded in medical texts such as the *rGyud bZhi*. In Darjeeling, the majority of discussions around mental illness focused on the role of a small handful of entities. In addition, in discussions around some of these deities, there was often an emphasis on the role of the 'connection' between individuals and the deity involved. Some of these narratives of spirit possession from Darjeeling clearly reflect notions of spirit affliction found across the Himalayan region and beyond, where possession can cause *smyo nad*, and the path towards spirit-mediumship often commences with a period of 'madness' caused by spirits and/or deities. Others are more specific to the Tibetan context, based as they are on the narrative of Guru Rinpoche's taming of the Tibetan landscape through the superior power of the Buddhist dharma, which is fundamental to Tibetans' views of themselves and their world, and where, for Tibetans, the spirits can thus be said to be integral to the justification of Buddhism's existence (Samuel 2007, 222).

In the midst of this, Dechen's narrative is perhaps hard to place. Affected by a *lha* rather than a *gdon*, unable to either exorcise or control her possession and yet viewed as 'lucky' by some in her community, and suffering from a condition not recognised by the biomedical doctors she consulted, hers does not easily fit anthropological analyses of social and/or political contexts of possession and mediumship, such as those discussed in Chapter Four. Dechen's situation is perhaps best described by Diemberger's depiction of uncontrollable possession caused by the energy channels through which the *lha* normally enter not being 'purified' (2005, 120). However, what this meant for Dechen in practice was merely that there was little help for her condition, despite her consultations of a number of different medical and religious specialists. In the other cases I have described here, 'treatment' had also demonstrated mixed results and, even when a cure was effective, there were sometimes significant consequences for those involved in this often rather complex and difficult situation. We saw this in the case of Lhakpa, where the lama who attempted to deal with her spirit affliction is understood to have died as a result of his interactions with the spirit, and Lhakpa was, to some extent, blamed for this.

In contemporary Darjeeling, much health-seeking behaviour in the event of spirit affliction was focused on ritual intervention, and overall there was little discussion of medicine—either Tibetan or Western. Here, where there were no longer any working Tibetan *lha pa* who deal with spirit afflictions, a number of Tibetans described consulting Nepali spirit-mediums, whilst others relied predominantly on monastic and/or Tantric practitioners and their rituals, often recommended by amchi. I have briefly discussed here some consequences of the meeting of diverse worldviews and their accompanying explanatory models, for example in Gyaltsen's attempt to explain the change of consciousness—from Dechen to the *lha*—through biomedical notions of the brain. As we have seen across the case studies, when local explanatory models come up against biomedical models of health and illness, this can sometimes lead to difficulties for patients, their families and practitioners. For example, Migmar's family received conflicting advice from different religious and medical specialists. These examples give us some idea of what it means for patients in a pluralistic medical context such as this to navigate their way through diverse worldviews and their attendant explanatory models of mental illness and treatment methods, a topic examined further in the Conclusion. However, in some cases, such as Dechen's, none of these explanatory models seem able to afford much in the way of treatment, and her situation remained very difficult.

CONCLUSION:
NAVIGATING A PLURALISTIC
MEDICAL SYSTEM IN
DARJEELING

Over the previous chapters, I have explored Tibetan perspectives on mental health, illness and healing through a number of case studies and a broad base of interview material. Building on previous research by Millard, Jacobson and others, I hope that the material I have discussed here has started to build up a picture of this Tibetan exile community in Darjeeling, illustrating the prevalence of Tibetan concepts in the explanation, management and treatment of different forms of mental illness. Here, for many people, religious explanations dominated discussions around causation and treatment, and notions of 'belief' and 'faith' interwove with Tibetan concepts of 'luck', 'merit' and karma. It is thus not surprising that, as we saw, health-seeking behaviour often encompassed religious activities such as blessings and rituals as either the primary or supplementary response to an episode of mental illness. Indeed, I am not sure I came across a single narrative of mental illness in Darjeeling where religious activities did not feature to some degree. In this conclusion, I will draw together the common threads which have recurred throughout these narratives, examining how individuals and their families navigate these different worldviews and medical systems in their attempts to make sense of and treat mental illness, in a context where competing explanatory models of illness may overlap and diverge to greater and lesser degrees in different cases. Here, pragmatic concerns are often at the forefront in health-seeking behaviour, as patients and their families seek treatment(s) which respond to the different causes and contributory factors understood to be at play in an episode of mental illness. Within this pluralistic context, where patients often 'mix and match' explanatory models and treatments from different medical and healing systems, I will also explore the issues of integrative medical systems and patient choice.

Conducting research in Dhorpatan, Nepal, Millard found that all the cases of *sems nad* he encountered were related to the action of harmful spirits (2007, 259–60), in contrast to the multitude of explanations that I have described in Darjeeling. However, Dhorpatan was a radically different context in terms of medical and healing facilities, where the main medical facility was the Sowa Rigpa clinic, school and pharmacy, and biomedical services were limited to a small 'sub-clinic' staffed by one woman who had received training in basic health care. In contrast, in Darjeeling, of course, there was an abundance of medical and healing facilities. During his research there in the 1990s, Jacobson found patients presenting at Sowa Rigpa clinics with 'affective, cognitive or behavioral disturbances' which were not severe enough to suggest spirit affliction, predominantly diagnosed with *srog rlung* by amchi (2007, 232–33). In this research project I took lay perceptions as my starting point, rather than necessarily the perspectives of those presenting at a Sowa Rigpa clinic, as examined by Millard and Jacobson. However, as Jacobson described, I found that lay perceptions of mental illness causation and healing amongst Tibetan informants in Darjeeling broadly reflected—but were not limited to—a number of concepts found in the Tibetan medical texts or delineated by amchi. In addition, in some instances, I found that both Tibetan and biomedical explanatory concepts were employed to explain and describe an experience of illness. As Williams and Healy have suggested, patients (and their families) often employ 'exploratory maps' in their search for meaning in the event of mental illness. We have seen that certain Tibetan notions of the individual and her relationship to the environment—and the spirits and deities that reside within it—can allow for a number of explanations of illness. In particular, Tibetan perspectives on the rather porous boundary between individuals and their environment can create both explanation and treatment pathways for those affected by certain kinds of *sems nad* and *smyo nad*. In Darjeeling, this was evident in informants' explanations of mental illness, which often included references to spirit activity. Furthermore, the Tibetan perspectives on 'controlling the mind' which I encountered reflect Tibetan notions of the mind and consciousness, highlighting the interrelationship between Tibetan cultural, religious and medical understandings of the world. Such perspectives are a result of enduring Tibetan cultural and religious concepts of not only the person and the mind, but also of the environment and an individual's relationship to it. Perhaps then, as suggested by Jacobson and Millard, some broad equivalences can be drawn, for example, between certain *rlung* conditions and DSM or ICD categories of 'depression' and 'anxiety', but I would argue that these particularly Tibetan perspectives on the individual and the broader environment only highlight the differences between the different systems. This is particularly the case in relation to the Tibetan notion of *rlung*, which holds a central role in Tibetan concepts of mental health and illness and links together a number of medical and religious concepts of the mind and body and the wider environment, and which is often the focus of mental health treatment in Sowa Rigpa. In addition, the concept of *rlung* is wrapped up with Tibetan understandings of spirit affliction and spirit-mediumship, and numerous other uniquely Tibetan concepts including *dbang thang*, *rlung rta*, *bsod nams*, *yid ches* and *dad pa* can come into play either in isolation or in conjunction with one another in the causation of illness. Here, they not only contribute to patients' and their families' exploratory maps of mental illness, but also provide paths to its healing. This material reflects the findings of previous research in the Tibetan context, which found similar explanations of non-psychiatric conditions encompassing Tibetan cultural and religious concepts (see for example Calkowski 1985; Gerke 2012a; Schrempf 2011). These local understandings of illness, which encompass a number of these uniquely Tibetan religious and cultural perspectives and activities, such as the notions of 'controlling the mind' or Buddhism's subjugation of spirits, also inform traditional coping and healing mechanisms, as we have seen.

The fieldwork material demonstrates some of the complexities, not only of the management of mental illness in a personal context, but also of the broader picture of mental illness and its healing in this medically pluralistic setting. Here, afflicted individuals and their families have a plethora of diverse medical and religious specialists to choose from, each with their own attendant worldviews, diagnostic categories and treatment pathways. Each religious and medical system has its own notions of mental health and ill-health, drawing the boundaries between these two states in different places. As we have seen in Darjeeling, for individuals experiencing mental illness and their families, multiple considerations often inform health-seeking behaviour: people need to be able to navigate the different treatment options available to them in a useful, cost-effective, and often prompt manner. In times when emergency medical care is required, this is even more important. Patients and their families need to be able to make sometimes rapid judgements about different treatment modalities, and a number of factors can come into play here, including the expected efficacy and geographical and financial accessibility of multiple healing systems. Before such treatment decisions are made however, judgements first need to be made about whether an individual is, in fact, mentally healthy or ill.

Mapping Out Boundaries of Mental 'Health' and 'Illness'

"[T]he normal" (whether described as a moral, psychiatric, or even biological concept) is not one thing; it is many. (Calabrese 2006, 25)

As patients and their families employ these kinds of exploratory 'maps' in their search for meaning and treatment, they are managing not only their own and their healing practitioners' (and perhaps also their community's) different perspectives on health and illness, but perhaps more fundamentally, the worldviews which underlie each system. The case studies described in the previous four chapters illustrate the often complex interplay between different medical systems in a medically pluralistic area such as Darjeeling, where explanatory models proposed by the different medical and healing systems may be complementary or contradictory. As has, I hope, become clear, one consequence of medically pluralistic contexts is the possibility—indeed likelihood—of being considered 'well' in one system, whilst simultaneously 'unwell' (or even 'mad') in another. Kleinman has described diagnostic interpretation as a 'culturally constrained activity' by practitioners (1991, 9), and of course this is true for patients too, as they attempt to make sense of their experience of mental illness. As we have seen, boundaries between 'sanity' and 'insanity' are inconsistent across both time and culture. Definitions, understandings and interpretations change and adapt in response to broader cultural shifts and changes. This process is a result of innumerable factors, such as current philosophical views on the mind and body and the relationship between them; scientific understanding(s), knowledge and trends; and contemporary cultural norms along with their historical background. Here, context is all: as we have seen, individuals possessed by spirits are considered 'ill' in some cultures but not in others and, even within one culture, sub-groups may view phenomena differently. The patient's own experience of her condition will be mediated by her own interpretation of it, which will be dependent—at least in part—on the views of those around her (both professional and lay) (Kleinman 1991, 7).

In Bali, Connor argued that an afflicted individual's identity could change from him being considered in possession of a 'divinely ordained state of knowledge' to a psychiatric inpatient, depending on which type of healing practitioner he consulted (1982, 784), and this was also evident in the case of Dechen, discussed in the previous chapter. In her case, different individuals within her community held fundamentally different perspectives on cultural 'norms'. For Kleinman, diagnostic interpretation—the fit of a patient's experience into a taxonomic slot—is good 'only insofar as it is therapeutically useful' (1991, 9). With one biomedical doctor claiming that there was nothing wrong with Dechen, another local biomedical practitioner suggesting that most cases of mediumship were a form of psychosis, and traditional methods of dealing with such a condition ineffective in this instance, Dechen found herself in a kind of 'limbo'. Here, her condition was explained by a number of different perspectives, but none of these were able to offer much in the way of treatment or resolution.

An appraisal of 'sanity' or 'insanity' then, is defined not only by the perceptions of the individual, but also those of other members of his community and also of the medical or religious professionals whose help he may seek. Alarcón et al. note the fundamental role a sick individual's family play in relaying 'cultural messages regarding the interpretation and explanation of events that cause behavioral disturbances, their actual presentation, and the strategies patients choose to handle them' (2002, 244). Does a Tibetan patient in Darjeeling exhibiting strange behaviour and hallucinations have *smyo nad* or psychosis? It will depend on which kind of healing practitioner(s) she consults. If we follow Kleinman's assertion that 'disease' is 'the way practitioners recast illness in terms of their theoretical models of pathology' (1991, 7), then *smyo nad* and 'psychosis' might either be equivalent (in terms of symptoms), or different (in terms of perceptions of cause and treatment). Kleinman argues that a psychiatric diagnosis is an '*interpretation* of a person's experience'. That interpretation may differ systematically for all of those involved, including the patient himself, the members of his family and the practitioners he consults. In addition to cultural changes in terms of philosophical and scientific understandings of the body and mind as we saw in Chapter Five, disease boundaries may also be manipulated and altered.[1] Conditions thus become 'medicalised' or 'normalised' according to prevailing interests.

Managing Diverse Worldviews in a Medically Pluralistic Context

Within this medically pluralistic context in Darjeeling then, there exist multiple definitions and explanations of mental health and illness, with the boundaries between them drawn in different places. As we saw, in some cases, such as Jigme's, common local explanations of illness were directly at odds with

---

1. Indeed, such 'alteration' may even occur at the instigation of outside interests with profits to be made—see, for example, work on the role of pharmaceutical companies in the 'making' of various forms of 'disease' by Cassels and Moynihan 2005; Moynihan, Heath and Henry 2002; Moynihan and Henry 2006.

professional perspectives—both those of amchi and biomedical doctors. In others, there were significant overlaps, for example in explanations of Lobsang's *srog rlung*/depression, which was understood to have been caused by stress and worry. Within this pluralistic context then, how do patients and their families make sense of their experience of mental illness? Loizzo, Blackhall and Rapgay have suggested that Tibetan medicine's 'models, methods, and predictions differ so dramatically from those of conventional Western medicine' as to render them 'completely incompatible' (2009, 224). In some cases, such as Lobsang's, the multitude of explanatory frameworks offered by different systems did not seem to present a problem. For him, the diagnoses of *rlung, sems nad* and depression seemed to be equally valid, and did not appear to present any contradictions. For Pema, her mother's condition, despite its apparent similarity (at least in terms of symptoms) to a psychotic episode, was mainly described through the Tibetan term of *sems nad* and the rather generic English term 'madness'. A biomedical doctor well-known to the family was consulted, and when the prescribed treatment did not help, treatment ceased and a religious practitioner was consulted, with no apparent conflict in using these two different systems.

Hepburn argues that 'inadequate communication' between practitioners and patients who do not share a common background or mutual expectations 'directly contributes to low rates of patient compliance', suggesting that such problems are 'greatly magnified' where patients 'do not understand biomedicine and may operate with a plethora of other theoretical systems and expectations' (1988, 64). In Darjeeling, in some cases, this did not seem to be a problem, and we saw for example that Lobsang engaged with his prescribed biomedical treatment without any apparent concerns. In other cases, the situation was rather different, and fundamental differences between Western and non-Western treatment approaches and practitioner-patient interactions may create misunderstandings and tensions, so that even where biomedicine has been effective, a lack of understanding with regard to expectations (or limitations) of the treatment may lead to difficulties. We saw this in Migmar's case, where he ceased his biomedical treatment—which had been working—on the advice of another practitioner, a local *jhānkri* with a different perspective on the cause of his condition. A rather more extreme example of this was discussed by Dr. Sharma in Gangtok. He described the case of a patient of his whom he had diagnosed and treated as 'bipolar' (an abbreviation of 'bipolar affective disorder', (F31), grouped under 'mood [affective] disorders' in the ICD-10 (WHO 2010a)[2]). The patient, a university student, had responded very well to the

---

2. http://apps.who.int/classifications/icd10/browse/2010/en#/F30-F39.

prescribed pharmacological treatment but had then relapsed due to stress, leading her parents to conclude that the biomedical treatment was no longer working, and her ceasing to take it. Instead, her parents had taken her to a local
monastery where, he told me, she had been 'beaten black and blue' with a stick
by a monk's assistant.[3] When this 'treatment' was also unsuccessful in treating
their daughter, they brought her back to Dr. Sharma, who reported that she
had turned up covered in bruises, whereupon he adjusted her medication to
good effect. Whilst this sort of violent treatment is unusual (as far as I could
work out), it is a good illustration of some of the difficulties of navigating a
path to health within an arena of competing worldviews and their
accompanying explanatory frameworks, where patients and their families may
not be clear on expectations or prognoses. Here, a misunderstanding about
what to expect from illness and its treatment (for example, the notion of 'stress'
as a trigger for the relapse) led to some quite drastic, and harmful, action from
the religious practitioner whom they consulted for help. This rather upsetting
narrative is a—quite extreme—indication of the contemporary situation for
Tibetans in ethnically and medically pluralistic communities such as this, where
'exploratory maps' may include numerous threads of—sometimes conflicting—causative explanations through which they must navigate a path for treatment. At the biomedical Delek Hospital in Dharamsala, Dr. Sadutshang
suggested to me that some traditional perceptions of health and illness amongst
Tibetans could cause problems, explaining that sometimes, 'spiritual beliefs'
might prevent patients from consulting doctors: 'Not being educated, they
don't have the concept that this is an illness'. In fact, in Darjeeling, I found
that a number of affected individuals did indeed perceive their condition as an
illness, but subsequently found biomedicine to be an ineffective treatment for
them. We saw that Wangmo, for example, initially consulted a biomedical doctor, but found that the prescribed medicines did not help sufficiently, and she
sought religious help, which was far more successful. Similarly, Lhamo
described the ineffectiveness of biomedicine in treating Lhakpa's spirit possession, which had ultimately been successfully treated by her friend, a lama. In
Dechen's case, she had found that biomedical practitioners declared there to
be nothing wrong with her and could do nothing to help, despite her feeling
that she might be 'going mad'. In other cases, it was explained by informants

---

3. The Tibetan amchi and author Khangkar describes 'beating' as a possible treatment
for some cases of 'insanity': 'not enough to hurt the person but to give a sense of fright'
(2009, 119) I should note however, that I did not come across any other stories of this, and
Amchi Sonam Dolma was clear in assuring me that this is not an accepted treatment in Tibetan medicine.

that biomedical doctors were unable to help because they did not understand the cause of an illness. Earlier, I briefly described the case of Nyima's neighbour, whom he reported had died as a result of a Rai spirit affliction. In this case, he explained, biomedical doctors—unaware of the spirit cause—were unable to treat her. Calabrese has described the 'increasingly multicultural composition of contemporary societies' which has led to healthcare providers and other institutions facing a 'plethora of unfamiliar voices and claims that they are often ill equipped to comprehend' (2006, 24). In cases such as these in Darjeeling, however, the health care provider—who may very well be from the same community as the patient—is not necessarily 'unfamiliar' with such perspectives, but may instead find himself working within a system which allows no space for them.

Within this medically pluralistic context, as practitioners, patients and their families attempt to find ways to make sense of and manage their—often very distressing—symptoms, perceptions of the different medical systems and their utility and limitations will feed into this process. For example, a number of Tibetan informants in Darjeeling described a general delineation between biomedicine and Tibetan medicine as best for the treatment of 'acute' and 'chronic' conditions respectively, and I found some aspects of biomedical treatment to be more well-known than others. For example, when I discussed biomedical treatments for mental illness with Tibetan informants, several individuals immediately mentioned ECT, describing it as 'torture' or 'shock'. When I discussed the use of biomedicine for cases of *smyo nad* with Dolkar (55) she responded that 'it sometimes works, sometimes again goes bad [in other words, the person relapses].... Maybe because of torture—electric'. She mimed someone receiving ECT, explaining, 'Tibetans don't like to go to hospital, because of this [ECT]—it makes it worse'. Metok (63), a former biomedical nurse, agreed; 'If a person goes to [biomedical] hospital, the hospital will do shock—then they [the patient] get much worse'.[4]

Several interviewees felt that mental illnesses experienced by Tibetans were different from those experienced in the West, making Western-derived treatments inappropriate in such cases. When I asked Metok about 'schizophrenia' and 'psychosis', and whether she felt they were equivalent conditions to *smyo*

---

4. I noted previously that one local psychiatrist regarded this as a 'wonder treatment'. However, research has found that while ECT can be effective in the short term for depression, there is little evidence of long term efficacy, and even less evidence of its efficacy in treating psychotic illnesses such as schizophrenia or mania (Greenhalgh et al. 2005). Despite this, as we can see here, it was a treatment which was not only familiar to a number of my informants, but had even come to define 'Western medicine' for some of them.

nad (knowing that she was familiar with these English terms from her former nursing training in the UK), she answered,

> No—I don't think so. I never heard of this [psychosis] among Tibetans—I think we don't have this because of Buddhism.... The moment you feel not well your family take you to a monastery, do blessings, Tibetan medicine, *smyung gnas* [fasting] retreat, [do] *mani* [prayers] for many days.... [Your family] treat you very gently and smoothly—there is always someone looking after you.... They don't take you to Western hospital for medicines, or ECT.

Others too were sure that biomedicine could not help in such cases, with Tibetan approaches likely to be more successful. Norbu (35) explained, 'There's no Western medicine for this [*smyo nad*] ... [but] Tibetan medicine and *rinchen rilbu* can be successful for this'. His opinion was echoed by Phurpu (50), who discussed the case of a young neighbour with *smyo nad*, and concluded definitively that, 'There's no Western medicine for this—[you must] do *pūjā*, mantra, prayers'. Urgen (39) agreed: 'Lamas can treat your illness—you don't need to go to a doctor.... Some lamas can help with treatment for *smyon pa*.... Medicine probably—usually—doesn't work'. I asked if he was referring to 'Tibetan medicine' or 'Western medicine', and he replied, 'Both. I have seen this place where patients stay [a biomedical psychiatric unit]. I don't think they are giving medicines—just teaching them how to be.... I think Western medicines only work for ten percent [of patients]'.

However, in contrast to views such as these, in Darjeeling, as we saw, a number of individuals and their families did in fact consult biomedical practitioners. Some sought the help of biomedical doctors early on in the event of mental illness—particularly in situations of acute illness, such as was the case with Wangmo and Dechen—whereas others consulted such medical specialists only after other treatments had not significantly helped, for example in the case of Lobsang. I would argue that whilst the majority of informants held a fairly pessimistic view of biomedicine's ability to treat cases of *sems nad* in theory, in practice, when faced with an acute case, they may in fact be likely to consult a biomedical practitioner anyway, as part of their broad-ranging efforts to manage this very difficult situation. Indeed, lay individuals' approaches to health-seeking behaviour appeared to be highly pragmatic, at times consulting a number of practitioners whose perspectives appeared to be situated in apparently opposing systems, and I will examine these aspects of health-seeking behaviour next.

Pragmatism and the Myth of 'Rationality':
Health-Seeking Behaviour in Darjeeling

In Darjeeling, as we saw, individuals' treatment choices were often con-strained to different degrees by factors such as personal finances and/or the availability of local services. This was particularly evident in the availability of biomedical treatments in the area—where interventions were predominantly limited to medication—and the lack of Tibetan spirit-medi-ums, which was mentioned by a number of informants. Previous research within Tibetan communities has demonstrated that patients' health-seeking behaviour is often driven by pragmatic rather than ideological concerns, such as perceived efficacy and practicalities such as cost and geographical proximity. For example, in Darjeeling, Jacobson found the cost of biomedical treatment often mentioned as a factor in its abandonment by patients (2000, 509). Sim-ilarly, working in Amdo, Schrempf argued that particularly in rural areas, Ti-betans' 'pragmatic concerns'—such as the accessibility of certain types of medicines, consultation of a 'trusted' doctor, or the 'success or failure of a particular medical technique or system after an initial unsuccessful resort'—overrode any others (2011, 165). In addition, she suggested that financial or social constraints, or a knowledge or lack of Chinese language might also be factors, where rural Tibetan patients 'rarely seem to seek out a particular med-ical system for ideological reasons' (Schrempf 2011, 165–66). I too found that these factors were clearly a consideration for patients and their families in Darjeeling. Many Tibetans in the area were not well off financially, and the costs of different treatments therefore often had a significant bearing on their likely uptake.

As in many societies, a number of Tibetan informants narrated the use of multiple (religious and/or medical) treatment options simultaneously, as Metok explained: 'When we get sick we do *pūjā* and treatment together'. However, others narrated stories more similar to Wangmo's and Lobsang's, where the consultation of different healers was undertaken consecutively, and patients (and their families) often clearly delineated the different remits of the healers and their treatments. In addition, a number of Tibetans discussed the need to consult a diviner to determine which kind of practitioner to visit, or at which hospital to have a needed operation, in a reflection on Schrempf's findings (on non-psychiatric illness) in Amdo (2011). Such descriptions of health-seeking behaviour echo Jacobson's findings in relation to *srog rlung*, where most of his Tibetan informants with this diagnosis combined a number of different 'treat-ment modalities', with four out of the six informants consulting both biomedical doctors and amchi, and four consulting both lama and amchi (2000, 494–97).

Many of the Tibetans I spoke to in Darjeeling had strongly held perceptions of the appropriateness of different healing methods for different types of illness. For example, as has been reported by others (see, for example, Samuel in Dalhousie 2009; Wangda 1996), biomedicine was viewed by many as a fast-acting treatment for conditions such as colds and coughs or sleeping problems. In comparison, Tibetan medicine was often seen as a slower-acting, longer-term treatment, with many people explaining to me that it 'cuts the roots of the disease', treating the cause of an illness. It was especially mentioned in relation to chronic conditions such as arthritis, digestive problems or *rlung*-related illnesses. As Samten (42) explained, 'For emergency, I take allopathic medicine; for non-emergency, definitely take Tibetan medicine — Tibetan medicine is especially good for old diseases … chronic diseases'. Thus for an acute episode of mental illness, such as Wangmo's sudden-onset 'madness', it is perhaps not surprising for family members to initially consult a biomedical doctor, as her family did for her. Nonetheless, in a number of the cases of mental illness that I have discussed, religious practitioners were the first point of call for patients and their families, and the fieldwork material demonstrates how religious perceptions of causation often predominated in conditions such as *sems nad* and *smyo nad*. In addition, even when there was not understood to be a particular religious cause of a mental health condition, patients and/or their families often still consulted a religious practitioner, sometimes alongside other medical practitioners. In Migmar's case, his parents had consulted a number of healing practitioners one by one, whose treatments had helped to different degrees. Interestingly however, he had ceased his biomedical treatment when advised to do so by a *jhānkri*, suggesting that he and his family placed a significant amount of faith in this local religious practitioner's advice, even when the biomedical treatment appeared to be helping to at least some degree. When I asked Migmar's neighbour, Tsering (59), which treatment he thought had helped, he said he was not sure: perhaps the *jhānkri* had helped, but so had the rinpoche's blessings, in addition to the application of a nutmeg poultice, which had certainly helped him to sleep. Similarly, when I asked Phurpu how he and his family navigated the numerous treatment options in the event of illness, he laughed, telling me, 'It's not a problem — you just go to them all!' Whilst there was certainly an element of jest in his response, it does highlight the fact that generally speaking, in such discussions with Tibetan informants, the emphasis was not on the question of which treatment had been successful, but rather on the very fact of the successful outcome. Indeed, the often numerous treatments may all be understood to have been of some utility.

Hepburn claims that in non-Western countries health-seeking behaviour often involves 'a pattern of healer consultation that is usually explicitly pluralistic, with many types of healers considered to be legitimate' (1988, 64), and this was certainly evident in a number of cases I saw. Furthermore, practitioners do not operate in a vacuum of course, and in Darjeeling it was not uncommon for one medical or healing specialist to refer patients to another practitioner or healing system when they felt it might be more efficacious for the patient. For example, at the MTK clinic in Sonada, I listened as Amchi Lobsang Thubten advised one elderly man to take some biomedicine for his very high blood pressure (alongside the Tibetan medicine he prescribed for his osteoarthritis), explaining that 'it works very quickly' to bring the blood pressure down. Indeed, concepts regarding the differing 'remits' of Tibetan medicine and biomedicine as described above are often shared by Tibetan practitioners and, in Lhasa, Adams and Li claim that the practitioners of both Tibetan medicine and biomedicine were able to integrate the practices of the other tradition into their care of patients (despite simultaneously claiming that the two traditions were incommensurable) (2008, 106).

This delineation of the boundaries of Tibetan medicine (as good for 'chronic' conditions) and biomedicine (as good for 'acute' conditions), can aid in swiftly and pragmatically navigating the plural medical environment in Darjeeling. Hepburn argues that such a pattern of 'differential choice of traditional and biomedical practitioners for chronic and acute conditions respectively' is common in many non-Western societies (1988, 69). However, such pluralistic thinking in regard to medicine, of course, is also evident in Western societies, as we saw in Chapter Five. There, despite the predominance of biomedicine, there remains a broad diversity in individuals' motives with regard to health-seeking behaviour (Hepburn 1988, 70).

For some of my informants in Darjeeling then, health-seeking behaviour was quite pragmatic, and individuals and their families often appeared to move easily between the different medical and healing systems. This reflects Ruwanpura et al.'s findings in Dharamsala, where they described the 'ease' with which Tibetan informants combined 'diverse coping strategies' in the treatment of mental illness (2006, 198). They found that most of the Tibetan torture survivors they spoke to utilised diverse — often 'fundamentally different' — treatment strategies to alleviate their distress with little or no conflict (2006, 194–95). In Amdo, Schrempf observed that Tibetan patients' health-seeking behaviour was also a method of making meaning of their situation (2011, 172–73), echoing Evans-Pritchard's classic analysis of health and illness among the Azande where, while 'practical reasons' were frequently given to explain the immediate causes of an illness, supernatural causes were often invoked to answer the question of 'Why me?' (1937). Indeed, Summerfield argues that when a biomedical diagnosis such as 'depression' is given to non-Western populations, it may have 'little power to explain their problems' (2008, 993). For example, 'loneliness' might explain in part why Wangmo became ill, but it does not explain why it was she—and not any of the other mothers of children who had moved away—who was particularly affected by this. Similarly, whilst it was agreed that Dechen's condition was the result of the activity of a *lha*, this does not explain why the spirit affected *her* rather than anyone else.

I discussed in Chapter Eight some of the different—often co-occurring—*rgyu* and *rkyen* which can cause and contribute to illness. Bearing in mind the coexistence of such multiple causative and contributory factors, it of course makes sense to utilise different treatment methods to address the various factors involved in a case of illness. Thus, in the event of mental illness, biomedicine may be ingested for its ability to deal with the symptoms of an illness or calm down an acute episode, Buddhist practices might be conducted for their role in improving one's karma or *dbang thang*, rituals might be conducted by a local *lha bzhugs mkhan* or monastic practitioner to appease local spirits or to improve one's *rlung rta* and Tibetan medicine may be taken to 'cut the roots of the disease'. In fact, as Wagner et al. argue, in relation to ways of thinking about mental illness (in this context, in a large north Indian city),

> [I]t is not unusual for people to express contradictions in discourse, because they do not live in a single homogenous world, but in many worlds each of which requires its own distinct form of discourse and thought. It is in the context of different life-worlds that holding on to 'contradictory' representations makes sense (2000, 303–04).

This notion of 'cognitive polyphasia' that they discuss (2000, 310–11) was originally proposed by Moscovici (1961). Described by Provencher, Arthi and Wagner as implying a 'dynamic coexistence of different modalities of knowledge within the same group and, even, within the same individual vis-à-vis a given social object' (2012, 1.1), it was perhaps a precursor to Williams and Healy's notion of 'exploratory maps', illustrating why patients are likely to employ a number of explanations simultaneously or in short succession. Provencher, Arthi and Wagner point to Lévy-Bruhl's argument that 'different logics can, and indeed do, co-exist side by side because of the different functions they play' (2012, 1.4), particularly in a 'world characterised by the co-existence of different modes of knowledge, each representative of different ways of life and different traditions' (2012, 1.9). I would argue that this is even more evident in cases of mental illness, which is inherently hard to categorise and where, as we have seen, traditional causative explanations and treatment methods may span the spheres of both medicine and religion.

Nevertheless, it was apparent that in many cases in Darjeeling, there was no straight line evident between the perceived cause(s) of the illness and the treatments sought. Specifically, sometimes there appeared to be a greater number of healing methods employed than there were thought to be causes. For example, while Wangmo's family felt that her condition was most likely caused by 'sadness' and 'worry', we find the perceived cause of the illness little related to the medical and healing strategies which were sought out. Presumably it was not possible for Pema to move back home (her absence having been perceived as the precipitator of her mother's illness), and instead her family consulted a biomedical doctor and then a religious practitioner. Similarly, in Dharamsala, Ruwanpura et al. found that Tibetan interviewees' coping strategies for mental illness or distress were 'notably more varied' than their causative explanations (2006, 197). They suggest that generally, 'holding fundamentally different beliefs about causation but seeking a form of treatment which did not coincide with those beliefs did not seem to cause any problems' for their Tibetan informants (2006, 200). Where such an approach might be viewed as rather 'non-rational' in Western scientific discourse, Hepburn argues that such actions are 'non-rational' 'only in terms of Weber's very narrow definition of rationality, which expressed the sentiment of his and our age that the most technically efficient action is the most rational' (1988, 67). Hepburn follows Habermas' (1971) claim that individuals have many goals, which may be pursued separately or simultaneously, where people are 'seeking a full understanding of their sickness experience as it relates to their many diverse interests' (1988, 67). A pluralistic system thus reflects the way that people think in complex ways about mental illness, as they explore their way through their experience of illness. This was evident in Tibetan informants' explanations of *sems nad* which included reference to a number of specifically Tibetan and more general concepts, including *rlung*, *dbang thang*, sadness and worry. Similarly, in Patna, north India, Wagner et al. found that traditional and biomedical explanations of madness 'have their place in different contexts. Each of the two representations is situated at different nodes of the respondents' social world' (1999, 441). Individuals hold personal and sometimes perhaps idiosyncratic perspectives on their illness which inform their health-seeking behaviour to a greater or lesser extent depending on the circumstances. These may not be 'rational' in the Weberian sense, but are in fact perfectly 'rational' from the perspective of the afflicted individual. If a sickness is the result of multiple factors (such as financial worries, bereavement or family history of depression in the Western context, or *rlung* or karma in the Tibetan context), then it actually makes perfect 'rational' sense to seek treatment from a variety of practitioners with different remits, each able to deal with different aspects of the illness.

'Integration' and Patient Choice

Evidently then, lay Tibetan informants in Darjeeling were often integrating a number of different worldviews and their attendant classification and treatment systems, consulting multiple specialists (both religious and medical) and incorporating several different treatment methods concurrently in their endeavours to make sense of and treat episodes of mental illness. In Chapter Nine, for example, I described Gyaltsen's attempt to explain Dechen's experience of mediumship through biomedical notions of the brain. Similarly in Dharamsala, Prost described some complex explanations given by informants regarding their illness, such as the case of tuberculosis (TB), where concepts of *'bu* (insect), 'bacillus' and the *nyes pa* were combined to explain its causation (2007, 49). In Darjeeling, as I have described here, several informants demonstrated a more or less integrative approach to health-seeking behaviour, consulting a number of practitioners from different medical and healing systems concurrently or consecutively. Unfortunately, but perhaps not surprisingly, more formal attempts at integration have often proved more problematic.

Back in 1978, the WHO suggested that the integration of biomedical and traditional healing systems 'offered reciprocal benefit to each system' (1978, 18), and argued that effective integration in medicine entailed a 'synthesis of the merits of both the traditional and the so-called "Western" or modern systems of medicine', suggesting that this 'requires a flexible system capable of accommodating individual skills and varying levels of knowledge and education', where 'mutual respect, recognition and collaboration' between the practitioners from the different systems is ensured (1978, 16). In Dharamsala, I interviewed Dr. Sadutshang, Chief Medical Officer of the biomedical Delek Hospital, located just below the town. He was keen to stress the 'integrative' approach he said existed between the different healing systems in the area, describing the hospital's 'long-standing interaction' with the MTK, and their 'aim to provide some sort of integrated care to our patients'. This also extended to the medical staff, with hospital doctors 'teaching MTK doctors and medical students on Western medicine topics', and MTK students interning at the Delek Hospital. He told me that a MTK doctor came regularly to the hospital to treat TB patients, as Tibetan medicine was particularly good at treating the side effects and co-morbidity of TB.[5] He explained that they were 'developing a trusting relationship with Tibetan medicine and Western medicine', in which

---

5. TB is perhaps a special case, due to its high prevalence in the Tibetan community (which was also mentioned by Tibetan informants in Darjeeling) and the Indian government's explicit strategy to deal with it.

he encouraged spiritual practice in the hospital, such as allowing monks to
come in and conduct rituals for patients and their families. He described how
they had collaborated on the (now defunct) Transcultural Psychosocial Organisation (TPO) Tibetan Torture Survivors' Project, which had utilised 'every resource we had on an equal level', in addition to integration which was occurring
on a more 'informal basis'. He explained:

> It's all about respecting each other—you just can't rubbish away cen-
> turies of belief.... You shouldn't be tunnel-visioned ... I would like
> to see the bigger picture with mental problems—you have to see the
> whole picture.... As the Dalai Lama says—the science of the mind is
> in an infantile stage—we don't know yet—we know very little—there
> is a lot to learn.

In addition, a certain amount of integration of medicine has been promoted
by the MTK in some areas in, for example, amchi's use of sphygmomanometers
alongside pulse diagnosis in Spiti (Besch 2006, 292).[6] But the situation is often
rather complex—especially where Tibetan medicine and biomedicine start to
contradict each other and practitioners may have to 'choose a side', and where
patients may bring their own expectations of treatment. In Qinghai in the PRC,
for example, Adams, Dhondup and Le describe the interesting situation at the
Arura Tibetan Medical Hospital, whereby amchi utilised both biomedical and
Tibetan diagnostic methods, ignoring biomedical diagnostic information in one
situation and Tibetan in another. Here, one amchi described overlooking blood
pressure readings when they contradicted his own Tibetan pulse diagnosis. In
contrast, in cases where ultrasound scan results contradicted his Tibetan
diagnoses, he sometimes gave preference to this Western system. Another amchi
described biomedical tests as sometimes 'not very useful in diagnosing accurately',
but useful for 'appeasing and instilling confidence in [Chinese] patients who expected this kind of medical encounter' (2011, 113–15). And, in the context of
India, I would suggest that the kind of considered but informal integrative approach which Dr. Sadutshang described was fairly unique to Dharamsala. It was
likely a result of a combination of factors, such as the area's overtly political backdrop, Tibetan exile identity politics, and the influence of outside funding and
interests. A more formal attempt at an integrative health project in Dharamsala
had been less successful, and several researchers have discussed the problems encountered by those who set up the Tibetan Torture Survivors' Project in Dharam-

---

6. In fact, the use of sphygmomanometers seems to be common amongst many amchi.
Samuel notes its use in Dalhousie (2001, 252–53), and I have described already its use by
amchi in Darjeeling.

sala. Founded in 1995 by a Western NGO in collaboration with the Tibetan government-in-exile, it sought to integrate Western and traditional Tibetan approaches to healing, specifically through Western-style 'counselling' methods and Tibetan herbal medicines (Mercer, Ager and Ruwanpura 2004). The project encountered resistance from the outset from high level Tibetan officials, with some viewing it as a threat to traditional Tibetan culture and coping mechanisms (Mercer, Ager and Ruwanpura 2004, 181–86). In addition, the founders were beset with practical problems related to cultural norms of expected and acceptable behaviour and the training of Tibetan staff in the entirely unfamiliar practice of Western-style counselling. Indeed, Calabrese argues that the 'calm, rational discussions characteristic of Euro-American talk therapy' are not widely-used in healing in the majority of human societies (2006, 29; see also Kirmayer 2007). Instead, 'psychotherapeutic intervention' is 'typically communal', utilising 'dramatic ritual ordeals' and altered states of consciousness (Calabrese 2006, 175). Certainly, this seems to have been the case here: some of the Tibetans who accessed the project in Dharamsala struggled with this Western approach, with one recipient of the service, an ex-political prisoner, likening the counselling to 'interrogation'. Nevertheless, the individual in question did report a positive experience overall, concluding that the treatment was 'quite effective' (Mercer, Ager and Ruwanpura 2005, 182–85).

In Darjeeling, despite Indian government support for 'traditional' medical systems, there have been no formalised attempts at integrative medicine that I am aware of, and practitioners may or may not refer patients to other healing specialists, depending on their own personal views. Thus, whilst some amchi and one local *mata-ji* described referring patients to biomedical doctors when they felt biomedical treatment would be more suitable or efficacious, it was notable that none of the biomedical doctors I interviewed discussed referring their patients to any non-biomedical practitioners. Talking to Dr. Ghosh, the resident psychiatrist at the government hospital in Darjeeling, it was clear that his view on mental illness was entirely biomedical. He mentioned only that sometimes when someone starts to 'behave strangely', often the individual or their family go initially to a monastery, temple or church, leading to a delay before they seek medical help, and thus rendering it much harder to treat them with biomedicine. Similarly, when I related the common explanation of Jigme's illness being the result of his father's actions to Dr. Sharma in Gangtok, he described this belief as a 'shared religious delusion … carried and shared by the whole community', to which the only solution was anti-psychotic medication for the patient. In addition, there was simply not the infrastructure in place for collaboration between different healing practices in Darjeeling, where psychiatrists (particularly those not local to the area) may be unfamiliar with local and/or Tibetan healing practices and medical theory. And, as we saw in Chapter Five, different notions of 'efficacy' and 'cure' can mean that when discussing health or the effects of healing, different practitioners may be referring to quite divergent or contradictory factors (Geest 1995, 362). Tibetan amchi I spoke to in Darjeeling and Dharamsala were divided over whether Tibetan medicine needed to 'prove' its efficacy through 'Western science', as they described it, or whether it was enough for Tibetan medicine to 'prove' itself through its own scientific method. In Darjeeling, Amchi Teinlay argued, 'some young Tibetan doctors try to explain Tibetan medicine according to Western science. Actually I think it's better if you keep it pure, and do not "dilute" it'.

Integrative health projects may also have unintended negative effects on traditional healing systems. Besch argues that in Spiti, the very existence of an alternative diagnostic system has devalued the local amchi's authority (as well as his social standing) and brought a power-shift in the relationship between amchi and patient (2006, 292, 314). In Bali, Connor noted that 'cultural and political pressures which reinforce present psychiatric practices are so great that they threaten not only to overwhelm recognition of the pragmatic value of traditional therapies, but also the very survival of such practices' (1982, 791). And in Lhasa, Adams and Li found that 'integration' at the Mentsikhang 'most often means adopting biomedical standards and authority and eliminating perceptions that Tibetan medicine is capable of advancing on its own, by its own rules or standards', thus rendering Tibetan medicine 'a second-best option—effective but limited, inexpensive but time-consuming' (2008, 128). Perhaps through a similar process, Prost notes that where they *are* compatible with biomedical concepts, a number of Tibetan medical concepts have been given a new salience (2007).

Traditional healers and Western health planners may go into an integrative health project with very different objectives, thus concurrently following their own—perhaps divergent—agendas, where even those health planners with the best intentions are sometimes inadvertently driving this process of 'biomedicalisation' through such projects (Geest 1995, 363). Kirmayer asserts that in reality, 'international collaborations have largely amounted to concerted efforts to export the practices of British and Anglo-American psychiatry to far corners of the world, including some of the … bad ideas that plague Western psychiatry' (2006, 136). Indeed, Connor asks whether this sort of integration should take place at all 'if the consequences are the expropriation of control from indigenous healers, both in their role as therapists and as influential members of their communities' (1982, 792). Such integrative projects then, can significantly impact on the availability of different treatments and patient choice. In Darjeeling, as we saw, patients often took a multi-faceted approach to health-seeking behaviour, employing a number of different explanatory frameworks and consulting several religious and medical practitioners concurrently, in response to the different causative and contributory factors understood to be involved in an episode of mental illness. Whilst a number of informants found biomedical treatment to be beneficial to greater or lesser degrees, they also valued other—more traditional—approaches. If traditional approaches to healing become limited, this may have a significant impact not only on patients' health-seeking behaviour, but also on their attempts to make sense of their illness experience in relation to the broader Tibetan perspectives on the person and the environment which underlie their understandings of mental health, illness and healing.

* * *

In the midst of this complex medically and culturally pluralistic situation in Darjeeling then, are patients—and their families—attempting to make sense of their illness experience and find ways to manage and/or treat it through the use of one or more of these different medical and healing systems. With mental illness often particularly difficult to understand and treat, perhaps a pluralistic medical system which includes a number of different models of mental illness can be an advantage for some patients as they explore different explanatory frameworks in their attempts to manage and treat their condition—allowing the creation of exploratory 'maps' as they navigate a path through their experience of mental illness within the context of their broader perspective of the world and their place within it. Clearly, for many lay Tibetan individuals in Darjeeling, the fact that the different models of mental illness offered opposing causative explanations was not necessarily a barrier to treatment. However, for others, this led to receiving contradictory advice from different specialists, which likely made an already distressing situation more difficult for patients and their families.

As we saw, for some Tibetan informants, differential diagnoses offered by different medical and healing systems did not cause any significant problems, and there were evidently some similarities between Tibetan and biomedical perspectives on mental illness in some cases. However, I would argue that—despite some valiant attempts, such as Jacobson's endeavour to locate *rlung* 'roughly on the nosological map' (2007, 236)—the Tibetan and biomedical categories remain difficult to correlate. We saw that in some cases of illness, such as Lobsang's, Tibetan and biomedical diagnoses were comparable, whilst in others, such as Dechen's, they were clearly not. Furthermore, I would argue that when these cases are situated in the wider context of Tibetan theories of anatomy, health and illness, these perspectives are incommensurable. Significantly different worldviews on the microcosm and macrocosm lead to very different understandings of the individual and the world around him—the 'embedded ecology' of Tibetan life—which inform perspectives on mental health and illness. The most obvious example of this in the Tibetan context is perhaps the Tibetan notion of spirits and deities and their relationships to humans, based upon the understanding of the eighth-century Buddhist 'transformation' of the Tibetan landscape. However, the Tibetan concept of *rlung* comes to mind here too—where notions of the mind, body and consciousness are mediated by this fundamental aspect of the anatomy which is so very different from biomedical concepts. Here, the *rlung* currents—particularly the *srog rlung*—are involved in mental health conditions from mild *sems nad*, 'depression' and sadness to severe *smyo nad* and hallucinations, in a continuum very different from the DSM and ICD categorisation into diagnoses such as 'depression', 'anxiety', 'bipolar' and 'schizophrenia'.

What is notable is that in some instances of mental illness in Darjeeling, despite the multitude of explanatory frameworks and available treatments, there appeared to be no efficacious treatment or resolution for the afflicted individual. In Jigme's case, for example, none of the treatments he had been prescribed had enabled him to partake in 'normal' Tibetan life within the community. In Dechen's case too, none of the biomedical or Tibetan (medical or religious) practitioners she had consulted had been able to improve her situation to any significant degree. Cases such as these only highlight the difficulties for patients and practitioners in dealing with these types of conditions involving *sems*— the 'mind' or 'consciousness'. I would therefore suggest that further ethnographic research on Tibetan understandings on *sems nad* and *smyo nad* is required, to elucidate in more detail the everyday reality for individuals affected by mental illnesses related to the different *nyes pa*, and to examine where these perspectives and experiences fit into the 'global mental health' arena.

Glossary of Tibetan Terms

'Dod chags: attachment, desire; one of the (afflictive) mental factors or afflictive emotions (Tib.: *nyon mongs*) of ignorance (Tib.: *gti mug*), attachment (Tib.: *'dod chags*) and aversion (Tib.: *zhe sdang*), which are often described as the ultimate underlying causes of both physical and mental diseases

'Brel ba: connection or relationship between phenomena and people. This is often used in relation to karma (Tib.: *las*)

'Khor lo: energy centres, chakras. Part of the Tibetan 'subtle body' anatomy, these are located along the central channel, which runs from the crown of the head to the base of the spine

Am chi, em chi: 'amchi', traditional Tibetan doctor. This Tibetan term is one of the most common to refer to practitioners of Sowa Rigpa, and it was the term most used by Tibetan informants in Darjeeling

Bad kan: phlegm, one of the three *nyes pa*, disturbance in which can lead to illness

bLa: vitality, life-force. Usually residing inside the body, this needs to be ritually recalled if it leaves, as its absence will leave the affected individual open to spiritual harm

bLa ma: lama, senior religious practitioner, spiritual teacher

Bod: Tibetan name for Tibet

Bod sman: Tibetan medicine (this was the most common term used by Tibetans in Darjeeling to refer to this)

bSangs: smoke-offering to local gods (often juniper)

bShad rGyud: Explanatory (Second) Tantra, the second treatise of the *rGyud bZhi*

bSod nams: merit, good karma

bTsan: a particular kind of unenlightened deity. Often understood to be the spirits of monks who lived in past times who were subdued by a Buddhist practitioner to act as guardians of Tibetan Buddhist sites

Byin rlabs: 'blessing' or 'spiritual power' received from a deity or lama

Dad pa: faith

dBang thang: spiritual power. Different human and non-human entities will hold 'stronger' or 'weaker' *dbang thang*. Religious specialists' practice (particularly the higher levels of Tantric practice which relate to enlightened Tantric deities) gives them access to *dbang thang* superior to that held by lay Buddhists and local worldly deities

dGon pa: gonpa, monastery

Dug gsum: three mental poisons

gDon: spirit, provocation (unenlightened)

gSo ba rig pa: 'Sowa Rigpa', lit. 'Science/knowledge of healing', this refers to a number of different traditions and practices across ethnically Tibetan areas in the Himalayan region. It is also known in different regions as 'Tibetan Medicine', '*Bod sman*' (Tibetan medicine), 'Amchi medicine', 'Mongolian medicine' and 'Buddhist medicine', and practices often vary significantly between the different regions

gTi mug: ignorance. This refers to the Buddhist notion of ignorance of the true nature of reality according to Buddhist thought; one of the (afflictive) mental factors or afflictive emotions (Tib.: *nyon mongs*) of ignorance (Tib.: *gti mug*), attachment (Tib.: *'dod chags*) and aversion (Tib.: *zhe sdang*), which are often described as the ultimate underlying causes of both physical and mental diseases

Gu ru Rin po che: 'Guru Rinpoche', Tibetan name of Padmasambhava, the eighth century Indian Tantric practitioner who travelled to Tibet and successfully subjugated local deities with the Buddhist Dharma

kLu: water spirit (although sometimes also used to refer to spirits residing in other parts of the natural environment, such as trees or rocks)

Kun gzhi: the basis of existence in Dzogchen thought

Las: karma, literally 'action', this is used to refer to the connection between action and result, often in a future life

Lha: god, deity (may be enlightened or unenlightened)

Lha pa, lha bzhugs mkhan (also *lha 'bab*): spirit-medium

Man ngag rGyud: Oral Instruction Tantra, the third treatise of the *rGyud bZhi*

mKhris pa: bile, one of the three *nyes pa*, disturbance in which can lead to illness

Mo: divination, conducted by a *mo pa* ('diviner') who may be a lay or monastic practitioner

Nyes pa: 'humour', 'fault'. This is a direct translation of the Sanskrit *doṣa*, and is usually translated into English as 'humour', although there are significant problems with this

Nyon mongs: (afflictive) mental factors, afflictive emotions. This often refers to three principal factors: ignorance (Tib.: *gti mug*); attachment (Tib.: *'dod chags*) and aversion (Tib.: *zhe sdang*), which are often described as the ultimate underlying causes of both physical and mental diseases

Phyi ma'i rGyud: Additional or Final Tantra, the fourth treatise of the *rGyud bZhi*

rDo rje Shugs ldan: 'Dorje Shugden', a controversial deity from the Gelugpa Buddhist tradition

rDzogs chen: 'Dzogchen', 'Great Perfection', the highest level Tantric teachings of the Tibetan Nyingma and Bon traditions

rGyal po: literally 'king', this is used to refer to a particular kind of unenlightened deity, often thought to have been religious specialists in previous lives, thus holding considerable spiritual knowledge and power

rGyu: cause, primary cause (in contrast to *rkyen*: condition or secondary cause). These two factors can work together to produce illness and/or misfortune

rGyud bZhi: 'Four Tantras' or 'Four Treatises', the principal medical text in the Sowa Rigpa medical tradition. The full title of the text is often given as **bDud rtsi snying po yan lag brgyad pa gsang ba man ngag gi rgyud**, although in practice the title varies somewhat between different editions

Rin chen ril bu: 'rinchen rilbu', precious (ritually empowered) pills

Rin po che: 'Rinpoche', the title for an individual recognised as the reincarnation of a previous Buddhist teacher

rKyen: condition, secondary cause (in contrast to *rgyu*: condition or primary cause). These two factors can work together to produce illness and/or misfortune

rLung: wind, one of the three *nyes pa* which resides in a number of channels (Tib.: *rtsa*) in the body. Disturbance in this can lead to illness. This is a translation of two Sanskrit terms: *vāta*, one of the three Ayurvedic *doṣa* (usually translated as 'wind') and *prāṇa* (usually translated as 'life force', 'life energy', or 'breath'), the manipulation of which is often a fundamental aspect of Tantric and yogic meditative practices

rLung rta: luck; this also refers to pieces of paper or fabric printed with prayers which are attached to high mountain passes and religious sites or tossed into the wind

rNam shes: consciousness

rTsa: channels, part of the Tibetan 'subtle body' anatomy, in which the *rlung* resides

rTsa rGyud: Root (First) Tantra, the first treatise of the *rGyud bZhi*

Sems: mind, consciousness

Sems nad: illness of the mind, mental illness

(Shi) 'dre: spirit, ghost (usually referring to the spirit of someone recently deceased)

sMan rtsis khang: Department/house of Medicine and Astronomy, this is often used to refer to a Sowa Rigpa hospital

sMyo byed kyi gdon: spirits that cause madness

sMyo nad: madness, psychosis (also *smyo(n) pa* to refer either to the condition or to an individual suffering from this condition)

sNgags pa: literally 'mantra healer', a particular kind of Tantric ritual specialist

sNying rlung: 'wind' in the heart. This refers to a condition where *rlung* has entered the heart area, causing physical and mental symptoms

sPrul sku: 'trulku', 'emanation body', refers to a lama who is a human manifestation of a Tantric deity, and is usually also an incarnation of a previous lama

Srog rtsa: central channel (part of the Tibetan 'subtle body' anatomy) which runs from the crown of the head to the base of the spine

Srog ('dzin) rlung: life-holding/sustaining wind, situated in the *srog rtsa*. One of the main *rlung* currents, the term *srog rlung* is also commonly used to refer to the condition resulting from disturbance in this *rlung* current

Srung ma: guardian deity

Thig le: internal 'drop' (part of the Tibetan 'subtle body' anatomy)

Yid ches: belief

Yul lha: local god

Zhe sdang: aversion; one of the (afflictive) mental factors or afflictive emotions (Tib.: *nyon mongs*) of ignorance (Tib.: *gti mug*), attachment (Tib.: *'dod chags*) and aversion (Tib.: *zhe sdang*), which are often described as the ultimate underlying causes of both physical and mental diseases

Reference List

Adams, V. 1996. Karaoke as modern Lhasa, Tibet: Western encounters with cultural politics. *Cultural Anthropology* 11(4):510–46.

———. 1998. Suffering the winds of Lhasa: Politicized bodies, human rights, cultural difference, and humanism in Tibet. *Medical Anthropology Quarterly* 12(1):74–102.

———. 2001a. The sacred in the scientific: Ambiguous practices of science in Tibetan medicine. *Cultural Anthropology* 16(4):542–75.

———. 2001b. Particularizing modernity: Tibetan medical theorizing of women's health in Lhasa, Tibet. In *Healing powers and modernity: Traditional medicine, shamanism, and science in Asian societies*, ed. L. H. Connor and G. Samuel, 222–46. Westport, CT: Greenwood Press.

———. 2002. Establishing proof: Translating 'science' and the state in Tibetan medicine. In *New horizons in medical anthropology: Essays in honour of Charles Leslie*, ed. M. Lock and M. Nichter, 200–20. London: Routledge.

———. 2007. Integrating abstraction: Modernising medicine at Lhasa's Mentsikhang. In *Soundings in Tibetan medicine: Historical and anthropological perspectives. Proceedings of the Tenth Seminar of the International Association of Tibetan Studies (PIATS), Oxford, 2003*, ed. M. Schrempf, 29–43. Leiden and Boston, MA: Brill.

———. 2005. Saving Tibet? An inquiry into modernity, lies, truths, and beliefs. *Medical Anthropology* 24(1):71–110.

———. 2011. Encounters with efficacy. *Asian Medicine* 6(1):1–21.

Adams, V., R. Dhondup and P. V. Le. 2011. A Tibetan way of science: Revisioning biomedicine as Tibetan practice. In *Medicine between science and religion: Explorations on Tibetan grounds*, ed. V. Adams, M. Schrempf and S. R. Craig, 107–26. New York: Berghahn Books.

Adams, V. and F.-F. Li. 2008. Integration or erasure? Modernizing medicine at Lhasa's Mentsikhang. In *Tibetan medicine in the contemporary world: Global politics of medical knowledge and practice*, ed. L. Pordié, 105–31. London: Routledge.

Alarcón, R. D., M. Alegria, C. C. Bell, C. Boyce, L. J. Kirmayer, K-M. Lin, S. Lopez, B. Üstün, and K. L. Wisner. 2002. Beyond the funhouse mirrors. In *A research agenda for DSM-V*, ed. D. J. Kupfer, M. B. First and D. A. Regier. 219–81. Washington, D.C.: American Psychiatric Association.

American Psychiatric Association. 1980. *Diagnostic and statistical manual of mental disorders: DSM-III*, 3rd ed. Washington, DC: American Psychiatric Association.

———. 1994. *Diagnostic and statistical manual of mental disorders: DSM-IV*, 4th ed. Washington, DC: American Psychiatric Association.

———. 2000. *Diagnostic and statistical manual of mental disorders: Fourth edition text revision (DSM-IV-TR)*, 4th ed. Arlington, VA: American Psychiatric Association.

———. 2013. *Diagnostic and statistical manual of mental disorders: Fifth edition (DSM 5)*, 5th ed. Arlington, VA: American Psychiatric Association.

Anand, D. 2000. (Re)imagining nationalism: Identity and representation in the Tibetan Diaspora of South Asia. *Contemporary South Asia* 9(3):271–87.

———. 2002. World politics, representation, identity: Tibet in Western popular imagination. PhD diss., University of Bristol.

———. 2008. *Geopolitical exotica: Tibet in western imagination*. Minneapolis, MN: University of Minnesota Press.

Andrews, G., T. Slade, and L. Peters. 1999. Classification in psychiatry: ICD-10 versus DSM-IV. *British Journal of Psychiatry* 174:3–5.

Angel, K. 2010. The history of 'female sexual dysfunction' as a mental disorder in the 20th century. *Current Opinion in Psychiatry* 23(6):536–41.

Arbuzov, A. 2013. Pharmacology in TTM psychiatry. Paper presented at: *International Academy of Traditional Tibetan Medicine (IATTM) 2nd International Congress on Traditional Tibetan Medicine, Innsbruck, September 2013*. http://attm-austria.at/download/kongress2013/DrArbuzov_TTMIC2013.pdf.

Arya, P. Y. Tibetan Buddhist psychology and psychotherapy. *Tibetan Medicine Education Centre*. http://www.tibetanmedicine-edu.org/index.php/psychology-and-psychotherapy.

Barnett, L. 24th March 2014. The play that wants to change the way we treat mental illness. *The Guardian*. http://www.theguardian.com/lifeandstyle/2014/mar/24/play-mental-illness-eradication-schizophrenia-western-lapland-open-dialogue-hallucination.

Bateson, G., D. D. Jackson, J. Haley and J. Weakland. 1956. Toward a theory of schizophrenia. *Behavioral Science* 1(4):251–64.

Bateson, G., D. D. Jackson, J. Haley and J. Weakland. 1963. A note on the double bind—1962. *Family Process* 2(1):154–61.

BBC. 19th September 2011. Deadly earthquake rocks India, Nepal and Tibet. *BBC.* http://www.bbc.co.uk/news/world-south-asia-14965598.

BBC. 6th July 2017. How a strike has paralysed life in India's Darjeeling. *BBC.* http://www.bbc.co.uk/news/world-asia-india-40491066.

Benedict, A. L., L. Mancini and M. A. Grodin. 2009. Struggling to meditate: Contextualising integrated treatment of traumatised Tibetan refugee monks. *Mental Health, Religion and Culture* 12(5):485–99.

Bentall, R. P. 2004. *Madness explained: Psychosis and human nature.* London: Penguin.

Beresford, P. and J. Wallcraft. 1997. Psychiatric system survivors and emancipatory research: Issues, overlaps and differences. In *Doing disability research*, ed. C. Barnes and G. Mercer, 66–97. Leeds: The Disability Press.

Berg, E. 2008. *The Sherpa Dumji masked dance festival: An ethnographic description of the 'great liturgical performance' as celebrated annually according to the tradition of the Lamaserwa clan in the village temple of Gonpa Zhung, Solu.* Lumbini: Lumbini International Research Institute.

Berglie, P.-A. 1976. Preliminary remarks on some Tibetan 'spirit-mediums' in Nepal. *Kailash* 4(1):85–108.

Besch, N. F. 2006. Tibetan medicine off the roads: Modernizing the work of the amchi in Spiti. PhD diss., University of Heidelberg.

Bhui, K. and D. Bhugra. 2002. Explanatory models for mental distress: Implications for clinical practice and research. *The British Journal of Psychiatry* 181(1):6–7.

Bjerken, Z. 2001. The mirrorwork of Tibetan religious historians: A comparison of Buddhist and Bon historiography. PhD diss., University of Michigan.

Blondeau, A.-M., ed. 1998. *Tibetan mountain deities, their cults and representations: Papers presented at a panel of the 7th Seminar of the International Association for Tibetan Studies, Graz, 1995.* Graz: Austrian Academy of Sciences Press.

Boddy, J. 1994. Spirit possession revisited: Beyond instrumentality. *Annual Review of Anthropology* 23:407–34.

Borras, L., S. Mohr, P-Y. Brandt, C. Gilliéron, A. Eytan and P. Huguelet. 2007. Religious beliefs in schizophrenia: Their relevance for adherence to treatment. *Schizophrenia Bulletin* 33(5):1238–46.

Bourguignon, E. 1976. *Possession.* San Francisco: Chandler & Sharp Publishers.

British Psychological Society. 2012. *DSM-5: The future of psychiatric diagnosis (2012—final consultation): British Psychological Society response to the American Psychiatric Association.* Leicester: The British Psychological Society.

Brock, D. 2008. Taming the mind: Current mental health treatments and obstacles to expanding the western-model in a Tibetan exile community. *Independent Study Project (ISP) Collection* Paper 209.

Burns, T. 2013. *Our necessary shadow: The nature and meaning of psychiatry.* London: Penguin Books.

Calabrese, J. D. 2006. Mirror of the soul: Cultural psychiatry, moral socialization and the development of the self in the Native American Church. PhD diss., University of Chicago.

_____. 2008. Clinical paradigm clashes: Ethnocentric and political barriers to Native American efforts at self-healing. *Ethos* 36(3):334–53.

Calkowski, M. 1985. Power, charisma, and ritual curing in a Tibetan community in India. PhD diss., University of British Columbia.

_____. 1993. Contesting hierarchy: On gambling as an authoritative resource in Tibetan refugee society. In: *Proceedings of the International Seminar on the Anthropology of Tibet and the Himalaya, Ethnographic Museum of the University of Zürich, September 1990*, 30–38. Zürich: Ethnographic Museum of the University of Zurich.

Cantwell, C. 1995. The Tibetan medical tradition, and Tibetan approaches to healing in the contemporary world. *Kailash: Journal of Himalayan Studies* XVII(4 & 5):157–84.

Cassani, M. 2011. Open Dialogue: A documentary on a Finnish alternative approach to healing psychosis. *Beyond Meds.* http://beyondmeds.com/2011/03/17/opendialogdoc/.

Cassaniti, J. and Luhrmann, T. M. 2011. Encountering the supernatural: A phenomenological account of mind. *Religion and Society: Advances in Research* 2(1):37–53.

Cassels, A. and R. Moynihan. 2005. *Selling sickness: How the world's biggest pharmaceutical companies are turning us all into patients.* New York: Nation Books.

Central Institute of Buddhist Studies: http://cibsleh.in/index.php/facilities/medical.

Central Tibetan Administration: http://tibet.net/about-cta/tibet-in-exile/.

Central Tibetan Administration Planning Commission. 2010. *Demographic survey of Tibetans in exile—2009.* Dharamsala: Central Tibetan Administration.

Chagpori Tibetan Medical Institute: http://www.chagpori.org/college.htm.

Chaudhuri, M. 2014. New mental health bill is tabled in the Indian parliament. *BMJ: British Medical Journal* 348:g1507.

Clark, B. 1995. *The quintessence Tantras of Tibetan medicine*. Ithaca, NY: Snow Lion Publications.

Clifford, J. 1986. Introduction: Partial truths. In *Writing culture: The poetics and politics of ethnography*, ed. J. Clifford and G. E. Marcus, 1–26. Berkeley and Los Angeles, CA: University of California Press.

Clifford, T. 1989. *Tibetan Buddhist medicine and psychiatry: The Diamond Healing*. Irthlingborough: Crucible, The Aquarian Press.

Clifton, T. 28th April 1997. Did an obscure Tibetan sect murder three monks close to the Dalai Lama? *Newsweek*.

Connor, L. 1982. Ships of fools and vessels of the divine: Mental hospitals and madness, a case study. *Social Science & Medicine* 16(7):783–94.

Cooper, R. 2004. What is wrong with the DSM? *History of Psychiatry* 15(1):5–25.

Cornu, P. 1997. *Tibetan astrology*. Boston, MA: Shambhala Publications.

Corrigan, P. W. and A. C. Watson. 2004. At issue: Stop the stigma: call mental illness a brain disease. *Schizophrenia Bulletin* 30(3):477–79.

Council for Evidence-Based Psychiatry. http://cepuk.org/.

Crook, J. H. 1997. The indigenous psychiatry of Ladakh, part I: Practice theory approaches to trance possession in the Himalayas. *Anthropology & Medicine* 4(3):289–307.

Crossley, N. 1998. R. D. Laing and the British anti-psychiatry movement: A socio-historical analysis. *Social Science & Medicine* 47(7):877–89.

Csordas, T. J. 1987. Health and the holy in African and Afro-American spirit possession. *Social Science & Medicine* 24(1):1–11.

————. 2002. *Body/meaning/healing*. Basingstoke and New York: Palgrave Macmillan.

Czaja, O. 2005 & 2006. Zurkharwa Lodro Gyalpo (1509–1579) on the controversy of the Indian origin of the rGyud bzhi. *The Tibet Journal* 30 & 31(4 & 1):131–52.

Dain, N. 1989. Critics and dissenters: Reflections on 'anti-psychiatry' in the United States. *Journal of the History of the Behavioral Sciences* 25(1):3–25.

Dasgupta, A. 1999. Ethnic problems and movements for autonomy in Darjeeling. *Social Scientist* 27(11–12):47–68.

Day, S. 1989. Embodying spirits: Village oracles and possession rituals in Ladakh, north India. PhD diss., London School of Economics and Political Science (University of London).

Deacon, B. J. 2013. The biomedical model of mental disorder: A critical analysis of its validity, utility, and effects on psychotherapy research. *Clinical Psychology Review* 33(7):846–61.

Dein, S. 2004. Working with patients with religious beliefs. *Advances in Psychiatric Treatment* 10(4):287–94.

Diemberger, H. 2005. Female oracles in modern Tibet. In *Women in Tibet*, ed. J. Gyatso and H. Havnevik, 113–68. London: Hurst & Company.

DiValerio, D. M. 2015. *The holy madmen of Tibet.* New York: Oxford University Press.

Dodin, T. and H. Rather, eds. 1996. *Imagining Tibet: Perceptions, projections, and fantasies.* Somerville, MA: Wisdom Publications.

Dolma, S. 2013. sNying rlung disorder: 'Wind in the heart'. Paper presented at: *International Academy of Traditional Tibetan Medicine (IATTM) 2nd International Congress on Traditional Tibetan Medicine, Innsbruck, September 2013.* http://attm-austria.at/download/kongress2013/08_sonam_dolma.mp3.

Donden, Y. 1997. *Health through balance: An introduction to Tibetan medicine.* Delhi: Motilal Banarsidass.

Dorjee, P. 2005. *The spiritual medicine of Tibet: Heal your spirit, heal yourself.* London: Watkins Publishing.

Dow, J. 1986. Universal aspects of symbolic healing: A theoretical synthesis. *American Anthropologist* 88(1):56–69.

Dreyfus, G. 1998. The Shuk-den affair: History and nature of a quarrel. *Journal of the International Association of Buddhist Studies* 21(2):227–70.

————. 2005. Are we prisoners of Shangrila? Orientalism, nationalism, and the study of Tibet. *Journal of the International Association of Tibetan Studies* 1(1):1–21.

Drungtso, T. T. 2004. *Tibetan medicine: The healing science of Tibet.* Dharamsala, HP: Drungtso Publications.

Ekman, P. 1999. Basic emotions. In *Handbook of cognition and emotion.* Vol. 98, ed. T. Dalgleish and M. J. Power, 45–60. Chichester: Wiley-Blackwell.

Ekman, P., R. J. Davidson, M. Ricard and B. A. Wallace. 2005. Buddhist and psychological perspectives on emotions and well-being. *Current Directions in Psychological Science* 14(2):59–63.

Emmerick, R. E. 1977. Sources of the rGyud-bzhi. *(Supplement, Deutscher Orientalistentag vom 28. Sept. bis 4. Okt. 1975 in Frieburg i. Br.) Zeitschrift der Deutschen Morgenländischen Gesellschaft (Wiesbaden)* III(2):1135–42.

Epstein, M. and J. D. Lieff. 1981. Psychiatric complications of meditation practice. *Journal of Transpersonal Psychology* 13(2):137–47.

Epstein, M. and S. Topgay. 1982. Mind and mental disorders in Tibetan medicine. *ReVision: A Journal of Consciousness and Change* 9(1):67–79.

Evans-Pritchard, E. E. 1937. *Witchcraft, magic, and oracles among the Azande.* Oxford: Clarendon Press.

Fernando, S. 2002. *Mental health, race and culture.* 2nd ed. Basingstoke, Hampshire: Palgrave.

Frances, A. J. 2nd December 2012. DSM 5 is guide not a bible—ignore it's ten worst changes. *Psychology Today.* https://www.psychologytoday.com/blog/dsm5-in-distress/201212/dsm-5-is-guide-not-bible-ignore-its-ten-worst-changes.

Ga, Y. 2010. The sources for the writing of the Rgyud bzhi, Tibetan medical classic. PhD diss., Harvard University.

———. 2014. The origin of the Four Tantras and an account of its author, Yuthog Yonten Gonpo. In *Bodies in balance: The art of Tibetan medicine,* ed. T. Hofer, 154–77. Seattle and London: Rubin Museum of Art, New York in association with University of Washington Press.

Gazmeri, D. 22nd May 2010. Gorkha leader Madan Tamang hacked in public. *The Times of India.* http://timesofindia.indiatimes.com/india/Gorkha-leader-Madan-Tamang-hacked-in-public/articleshow/5960365.cms.

Geekie, J. 2004. Listening to the voices we hear: Clients' understandings of psychotic experiences. In *Models of madness: Psychological, social and biological approaches to schizophrenia,* ed. J. Read, L. Mosher and R. P. Bentall, 147–60. Hove and New York: Brunner-Routledge.

Geest, S. van der. 1995. The efficacy of traditional medicine (and biomedicine). In *Health matters: Public health in north-south perspective.* Vol. 9, ed. K. van der Velden, J. K. S. Ginneken, J. P. Velema, F. B. Wall and J. H. Wijnen, 360–65. Houten/Diegem: Bohn Stafleu Van Loghum.

Gellner, D. N. 1994. Priests, healers, mediums and witches: The context of possession in the Kathmandu Valley, Nepal. *Man* 29(1):27–48.

Gerke, B. 1999. Mataji Kumari Cintury: Devi healer Priestess of Darjeeling: Wanderer zwischen den Welten: funktion und formen des heutigen schamanismus. *Curare* 22(2):157–64.

———. 2010. Tibetan treatment choices in the context of medical pluralism in the Darjeeling hills, India. In *Studies of Medical Pluralism in Tibetan History and Society (PIATS 2006: Proceedings of the Eleventh Seminar of the International Association of Tibetan Studies, Königswinter 2006),* ed. S. Craig, M. Schrempf, F. Garrett and M. Cuomu, 337–76. Andiast, Switzerland: International Institute for Tibetan and Buddhist Studies.

———. 2011. Correlating biomedical and Tibetan medical terms in amchi medical practice. In *Medicine between science and religion: Explorations on Tibetan grounds,* ed. V. Adams, M. Schrempf and S. R. Craig, 127–52. New York: Berghahn Books.

———. 2012a. *Long lives and untimely deaths: Life-span concepts and longevity practices among Tibetans in the Darjeeling Hills, India.* Leiden: Brill.

_____. 2012b. Introduction: Challenges of translating Tibetan medical texts and medical histories. In *Wurzeltantra und Tantra der Erklaerungen. Aus 'Die Vier Tantra der Tibetischen Medizin'*, ed. F. Ploberger, 17–29. Schiedlberg: Bacopa Verlag.

_____. 2013. On the 'subtle body' and 'circulation' in Tibetan medicine. In *Religion and the subtle body in Asia and the west: Between mind and body*, ed. G. Samuel and J. Johnston, 83–99. Abingdon and New York: Routledge.

_____. 2014. The art of Tibetan medical practice. In *Bodies in balance: The art of Tibetan medicine*, ed. T. Hofer, 16–31. Seattle and London: Rubin Museum of Art, New York in association with University of Washington Press.

Goleman, D. 2004. *Destructive emotions: A scientific dialogue with the Dalai Lama.* London: Bloomsbury Publishing.

Good, B. J. 1994. *Medicine, rationality, and experience: An anthropological perspective.* Cambridge: Cambridge University Press.

Govinda, A. B. 1974. *The way of the white clouds.* London: Rider.

Greenhalgh, J., C. Knight, D. Hind, C. Beverley and S. Walters. 2005. Clinical and cost-effectiveness of electroconvulsive therapy for depressive illness, schizophrenia, catatonia and mania: Systematic reviews and economic modelling studies. *Health Technology Assessment* 9(9).

Grof, C. and S. Grof. 1990. *The stormy search for the self: A guide to personal growth through transformational crisis.* New York: Jeremy P. Tarcher/Penguin.

Gutschow, K. 1997. A study of 'wind disorder' or madness in Zangskar, northwest India. In *Recent research on Ladakh: Proceedings of the 7th Colloquium of the International Association for Ladakh Studies, Bonn/Sankt Augustin, June 1995*, ed. T. Dodin and H. Räther, 177–202. Kröning: Asanger Verlag.

Gyatso, J. 2004. The authority of empiricism and the empiricism of authority: Medicine and Buddhism in Tibet on the eve of modernity. *Comparative Studies of South Asia, Africa and the Middle East* 24(2):83–96.

_____. 2013. Experience, empiricism, and the fortunes of authority: Tibetan medicine and Buddhism on the eve of modernity. In *The Tibetan history reader*, ed. G. Tuttle and K. R. Schaeffer, 363–85. New York and Chichester: Columbia University Press.

_____. 2015. *Being human in a Buddhist world: An intellectual history of medicine in early modern Tibet.* New York: Columbia University Press.

Gyatso, Y. 2005. Nyes pa: A brief review of its English translation. *Tibet Journal* 30 & 31(4 & 1):109–18.

Habermas, J. 1971. *Knowledge and human interests.* Trans. J. Shapiro. London: Heinemann.

Hacking, I. 1998. *Rewriting the soul: Multiple personality and the sciences of memory.* Princeton, NJ: Princeton University Press.

Halperin, D. 1996. Trance and possession: Are they the same? *Transcultural Psychiatry* 33(1):33–41.

Harland, R., E. Antonova, G. S. Owen, M. Broome, S. Landau, Q. Deeley and R. Murray. 2009. A study of psychiatrists' concepts of mental illness. *Psychological Medicine* 39(6):967–76.

Healy, D. 2004. Shaping the intimate: Influences on the experience of everyday nerves. *Social Studies of Science* 34(2):219–45.

Hepburn, S. J. 1988. W. H. R. Rivers Prize Essay (1986): Western minds, foreign bodies. *Medical Anthropology Quarterly* 2(1):59–74.

Hitchcock, J. T. and R. L. Jones, eds. 1976. *Spirit possession in the Nepal Himalayas.* New Delhi: Vikas Publishing House.

Hofer, T. 2008a. Socio-economic dimensions of Tibetan medicine in the Tibet Autonomous Region, China, Part One. *Asian Medicine* 4(1):174–200.

_____. 2008b. Socio-economic dimensions of Tibetan medicine in the Tibet Autonomous Region, China, Part Two. *Asian Medicine* 4(2):492–514.

_____. 2011. Tibetan medicine on the margins: Twentieth century transformations of the traditions of Sowa Rigpa in central Tibet. PhD diss., University College London (University of London).

Hofmann, S. G., A. T. Sawyer, A. A. Witt and D. Oh. 2010. The effect of mindfulness-based therapy on anxiety and depression: A meta-analytic review. *Journal of Consulting and Clinical Psychology* 78(2):169–83.

Holloway, F. 2008. Is there a science of recovery and does it matter? Invited commentary on ... Recovery and the medical model. *Advances in Psychiatric Treatment* 14(4):245–47.

Hussain, D. and B. Bhushan. 2011. Cultural factors promoting coping among Tibetan refugees: A qualitative investigation. *Mental Health, Religion & Culture* 14(6):575–87.

Jacobson, E. 2000. Situated knowledge in classical Tibetan medicine: Psychiatric aspects. PhD diss., Harvard University.

_____. 2002. Panic attack in a context of comorbid anxiety and depression in a Tibetan refugee. *Culture, Medicine and Psychiatry* 26(2):259–79.

_____. 2007. Life-wind illness in Tibetan medicine: Depression, generalised anxiety, and panic attack. In *Soundings in Tibetan medicine: historical and anthropological perspectives. Proceedings of the Tenth Seminar of the International Association of Tibetan Studies (PIATS), Oxford, 2003,* ed. M. Schrempf, 225–46. Leiden and Boston, MA: Brill.

Janes, C. R. 1995. The transformations of Tibetan medicine. *Medical Anthropology Quarterly* 9(1):6–39.

————. 1999a. Imagined lives, suffering, and the work of culture: The embodied discourses of conflict in modern Tibet. *Medical Anthropology Quarterly* 13(4):391–412.

————. 1999b. The health transition, global modernity and the crisis of traditional medicine: The Tibetan case. *Social Science & Medicine* 48(12):1803–20.

————. 2001. Tibetan medicine at the crossroads: Radical modernity and the social organization of Traditional medicine in the Tibet Autonomous Region, China. In *Healing powers and modernity: Traditional medicine, shamanism, and science in Asian societies*, ed. L. H. Connor and G. Samuel, 197–221. Westport, CA: Bergin & Garvey.

————. 2002. Buddhism, science, and market: The globalisation of Tibetan medicine. *Anthropology & Medicine* 9(3):267–89.

Jones, R. L. 1976. Spirit possession and society in Nepal. In *Spirit possession in the Nepal Himalayas*, ed. J. T. Hitchcock and R. L. Jones, 1–11. New Delhi: Vikas Publishing House.

Judith, A. 2011. *Eastern body, western mind: Psychology and the chakra system as a path to the self.* New York: Random House.

Kandel, E. R. 1998. A new intellectual framework for psychiatry. *American Journal of Psychiatry* 155(4):457–69.

Kay, D. 1997. The New Kadampa Tradition and the continuity of Tibetan Buddhism in transition. *Journal of Contemporary Religion* 12(3):277–93.

Keen, T. 1999. Schizophrenia: Orthodoxy and heresies. A review of alternative possibilities. *Journal of Psychiatric and Mental Health Nursing* 6(6):415–24.

Keller, A. D. Lhewa, B. Rosenfeld, E. Sachs, A. Aladjem, I. Cohen, H. Smith and K. Porterfield 2006. Traumatic experiences and psychological distress in an urban refugee population seeking treatment services. *The Journal of Nervous and Mental Disease* 194(3):188–94.

Khangkar, L. D. 1986. *Lectures on Tibetan medicine.* Dharamsala, HP: The Library of Tibetan Works and Archives.

Kirmayer, L. J. 2006. Beyond the 'new cross-cultural psychiatry': Cultural biology, discursive psychology and the ironies of globalization. *Transcultural Psychiatry* 43(1):126–44.

————. 2007. Psychotherapy and the cultural concept of the person. *Transcultural Psychiatry* 44(2):232–57.

Kleinman, A. M. 1977. Depression, somatization and the 'new cross-cultural psychiatry'. *Social Science & Medicine* 11(1):3–9.

_____. 1980. *Patients and healers in the context of culture: An exploration of the borderland between anthropology, medicine, and psychiatry.* Berkeley, CA: University of California Press.

_____. 1991. *Rethinking psychiatry: From cultural category to personal experience.* New York: Free Press.

_____. 2009. Global mental health: A failure of humanity. *The Lancet* 374(9690):603–04.

_____. 2010. Four social theories for global health. *The Lancet* 375(9725):1518–19.

Kloos, S. 2010. Tibetan medicine in exile: The ethics, politics and science of cultural survival. PhD diss., University of California, San Francisco with University of California, Berkeley.

Kressing, F. 2003. The increase of shamans in contemporary Ladakh: Some preliminary observations. *Asian Folklore Studies* 62:1–23.

Kruszelnicki, K. S. 16th September 2004. Schizophrenia & split personality. *ABC Science.* http://www.abc.net.au/science/articles/2004/09/16/1200266.htm.

Kvaerne, P. 1976. The genesis of the Tibetan Buddhist tradition. *Tibet Review* 11(3):9–15.

Larsson, S. 2012. *Crazy for wisdom: The making of a mad yogin in fifteenth-century Tibet.* Leiden: Brill.

Leff, J., N. Sartorius, A. Jablensky, A. Korten and G. Ernberg. 1992. The international pilot study of schizophrenia: Five-year follow-up findings. *Psychological Medicine* 22(1):131–45.

Lewis, S. E. 2013. Trauma and the making of flexible minds in the Tibetan exile community. *Ethos* 41(3):313–36.

Lichter, D. and L. Epstein. 1983. Irony in Tibetan notions of the good life. In *Karma: An anthropological inquiry,* ed. C. F. Keyes and E. V. Daniel, 223–59. Berkeley, CA: University of California Press.

Littlewood, R. 1991. From disease to illness and back again. *The Lancet* 337(8748):1013–16.

_____. 1992. DSM-IV and culture: Is the classification internationally valid? *Psychiatric Bulletin* 16(5):257–61.

Loizzo, J. J., L. Blackhall and L. Rapgay. 2009. Tibetan medicine: A complementary science of optimal health. *Annals of the New York Academy of Sciences* 1172(1):218–30.

Lopez, D. S. J. 1999. *Prisoners of Shangri-la: Tibetan Buddhism and the west.* Chicago, IL and London: University of Chicago Press.

Luhrmann, T. M. 2007. Social defeat and the culture of chronicity: Or, why schizophrenia does so well over there and so badly here. *Culture, Medicine and Psychiatry* 31(2)135–72.

_____. 2010. What counts as data? In *Emotions in the field: The psychology and anthropology of fieldwork experience*, ed. J. Davies and D. Spencer, 212–38. Stanford, CA: Stanford University Press.

_____. 2012. Beyond the brain. *The Wilson Quarterly* Summer 2012:28–34.

Lutz, C. 1985. Depression and the translation of emotional worlds. In *Culture and depression: Studies in the anthropology and cross-cultural psychiatry of affect and disorder*, ed. A. Kleinman and B. Good, 63–100. Berkeley and Los Angeles, CA: University of California Press.

McKay, A. 2005. The indigenisation of western medicine in Sikkim. *Bulletin of Tibetology* 41(2):25–48.

_____. 2011. Biomedicine in Tibet at the edge of modernity. In *Medicine between science and religion: Explorations on Tibetan grounds*, ed. V. Adams, M. Schrempf and S. R. Craig, 33–56. New York: Berghahn Books.

McKenzie, K., V. Patel and R. Araya. 2004. Learning from low income countries: Mental health. *British Medical Journal* 329(7475):1138–40.

Mehta, S. and A. Farina. 1997. Is being 'sick' really better? Effect of the disease view of mental disorder on stigma. *Journal of Social and Clinical Psychology* 16(4):405–19.

Men-Tsee-Khang Tibetan Medical and Astrological Institute: http://www.men-tsee-khang.org/branch/main.htm.

Mercer, S. W., A. Ager and E. Ruwanpura. 2005. Psychosocial distress of Tibetans in exile: Integrating western interventions with traditional beliefs and practice. *Social Science & Medicine* 60(1):179–189.

Merriam-Webster Medline Plus Medical Dictionary: http://www.merriam-webster.com/medlineplus/.

Merskey, H. 1992. The manufacture of personalities. The production of multiple personality disorder. *The British Journal of Psychiatry* 160(3):327–40.

Meyer, F. 1998. *The history and foundations of Tibetan medicine*. New York: Rizzoli.

_____. 2003. The golden century of Tibetan medicine. In *Lhasa in the seventeenth century: The capital of the Dalai Lamas*, ed. F. Pommaret, 99–117. Leiden and Boston, MA: Brill.

Middleton, T. 2013. Anxious belongings: Anxiety and the politics of belonging in subnationalist Darjeeling. *American Anthropologist* 115(4):608–21.

Millard, C. 2007. Tibetan medicine and the classification and treatment of mental illness. In *Soundings in Tibetan medicine: Historical and anthropological perspectives. Proceedings of the Tenth Seminar of the International Association of Tibetan Studies (PIATS), Oxford, 2003*, ed. M. Schrempf, 247–82. Leiden and Boston, MA: Brill.

_____. 2013. Bon medical practitioners in contemporary Tibet: The continuity of a tradition. *East Asian Science, Technology and Society* 7(3):353–79.

Miller, B. D. 1956. Ganye and kidu: Two formalized systems of mutual aid among the Tibetans. *Southwestern Journal of Anthropology* 12(2):157–70.

Miller, C. J. 1978. *Faith-healers in the Himalayas*. Kathmandu: Centre for Nepal and Asian Studies, Tribhuvan University.

Ministry of Ayurveda, Yoga and Naturopathy, Unani, Siddha and Homeopathy (AYUSH): http://ayush.gov.in/.

Mitchell, L. and S. Romans. 2003. Spiritual beliefs in bipolar affective disorder: Their relevance for illness management. *Journal of Affective Disorders* 75(3):247–57.

Moacanin, R. 1986. *The essence of Jung's psychology and Tibetan Buddhism: Western and Eastern paths to the heart*. Somerville, MA: Wisdom Publications.

Mol, A. and M. Berg. 1998. Differences in medicine: An introduction. In *Differences in medicine: Unraveling practices, techniques, and bodies*, ed. M. Berg and A. Mol, 1–12. Durham, NC: Duke University Press.

Moncrieff, J. 2010. Psychiatric diagnosis as a political device. *Social Theory & Health* 8(4):370–82.

Moncrieff, J. and M. J. Crawford. 2001. British psychiatry in the 20th century—observations from a psychiatric journal. *Social Science & Medicine* 53(3):349–56.

Morrison, A. P. et al. 2014. Cognitive therapy for people with schizophrenia spectrum disorders not taking antipsychotic drugs: A single-blind randomised controlled trial. *The Lancet* 383(9926):1395–403.

Moscovici, S. 1961. *La psychanalyse: Son image et son public*. Paris: Presses Universitaires de France.

Moynihan, R., I. Heath and D. Henry. 2002. Selling sickness: The pharmaceutical industry and disease mongering. *British Medical Journal* 324(7342):886–91.

Moynihan, R. and D. Henry. 2006. The fight against disease mongering: Generating knowledge for action. *PLoS Medicine* 3(4):425–28.

Myers, N. L. 2011. Update: Schizophrenia across cultures. *Current Psychiatry Reports* 13(4):305–11.

National Institute for Health and Care Excellence. 2014. *Psychosis and schizophrenia in adults: Treatment and management (NICE clinical guideline 178)*. London: NHS National Institute for Health and Care Excellence.

National Institute for Health and Clinical Excellence. 2009. *Depression in adults: The treatment and management of depression in adults (NICE clinical guideline 90)*. London: National Institute for Health and Clinical Excellence.

_____. 2011. *Generalised anxiety disorder and panic disorder (with or without agoraphobia) in adults: Management in primary, secondary and community care (NICE clinical guideline 113).* London: National Institute for Health and Clinical Excellence.

Nebesky-Wojkowitz, R. de. 1956. *Oracles and demons of Tibet: The cult and iconography of the Tibetan protective deities.* Kathmandu: Pilgrims Book House.

Noll, R. 1983. Shamanism and schizophrenia: A state-specific approach to the 'schizophrenia metaphor' of shamanic states. *American Ethnologist* 10(3):443–59.

Norbu, N. 1995. *Drung, deu, and Bön: Narrations, symbolic languages, and the Bön traditions in ancient Tibet.* Dharamsala: Library of Tibetan Works and Archives.

Nurani, L. M. 2008. Critical review of ethnographic approach. *Journal Sosioteknologi* 14(7):441–47.

Open Dialogue UK: http://opendialogueapproach.co.uk/.

Ozawa-De Silva, C. and B. R. Ozawa-De Silva. 2011. Mind/body theory and practice in Tibetan medicine and Buddhism. *Body & Society* 17(1):95–119.

Patel, V. 2002. *Where there is no psychiatrist: A mental health care manual.* London: Gaskell.

_____. 2007. Mental health in low-and middle-income countries. *British Medical Bulletin* 81(1):81–96.

Peters, L. G. 1987. The Tamang shamanism of Nepal. In *Shamanism: An expanded view of reality,* ed. S. Nicholson, 161–80. Wheaton, IL: Theosophical Publishing House.

Phuntsok, T. and T. Lhamo. 2009. *Study in elements of Tibetan medicine.* Beijing: China Tibet Publishing House.

Pilgrim, D. 2002. The biopsychosocial model in Anglo-American psychiatry: Past, present and future? *Journal of Mental Health* 11(6):585–94.

_____. 2007. The survival of psychiatric diagnosis. *Social Science & Medicine* 65(3):536–47.

Prost, A. 2004. Exile, social change and medicine among Tibetans in Dharamsala (Himachal Pradesh), India. PhD diss., University College London (University of London).

_____. 2006. Causation as strategy: Interpreting humours among Tibetan refugees. *Anthropology & Medicine* 13(2):119–30.

_____. 2007. Sa cha'di ma'phrod na ... Displacement and traditional Tibetan medicine among Tibetan refugees in India. In *Soundings in Tibetan medicine: Historical and anthropological perspectives. Proceedings of the Tenth Seminar of the International Association of Tibetan Studies (PIATS), Oxford, 2003,* ed. M. Schrempf, 45–64. Leiden and Boston, MA: Brill.

_____. 2008. *Precious pills: Medicine and social change among Tibetan refugees in India*. Oxford and New York: Berghahn Books.

Provencher, C., Arthi and W. Wagner. 2012. Cognitive polyphasia: Introductory article. *Papers on Social Representations* 21(1):1.1–1.15.

Rabgay [= Rapgay], L. 1984. Mind-made health: A Tibetan perspective. *Tibetan Medicine* 8:45–55.

_____. 1985. rLung diseases and their treatment. *Tibetan Medicine* 9:47–68.

_____. 1985. *Tibetan medicine: A holistic approach to better health*. New Delhi: Sona Printers.

Rapport, N. 1997. Edifying anthropology: Culture as conversation; representation as conversation. In *After writing culture: Epistemology and praxis in contemporary anthropology*, ed. A. James, J. Hockey and A. Dawson, 177–93. London and New York: Routledge.

Read, J. and R. P. Bentall. 2012. Negative childhood experiences and mental health: Theoretical, clinical and primary prevention implications. *The British Journal of Psychiatry* 200(2):89–91.

Read, J., N. Haslam, L. Sayce and E. Davies. 2006. Prejudice and schizophrenia: A review of the 'mental illness is an illness like any other' approach. *Acta Psychiatrica Scandinavica* 114(5):303–18.

Read, J., P. J. Fink, T. Rudegeair, V. Felitti and C. L. Whitfield. 2008. Child maltreatment and psychosis: A return to a genuinely integrated bio-psycho-social model. *Clinical Schizophrenia & Related Psychoses* 2(3):235–54.

Read, U. 2012. I want the one that will heal me completely so it won't come back again: The limits of antipsychotic medication in rural Ghana. *Transcultural Psychiatry* 49(3–4):438–60.

Richards, G. 2000. Britain on the couch: The popularization of psychoanalysis in Britain 1918–1940. *Science in Context* 13(2):183–230.

Rissmiller, D. and J. Rissmiller. 2006. Open forum: Evolution of the antipsychiatry movement into mental health consumerism. *Psychiatric Services* 57(6):863–66.

Rosenbush, E. 2013. Srog-rtsa—The vital channel in the context of mental health. Paper presented at: *International Academy of Traditional Tibetan Medicine (IATTM) 2nd International Congress on Traditional Tibetan Medicine*, September 2013, Innsbruck, Austria. http://attm-austria.at/download/kongress2013/09_eric_rosenbush.mp3.

Rösing, I. 2006. *Shamanic trance and amnesia: Traditional healing in Ladakh*, 201–2. New Delhi: Concept Publishing Company.

Ruwanpura, E., S. W. Mercer, A. Ager and G. Duveen. 2006. Cultural and spiritual constructions of mental distress and associated coping mechanisms of Tibetans in exile: Implications for western interventions. *Journal of Refugee Studies* 19(2):187–202.

Sachs, E., B. Rosenfeld, D. Lhewa, A. Rasmussen and A. Keller. 2008. Entering exile: Trauma, mental health, and coping among Tibetan refugees arriving in Dharamsala, India. *Journal of Traumatic Stress* 21(2):199–208.

Samuel, G. 1993. *Civilized shamans: Buddhism in Tibetan societies.* Washington: Smithsonian Institution Press.

_____. 2001. Tibetan medicine in contemporary India: Theory and practice. In: Connor, L. H. and G. Samuel. *Healing powers and modernity: Traditional medicine, shamanism, and science in Asian studies,* 247–68. Westport, CT and London: Bergin & Garvey.

_____. 2007. Spirit causation and illness in Tibetan medicine. In *Soundings in Tibetan medicine: Historical and anthropological perspectives. Proceedings of the Tenth Seminar of the International Association of Tibetan Studies (PIATS), Oxford, 2003,* ed. M. Schrempf, 213–24. Leiden and Boston, MA: Brill.

_____. 2009. Religion, health and suffering among contemporary Tibetans. In *Religion, health and suffering,* ed. J. R. Hinnells and R. Porter, 85–110. Abingdon and New York: Routledge.

_____. 2010. Healing, efficacy and the spirits. *Journal of Ritual Studies* 24(2):7–20.

_____. 2012. *Introducing Tibetan Buddhism.* Abingdon: Routledge.

_____. 2013. The subtle body in India and beyond. In *Religion and the subtle body in Asia and the west: Between mind and body,* ed. G. Samuel and J. Johnston, 33–47. Abingdon and New York: Routledge.

Sapey, B. and P. Bullimore. 2013. Listening to voice hearers. *Journal of Social Work* 13(6):616–32.

Saraceno, B., M. v Ommeren, R. Batniji, A. Cohen, O. Gureje, J. Mahoney, D. Sridhar and C. Underhill. 2007. Barriers to improvement of mental health services in low-income and middle-income countries. *The Lancet* 370(9593):1164–74.

Sartorius, N., R. Shaprio and A. Jablensky. 1974. The international pilot study of schizophrenia. *Schizophrenia Bulletin* 1(11):21–34.

Sartorius, N., A. Jablensky, A. Korten, G. Ernberg, M. Anker, J. E. Cooper and R. Day. 1986. *Early manifestations and first-contact incidence of schizophrenia in different cultures: A preliminary report on the initial evaluation phase of the WHO collaborative study on determinants of outcome of severe mental disorders.* Geneva: WHO.

Schrempf, M. 2007. Bon lineage doctors and the local transmission of knowing medical practice in Nagchu. In *Soundings in Tibetan medicine: Historical and anthropological perspectives. Proceedings of the Tenth Seminar of the International Association of Tibetan Studies (PIATS), Oxford, 2003*, ed. M. Schrempf, 91–126. Leiden and Boston, MA: Brill.

————. 2011. Between mantra and syringe: Healing and health-seeking behaviour in contemporary Amdo. In *Medicine between science and religion: Explorations on Tibetan grounds*, ed. V. Adams, M. Schrempf and S. R. Craig, 157–84. New York: Berghahn Books.

Schröder, N.-A. 2011. *Discussing psychotrauma with Tibetan healing experts: A cultural translation.* Berlin: WieBensee Verlag.

Seikkula, J. and M. E. Olson. 2003. The open dialogue approach to acute psychosis: Its poetics and micropolitics. *Family Process* 42(3):403–18.

Seikkula, J., J. Aaltonen, B. Alakare, K. Haarakangas, J. Keränen and K. Lehtinen. 2006. Five-year experience of first-episode nonaffective psychosis in open-dialogue approach: Treatment principles, follow-up outcomes, and two case studies. *Psychotherapy Research* 16(2):214–28.

Seligman, R. and L. J. Kirmayer. 2008. Dissociative experience and cultural neuroscience: Narrative, metaphor and mechanism. *Culture, Medicine and Psychiatry* 32(1):31–64.

Shah, P. and D. Mountain. 2007. The medical model is dead—long live the medical model. *The British Journal of Psychiatry* 191(5):375–77.

Shaw, I. 2002. How lay are lay beliefs? *Health: An Interdisciplinary Journal for the Social Study of Health, Illness and Medicine* 6(3):287–99.

Shorter, E. 1997. *A history of psychiatry: From the era of the asylum to the age of Prozac.* New York, John Wiley & Sons, Inc.

Shweder, R. A., J. Haidt, R. Horton and C. Joseph. 1993. The cultural psychology of the emotions: Ancient and renewed. In *Handbook of emotions*, 3rd ed, ed. M. Lewis, J. M. Haviland-Jones and L. Feldman Barrett, 417–31. New York & London: The Guilford Press.

Siegler, M. and H. Osmond. 1966. Models of madness. *The British Journal of Psychiatry* 112(493):1193–203.

Sihlé, N. 2002. Lhachö [lha mchod] and hrinän [sri gnon]: The structure and diachrony of a pair of rituals (Baragaon, Northern Nepal). In *Religion and secular culture in Tibet: (Tibetan Studies II): PIATS 2000 Tibetan Studies: Proceedings of the Ninth Seminar of the International Association of Tibetan Studies, Leiden, 2000*, ed. H. Blezer, 185–206. Leiden: Brill.

Silverman, D. 2000. *Doing qualitative research: A practical handbook.* London: Sage.

Silverman, J. 1967. Shamans and acute schizophrenia. *American Anthropologist* 69(1):21–31.

Singer, K. 1975. Depressive disorders from a transcultural perspective. *Social Science & Medicine* 9(6):289–301.

Smith, G., A. Bartlett and M. King. 2004. Treatments of homosexuality in Britain since the 1950s: An oral history: the experience of patients. *British Medical Journal* 328(7437):427–29.

Smith, W. C. 1977. *Belief and history*. Charlottesville, VA: University Press of Virginia.

Somer, E. 2006. Culture-bound dissociation: A comparative analysis. *Psychiatric Clinics of North America* 29(1):213–26.

Sonntag, S. K. 2003. Self-government in the Darjeeling hills of India. In *Emancipating cultural pluralism*, ed. C. E. Toffolo, 181–93. Albany, NY: State University of New York Press.

Southwold, M. 1979. Religious belief. *Man* 14(4):628–44.

Spanos, N. P. 1994. Multiple identity enactments and multiple personality disorder: A sociocognitive perspective. *Psychological Bulletin* 116(1):143–65.

Subba, T. B. 1988. Social adaptation of the Tibetan refugees in the Darjeeling-Sikkim Himalayas. *The Tibet Journal* 13:49–57.

_____. 1990. *Flight and adaptation: Tibetan refugees in the Darjeeling-Sikkim Himalaya*. Dharamsala: Library of Tibetan Works and Archives Dharamsala.

Summerfield, D. 2001. The invention of post-traumatic stress disorder and the social usefulness of a psychiatric category. *British Medical Journal* 322(7278):95–98.

_____. 2008. How scientifically valid is the knowledge base of global mental health? *British Medical Journal* 336(7651):992–94.

Szasz, T. S. 1960a. The myth of mental illness. *American Psychologist* 15(2):113–18.

_____. 1960b. *The myth of mental illness: Foundations of a theory of personal conduct*. New York: Hoeber-Harper.

Telegraph, The. 8th July 2011. Hill deal to be signed in 7 days. *The Telegraph*. https://www.telegraphindia.com/1110709/jsp/frontpage/story_14215656.jsp.

Terheggen, M. A., M. S. Stroebe and R. J. Kleber. 2001. Western conceptualizations and eastern experience: A cross-cultural study of traumatic stress reactions among Tibetan refugees in India. *Journal of Traumatic Stress* 14(2):391–403.

Thakker, J. and T. Ward, T. 1998. Culture and classification: The cross-cultural application of the DSM-IV. *Clinical Psychology Review* 18(5):501–29.

Thomas, P. and P. Bracken. 2004. Critical psychiatry in practice. *Advances in Psychiatric Treatment* 10(5):361–70.

Thomas, S. P., M. Groer, M. Davis, P. Droppleman, J. Mozingo and M. Pierce. 2000. Anger and cancer: An analysis of the linkages. *Cancer Nursing* 23(5):344–49.

Tomlinson, M., I. Rudan, S. Saxena, L. Swartz, A. C. Tsai and V. Patel. 2009. Setting priorities for global mental health research. *Bulletin of the World Health Organization* 87(6):438–46.

Tsarong, T. J. 1991. Tibetan psychopharmacology. *Integration: Zeitschrift für Geistbewegende Pflanzen und Kultur, Journal for Mind-moving Plants and Culture* 1, 43–60.

Tseng, W.-S. 2006. From peculiar psychiatric disorders through culture-bound syndromes to culture-related specific syndromes. *Transcultural Psychiatry* 43(4):554–76.

Tyler, S. A. 1986. Post-modern ethnography: From document of the occult to occult document. In *Writing culture: The poetics and politics of ethnography*, ed. J. Clifford and G. E. Marcus, 122–40. Berkeley and Los Angeles, CA: University of California Press.

Tyrer, P. and D. Steinberg. 2013. *Models for mental disorder*. 5th ed. Chichester: John Wiley & Sons.

Vahali, H. O. 2009. *Lives in exile: Exploring the inner world of Tibetan refugees*. New Delhi: Routledge.

Waddington, K. 2011. *An introduction to the social history of medicine: Europe since 1500*. London: Palgrave Macmillan.

Wagner, W., G. Duveen, M. Themel and J. Verma. 1999. The modernization of tradition: Thinking about madness in Patna, India. *Culture & Psychology* 5(4):413–45.

Wagner, W., G. Duveen, J. Verma and M. Themel. 2000. I have some faith and at the same time I don't believe: Cognitive polyphasia and cultural change in India. *Journal of Community and Applied Social Psychology* 10(4):301–14.

Walker, G. 2005. Modernization. In *Writing early modern history*, ed. G. Walker, 25–48. London: Bloomsbury.

Wangda, J. 1996. Health seeking behaviours of Tibetan refugee community in Dharamsala, India. MSc diss., Queen's University (Ontario).

Wangyal, T. (ed. M. Dahlby). 2002. *Healing with form, energy and light: The five elements in Tibetan shamanism, Tantra, and Dzogchen*. Ithaca, NY and Boulder, CO: Snow Lion Publications.

Williams, B. and D. Healy. 2001. Perceptions of illness causation among new referrals to a community mental health team: 'Explanatory model' or 'exploratory map'? *Social Science & Medicine* 53(4):465–76.

Wilson, M. 1993. DSM-III and the transformation of American psychiatry: A history. *American Journal of Psychiatry* 150:399–410.

Winkelman, M. 1997. Altered states of consciousness and religious behavior. In *Anthropology of religion: A handbook of method and theory*, ed. S. D. Glazier, 393–428. Westport, CN: Greenwood Press.

WHO Mental Health Gap Action Programme (mhGAP): http://www.who.int/mental_health/mhgap/en/.

World Health Organization. 1974. *Report of the international pilot study of schizophrenia, volume I: Results of the initial evaluation phase.* Geneva: World Health Organization.

————. 1975. *Schizophrenia: A multinational study. A summary of the initial evaluation phase of the International Pilot Study of Schizophrenia.* Geneva: World Health Organization.

————. 1978. *The promotion and development of traditional medicine.* Geneva: World Health Organization.

————. 1979. *Schizophrenia: An international follow-up study.* Chichester: Wiley.

————. 1993. *The ICD-10 classification of mental and behavioural disorders: Diagnostic criteria for research.* Geneva: World Health Organization.

————. 2001. *World health report 2001. Mental health: New understanding, new hope.* Geneva: World Health Organization.

————. 2002. *WHO policy perspectives on medicines. Promoting rational use of medicines: Core components.* Geneva: Wold Health Organization.

————. 2005. *The ICD-10 classification of mental and behavioural disorders: Clinical descriptions and diagnostic guidelines.* Geneva: World Health Organization.

————. 2010a. *ICD-10 Version: 2010, International statistical classification of diseases and related health problems 10th Revision (ICD-10) version for 2010.* WHO. http://apps.who.int/classifications/icd10/browse/2010/en#/.

————. 2010b. *mhGAP intervention guide for mental, neurological and substance use disorders in non-specialized health settings: Version 1.0.* Geneva: World Health Organization.

————. 2010c. *Mental health and development: Targeting people with mental health conditions as a vulnerable group.* Geneva: World Health Organization.

Yoeli-Tlalim, R. 2010. Tibetan 'wind' and 'wind' illnesses: Towards a multicultural approach to health and illness. *Studies in History and Philosophy of Science Part C: Studies in History and Philosophy of Biological and Biomedical Sciences* 41(4):318–24.

INDEX

Acupuncture, 71
Additional Tantra. *See Phyi ma'i rGyud*
Afflictive mental factors, 53. *See also
  nyon mongs*
A gar 35, 71
Amchi, 73
  in Darjeeling, 42–5
  practice, 68–9, 77, 214
  training, 53, 62–3, 65–8, 76
Amulet. *See srung nga*
Anger, xviii, 138, 141. *See also rlung
  langs, zhe sdang*
  as a cause of illness, 136, 140–1,
    142, 147, 155, 187–8
  as a symptom, 55, 59, 64, 136, 140
Anxiety, 6, 54,128, 136
  and *rlung* conditions, 60, 79–80,
    131–2, 136, 138, 198–9
  causes of, 132
  generalised anxiety disorder, 6,
    79–80
  Tibetan concepts relating to, 78,
    79, 80, 115, 132
  treatment of, 77
Aṣṭāṅgahṛdayasaṃhitā, 64
Astrology, 193

Attachment, 146, 150, *see also 'dod
  chags*
Aversion. *See zhe sdang*
Ayurveda, 39, 42, 53, 54, 57, 64

'Brel wa, 161, 163–6, 185–6, 188
'Bum bZhi, 70
Bad kan, 55, 57, 58, 59–60, 167
Bad kan smyo nad, 133
Belief. *See yid ches*
Bhaisajyaguru. *See* Medicine Buddha
Bhutia, 15, 19, 21, 26–7, 29
Bile. *See mkhris pa*
Biomedicine. *See also* psychiatry
  clinics and hospitals, Darjeeling,
    213
  history of in Tibetan contexts,
    118–23
  hospital, Gangtok, 41–2
  model of mental illness, 5, 102–7
  Tibetan perspectives on, 207, 118,
    119, 120–1, 138, 157, 202–5,
    206, 207–9, 212–3
Biopsychosocial model, 104
Bipolar disorder, 79–80, 178, 202–3.
  See also manic depression
bKa' sgo, 161

bLa, 87, 88, 170

bLa ma smyon pa, 151

Blessing, 3, 46, 48, 61, 128, 129, 146, 156, 157, 161–2, 163–4, 176, 184, 197, 205

Bloodletting, 9, 44, 69

Bon, 48, 69–70. *See also 'Bum bZhi*

brGya bzhi, 193, 194

British Psychological Society, 5

bShad rGyud, 64, 73

bSo nams, 73, 88, 167–8, 170, 199

bTsan, 85, 86–7, 88, 165, 182, 185–6

Byin rlabs. See blessing

Cause. *See rgyu, rkyen*

Central Council of Tibetan Medicine (CCTM), 68

Central School for Tibetans, 29

Central Tibetan Administration (CTA), 21, 22, 26, 27, 28

Chagpori medical institute, Lhasa, 65, 66–7

Chagpori Tibetan Medical Institute, Darjeeling, 42, 44–5, 67–8, 69

Chakra. *See 'khor lo*

Channels. *See rtsa*

Clifford, T., 61, 95, 167

Cognitive behaviour therapy (CBT), 41, 106, 122

Cognitive polyphasia, 209

Connection. *See 'brel wa*

Coping strategies, 16, 117, 208, 210, 213

Counselling, 41, 60, 121, 122–3, 138, 213

Critical psychiatry, 105

Cultural Revolution, 67, 74–5, 186

'Culture-bound disorder/syndrome', 97, 116–7

'Dod chags, 72, 167

'Dre. See (shi) 'dre

Dad pa, 163–6, 199

Dalai Lama, V[th], 65

Dalai Lama, XIIIth, 22, 67, 74

Dalai Lama, XIVth, 15, 22, 26, 67, 176, 186–7, 212

Dali Gonpa. *See* Drug Sangak Choling monastery

Darjeeling

climate in, 17, 19

history of, 19–21, 22

medical facilities in, 23, 28, 43, 39–45

political situation in, 16, 20–1

population of, 18

Tibetan population in, 21–9

tourism in, 17–19

dBang thang. See spiritual power

Deities. *See also btsan, lha, rgyal po, srung ma, yul lha*

classification of, 86

guardian/protector deities, 86, 185

possession by, 87–9, 93, 175–182

relationship with Buddhism, 185, 195

relationship with humans, 167, 169–70, 185–9, 198

Delusion. *See gti mug*

Depression

as causative factor, 61, 81

case study of, 127–30

classification of, 115

Tibetan concepts relating to, 7, 78, 79, 80, 115, 130–3, 154, 198–9

treatment for, 77, 128–9, 141

Desire. *See 'dod chags*

Desi Sangye Gyatso, 65, 66, 68

Diagnosis (in Sowa Rigpa), 44, 60, 65, 69, 91, 212

Diagnostic and Statistical Manual of Disease (DSM), 5, 53
  DSM-III, 95
  DSM-IV, 79, 116
  DSM-IV TR, 32, 116
  DSM-5, 5, 96–7, 98, 102, 116, 171
  utilisation of, 101, 107

Diet
  as causation of illness, 57, 61, 81, 139
  as treatment, 68, 142

Dissociation, 7, 94–5, 96–8

Dissociative identity disorder, 96–8. *See also* possession-form dissociative identity disorder

Divination, 87, 91, 157, 180, 206

dNgags skrag, 78

Dorje Shugden, 46, 186–8, 190

Drug Sangak Choling monastery, 45, 46, 182, 193, 194

Dug gsum, 167

Efficacy, 117–8, 163–5, 170–1, 214

Electro-convulsive therapy (ECT), 41, 122, 204–5

Emotion, 72, 74, 131, 138–42, 151, 154, 155, 187

Enema, 68

Epilepsy, 44, 90, 96, 108, 169

Exorcism, 48, 84, 87, 92–3, 168–9, 178, 179, 188

Explanatory Tantra. *See bShad rGyud*

'Exploratory map', 9, 76, 108, 148, 170, 184, 198, 200, 209, 215

Exposure and response therapy (ERT), 41

Faith. *See dad pa*

Five elements, 56, 62, 167

Four Tantras. *See rGyud bZhi*

Freud, S., 104

gCod, 156

gDon
  'byung po'i gdon, 90
  affliction by, 55, 81, 84, 87–8, 91, 164, 182–5, 185–6
  brjed byed kyi gdon, 90
  classification of, 86, 90–1
  gza' yi gdon, 90, 92
  possession by, 90, 95, 148, 151, 178–80, 182–4
  smyo byed kyi gdon, 61, 64, 83, 90, 178–9
  treatment for afflictions related to, 87, 91–3
  see also gson 'dre, klu, spirits

Ghost. *See (shi) 'dre*

Golden needle therapy, 44, 68

Gorkhaland, 20–1

gSon 'dre, 88, 182

gTi mug, 72, 167

Guru Rinpoche, 85, 87, 185, 195. *See also* Padmasambhava

gZa', 85, 90

Hallucinations, 60, 62, 80, 151, 155, 160

Humour/humor, 53, 58, 72. *See also nyes pa*

Ignorance. *See ma rig pa*

Insanity, 5, 60, 61, 71, 80, 149, 150–7, 178, 200–1. *See also* madness

Integration (of Sowa Rigpa and biomedicine), 68–9, 75, 119–21, 123, 208, 211–5

International Classification of Disease (ICD), 5, 53, 101, 102–3, 107

International Pilot Study of Schizophrenia, 5

'Jig skrag zhad snang, 78

Jacobson, E. E., 6, 60–1, 77, 79–80, 115, 132, 151, 198–9

Jhānkri, 45, 47–8, 49, 162, 176, 180, 184, 192

Jungian theory, 79

'Khor lo, 59

Karma, 74, 137, 140, 146, 152, 164, 167–71, 197, 209

Kleinman, A., xix, 3, 6, 7, 9, 107, 112, 115, 200–1

kLu, 85, 90, 180

Kraepelin, E., 103–5.
 Kraepelinian model of mental illness, 105, 106

Lamas, crazy. *See bla ma smyon pa*

Las. See karma

Lha. See deities

Lha bzhugs mkhan, 47, 87, 88–9, 93, 175–81, 191–2, 209

Lha pa. See lha bzhugs mkhan

Life channel. *See srog rtsa*

Life force. *See bla*

Life-sustaining wind. *See srog ('dzin) rlung*

Local deities. *See yul lha*

Luck. *See rlung rta*

Madness, 159–62, 184–5. *See also bad kan smyo nad,* insanity, *smyo byed kyi gdon, smyo nad*
 causes of, 150–5, 176–9, 185–6
 prevention of, 155–6
 rGyud bZhi classifications of, 150
 rlung-related madness, 71, 139, 141, 154–5
 spirit/deity-caused madness, 88–9, 96, 150, 178–9, 182, 184–9
 Tibetan concepts relating to, 78–80, 171–2
 treatment of, 156–7, 186, 207

Manic depression, 104, 111. *See also* bipolar disorder

Manjushree Center of Tibetan Culture, 29, 30

Man ngag rGyud, 61, 64, 73, 90

Ma rig pa, 167

Massage, 68, 71

Mataji, 45, 47–8, 176, 180, 192, 213

Medical pluralism, xvii–xix, 4, 7–11, 49–50, 49, 77, 110, 123, 173, 184, 197–216

Medicine Buddha, 64, 66, 73, 92

Meditation, 74, 132, 142, 153–4

Mental Health Gap Action Program (mhGAP) for Low- and Middle-Income Countries, 101, 110–11, 112

Men-Tsee-Khang (MTK) Tibetan Medical and Astrological Institute, Dharamsala, 62–3
 branch clinics, 67
 Darjeeling branch clinic, 42–4, 69
 history of, 67, 76
 museum, Dharamsala, 71, 91

Mentsikhang, Lhasa, 67, 70, 74–5, 76

Me rgyab. See rdo me

Merit, 167–8. *See also bsod nams*

Millard, C., 6, 61, 78–80, 88, 115, 132, 198

Mindfulness, 106, 153

mKhris pa, 55, 57, 58, 59–60, 167

Mo. See divination

Moxibustion, 9, 60, 68, 71

Multiple personality disorder. *See* dissociative identity disorder

Nam mkh'a, 92

Nechung Oracle, 87

Neurosis, 78, 80

Nutmeg, 141, 207

Nyams yig, 65

Nyes pa, 53, 55, 56–7, 58–62. *See also* humour
  arising of, 72, 73–4
  disturbance in, 74, 89

Nyon mongs, 72–4, 76, 78, 140, 141. *See also* afflictive mental factors

Obsessive-compulsive disorder (OCD), 41

Open dialogue, 106

Oracle, 87–8, 178, 180, 192. *See also* Nechung Oracle

Oral Instruction Tantra. *See Man ngag rGyud*

'*Phra ba. See* subtle body

Padmasambhava, 99, 154. *See also* Guru Rinpoche

Panic
  panic attack, 60, 132
  panic disorder, 6, 115
  Tibetan terms relating to, 78

Pehar, 87, 185

Phlegm. *See bad kan*

Phlegm madness. *See bad kan smyo nad*

Phyi ma'i rGyud, 64, 91

Planets. *See gza'*

Poison, 61, 140, 150

Population
  Tibetan population in Darjeeling, 21
  Tibetan population in India, 21

Possession, 83, 93, 175–9, 180–1. *See also* dissociation, *gdon, lha, lha zhugs mkhan*, spirit-medium,
  treatment of, 48, 91, 190–5
  western interpretations of, 7–8, 93–8, 178, 181, 200–1

Possession-form dissociative identity disorder, 96

Post-traumatic stress disorder (PTSD), 54, 80, 132, *See also* trauma

Psychiatry (biomedical), 5–7, 101–23. *See also* biomedicine, critical psychiatry, *Diagnostic and Statistical Manual of Disease, International Classification of Disease*
  access to, 9, 111–3, 121–2, 206
  anti-psychiatry movement, 105
  classification in, 5, 103–4, 107, 117
  clinics and hospitals, India, 23, 28, 39–42, 45, 119, 122
  costs of, 9, 40, 41–2, 206
  criticism of, 105, 112, 116
  history of, 102–6
  in cross-cultural context, 8–11, 108–9, 110–8, 118–23
  in Darjeeling, 25, 41
  post-psychiatry, 105
  treatment, 104, 106–7, 109, 111, 117–8, 122

Psychoanalysis, 104

Psychosis, 94, 118
  causes of, 89, 108–9
  classification of, 171–2
  symptoms of, 200–1
  Tibetan concepts relating to, 6,
    60, 61, 79, 80, 132, 149–50,
    162, 204–5
  treatment for, 71, 77, 106–7, 111
Psychotherapy, 104, 122
Pulse diagnosis. *See* diagnosis

Rai, 20, 185
rDo me, 192
Referral, 45, 208, 213
rGyal po, 85–7, 88, 92, 165, 179,
  182, 185–6
rGyu, 152, 167–8, 209
rGyud bZhi, 3, 53, 62, 71–2, 73, 77
  classification of mental disorders
    in, 72
  classification of spirits in, 90–1
  history of, 63–5
  treatment in, 74
Rin chen ril bu, 92, 157, 205
Ritual
  medicine production, 76
  practitioners, 76, 84,
  to increase *dbang thang*, 169
  treatment for mental illness, 73,
    74, 75, 146, 156, 197
  treatment for spirit/deity affliction,
    61, 92–3, 186, 191–5, 209
  see also *brgya bzhi, lha bzhugs
    mkhan, sngags pa*
rKyen, 152, 167–8, 209
rLung, 53, 55–7, 58–9, 61–2, 73, 199
  '*khrag rlung*, 132
  khyab byed rlung, 60
  snying rlung, 60, 135

thur sel rlung, 60
  see also *srog ('dzin) rlung*
rLung disturbance
  biomedical interpretations of, 6–7,
    79, 132–3, 198–9, 215
  causes of, 77–8, 80–1, 136–7,
    139–40, 153–5
  classification of, 72, 138–9
  politicisation of, 4, 16, 54, 56,
    133–5, 136
  prevention of, 142
  symptoms of, 6, 60, 61–2, 80, 131,
    135–6, 139–40, 151, 154–5
  Tantric practice related to, 57, 62,
    139, 153
  treatment of, 60, 71, 92, 137–8,
    141–2, 156, 207
  see also *srog 'dzin rlung*, disturbance
rLung langs, 141
rLung mtho po, 56
rLung rta, 88, 152, 167–71, 179–80,
  199, 209
Root Tantra. *See rTsa rGyud*
rTsa, 58–9, 78, 89, 178
rTsa rGyud, 64

Samuel, G., 57, 68, 71, 73, 79, 85, 87,
  90, 91, 92, 93–4,189, 195, 207
Schizophrenia, 41, 79–80, 96, 108,
  114, 132, 149, 171, 204–5
  symptoms of, 114
  treatment of, 106, 111, 122
  western models of, 104–5, 108
  see also *International Pilot Study of
    Schizophrenia*
Sems khrel, 78
Sems ma bde ba, 128, 150
Sems nad, 3, 11, 53, 59, 130, 133,
  140, 154, 160–2, 172, 202

causes of, 61, 74, 76–7, 142, 155–
6, 185–6, 198, 207, 210, 216
in the *rGyud bZhi*, 62, 64
treatment of, 68 77, 137, 142,
198, 205
Sems ngal, 78
Sems pham pa, 78
Sems rnyog dra, 79, 150
Sems sdug, 78
Sems skyon nad rigs, 79
Sems tshab pa, 78
(Shi) 'dre, 84, 86, 95, 164. *See also*
spirits
affliction related to, 182–5
possession by, 84, 148, 179–80,
182–5, 192
ritual for affliction related to,
193–4
Shing kun 25, 71
Shiva, 48
Sikkim, 30
sKu rim, 170
sKyo snang, 78
sMyod byed kyi gdon, 61, 64, 90–1,
178–9. *See also* madness, spirit
affliction, spirits
sMyo nad, 145–50, 159–62. *See also*
bad kan smyo nad, madness
biomedical interpretations of, 6,
79–80, 149–50, 171–2, 201
causes of, 61, 81, 88, 141, 146–8,
150–6, 167, 185–6, 198, 216
prevention of, 155–6
symptoms of, 61, 80, 145–6, 149,
150–1
treatment of, 61, 68, 71–2, 146,
148, 156–7, 198, 205
sNgags pa, 32, 46–7, 47, 72, 84, 92–
3, 165, 176, 191, 194

Somatisation, xix, 6, 55, 79, 115–6,
132–3, 135
Sowa Rigpa
biomedical interpretations of Sowa
Rigpa theory, 59, 78–81
clinics, Darjeeling and Gangtok,
42–5, 69, 198
costs of, 42–3, 44
diversity in practice of, 62–3, 67,
69, 71–2, 73
history of, 62–4, 65–8
legal recognition of in India, 54
relationship to Buddhism, 73–8,
164
secularisation of, 74–5
see also amchi, *rGyud bZhi*
Spirit affliction, 74, 88–90, 129, 184–
5, 198. *See also gdon, shi 'dre,*
smyo byed kyi gdon
cases of, 182–5, 189–90
causation of, 147, 165, 170, 179–
80, 198
diagnosis of, 91, 200–1
prevention of, 190–5
symptoms of, 150, 182, 184
treatment of, 46–8, 72, 77, 87, 91–
3, 156, 182, 184, 190–5, 204
Spirit-medium, Nepali. *See jhānkri,*
mataji
Spirit-medium, Tibetan, 84, 87, 92,
96, 180–2, 192, 206. *See also lha*
bzhugs mkhan
Spirits
classification of, 85–6, 90–1
relationship with Buddhism, 85–
7, 163, 195
relationship with humans, 87,
163–6, 190–5
see also gdon, shi 'dre

Spirits that cause madness. *See smyo byed kyi gdon*

Spirit trap. *See nam mkh'a*

Spiritual crisis, 8

Spiritual power, 85–7, 162, 163–6, 167–71, 179, 183, 195, 199

Srog 'dzin 11, 71

Srog ('dzin) rlung, 55, 59, 60, 80

Srog ('dzin) rlung disturbance, 60, 89, 127–30

    biomedical interpretations of, 79, 80, 132

    causes of, 131, 132, 136, 141, 155

    symptoms of, 60, 130–2, 140, 153, 198

    treatment of, 77, 132, 206–7

Srog rtsa, 55, 59

Srung ma, 185

Srung nga, 129, 176

Stigma, 108, 115, 148–9, 187, 189

Stress, 6, 7, 56, 130–2, 135–7, 155, 171–2, 202–3

Subtle body, xviii, 55–9, 61–2. *See also rlung*

'Symbolic healing', 94

T'ai chi, 57, 154

Three poisons. *See dug gsum*

Tibetan Department of Health, Dharamsala, 42

Tibetan government-in-exile, *See Central Tibetan Administration*

Tibetan Medicine. *See* Sowa Rigpa

Tibetan Refugee Help Centre (TRSHC), Darjeeling, 21, 23–5, 31, 33, 40, 43

Tibetan Settlement Office, Darjeeling, 28

Torture, 121, 208, 212–3

Transcultural Psychosocial Organisation (TPO) Torture Survivors Project, Dharamsala, 212–3

Trauma, 4, 34, 134, 139, 167–8. *See also* post-traumatic stress disorder

Trogawa Rinpoche, 42, 67–8

Williams, B. and Healy, D., 7, 9, 76, 108, 198

Wind. *See rlung, srog ('dzin) rlung*

World Health Organization, 5, 101, 211

Yid ches, 163–6, 199

Yul lha, 86, 164, 185–6

Yutok Yanton Gonpo, 64

Zhe sdang, 72, 167